Bob
Willis

A Cricketer and
a Gentleman

Bob
Willis

A Cricketer and a Gentleman

Edited by David Willis

HODDER &
STOUGHTON

First published in Great Britain in 2020 by Hodder & Stoughton
An Hachette UK company

5

Copyright © Beneficiar y of the Estate of Bob Willis 2020

A CIP catalogue record for this title is available from the British Library

Hardback ISBN 978 1 529 34134 8
eBook ISBN 978 1 529 34135 5

Typeset in Adobe Caslon Pro by Hewer Text UK Ltd, Edinburgh
Printed and bound in Great Britain by Clays Ltd, Elcograf S.p.A.

Hodder & Stoughton policy is to use papers that are natural, renewable
and recyclable products and made from wood grown in sustainable
forests. Theloggingandmanufactur ing processes are expected to conform
to the environmental regulations of the country of origin.

Hodder & Stoughton Ltd
Carmelite House
50 Victoria Embankment
London EC4Y 0DZ

www.hodder.co.uk

This book is dedicated to those whose lives
have been devastated by prostate cancer.

CONTENTS

'It's all over. And it is one of the most fantastic victories ever known in Test cricket history.'

Richie Benaud, Headingley, 1981

FOREWORD
By Sir Ian Botham

Not a day goes by when I do not think of Bob Willis, someone so central not just to my career, but to my whole life. I think of Bob the cricketer, the fellow commentator and pundit, the wine lover, music fan and enthusiast for so many of the finer things in life. Most of all, however, I think of Bob the man, and the enduring friendship that was to be a constant through almost all my adult years.

Among the vast store of memories, one that stands out above most others is when I first properly met him, just prior to my Test debut in 1977 at Trent Bridge as a twenty-one-year-old. Never one to be overcome with nerves, I was nonetheless slightly anxious. I was walking out to our net session the day before when I felt this big hand on my shoulder, belonging to someone I barely knew.

'Just relax and enjoy it. You're going to be fine,' Bob told me.

As the day, and the match, progressed he went out of his way to make me feel comfortable. Him being a senior player, it left quite an impression. This sort of thing gets passed down the generations, and I resolved that when I got some kind of seniority I would try and behave in the same way to the new lads coming into the team.

Almost exactly forty years later, to the day, I was delighted to see Bob had been named by the ICC in the all-time England

Test team, as voted by the fans to mark the 1,000th match being played.

Make no mistake, Bob was one of the very finest bowlers and that rarity, a genuine English quick. He used his height well and had real pace – if there was any bounce in the wicket he would extract it. I used to stand in the slips to him and very quickly I recognised that you needed to position yourself a couple of extra steps back. He was different from those other great England bowlers, Jimmy Anderson and Stuart Broad, in that he was a bang-it-in-the-wicket fast bowler. While he had that monster run-up for a lot of his career, it was also noticeable that he could be quick off fewer paces as well.

We would play 60 Tests together and take 476 wickets between us over a seven-year period. I loved opening the bowling with Bob. You could never complain when you had someone like that bowling at the other end. It is worth remembering that he would have taken even more wickets had there been neutral umpires for his whole career, especially as he played so many Tests in Australia, although we could all claim to have suffered a bit through that.

The fact that he played at a high level for so long was a testament to what a fighter he was, and not just in the sense that you knew he was always up for the battle. Bob was a bit wary of his own body and, because of the pounding his knees took on his approach to the crease, he often had to play through pain. I used to refer to his knees as Spaghetti Junction, as there were that many lines criss-crossing them, thanks to his operations. The surgical techniques were not as sophisticated at the time: it was more 'get the carving knife out and off we go'. It is often forgotten that he nearly died because of a thrombosis caused by one of the operations.

His batting was brave, too. It gave hours of amusement watching him, and whenever he got to 20 it felt like a hundred. It was not elegant, but lacked nothing in determination.

Of course, to me he was much more than a bowling partner, and often he served as a mentor and big-brother figure. If I had a problem, on or off the field, we could sit down with a bottle of wine and talk it through. I did not lack self-confidence, whereas Bob was maybe a bit the other way, so we were quite good for each other like that. We could talk about the game or about our lives away from it, the good and the bad. I trusted him and he was always there.

In these pages the many dimensions of Bob's character emerge, some of them less obvious to people who did not really know him. He was a relatively shy person by nature, and did not suffer fools. Some might have thought he was opinionated or miserable, but he was not like that at all and had this wonderful dry humour.

He also had a great sense of curiosity and was always up for organising things or doing something new. On one tour of Pakistan he decided not to take the team bus to the ground but instead rode as a pillion passenger on one of the police motorbikes. There he was, towering over the driver, a good yard taller. When he got to the ground, his hair was like a giant cobweb and the police rider was grinning from ear to ear.

That was another thing about Bob: he was great with ordinary people and had no airs and graces. Although he could count lots of famous friends from the world of cricket and way beyond that, he was always interested in people and their lives, whatever they did. I recall us driving up north around the time of the miners' strike and being held up at a roadblock – we had to wait for an extra half-hour while Bob talked to everyone because he wanted to find out what was going on.

He was a lot of fun to be around. In our playing days, we had our regular watering holes to relax in all round the country, whether it was pints of Timothy Taylor's at The Junction in Otley during Headingley matches, or the Number 15 wine bar in Manchester for Old Trafford games. Wherever we were in the world, if Bob Dylan was playing within a 300-mile radius, I would get dragged along.

After our playing days were over and we worked on television together, there were rounds of golf at Wentworth or Sunningdale – unlike his bowling action, nobody ever copied Bob's swing – followed by some very long lunches. On tour for Sky, there was the simple pleasure of playing cards during rain delays, or exploring what the local wine producers had to offer. He knew his stuff about a lot of subjects and had a proper knowledge of wine.

The thing he knew more about than anything, though, was cricket. Not just the technical side of the game – he was also well ahead of his time with his ideas about how it should be run. He would write these papers and get me to read them to see what I thought about his vision for four-day cricket, different divisions or other matters. I felt it was a great shame that the authorities did not listen to him enough, because usually what he came up with was pretty sound.

Just as he was irreplaceable as a player, he was unique as a commentator and pundit on TV. Some may have thought he was negative, but I knew how much he cared, and how proud as punch he was when England did well. *The Verdict* became his niche, and it built up a large cult following, with lots of people I know making sure they recorded it if they could not see it live. Players would watch it, and doubtless some of them would be hoping that it was not their number coming up that night. It was born out of his passion for the game.

The time in 2015 when Andrew Strauss asked him to speak to the current crop of England pace bowlers – Bob was as nervous about that as he would have been going in to face Dennis Lillee or Jeff Thomson. 'Don't worry, the worst that can happen is that they lynch you,' I told him. In the end he enjoyed it tremendously, and I am sure they found it worthwhile, once they saw there was more to him than putting a wig on and acting the judge.

Of course, the abiding memory most people will have of Bob is Headingley 1981, and I am not much different. He was under huge pressure going into that, playing for his England career. When Mike Brearley told him to let it rip as he ran in down the hill, it became a masterclass of delivering the highest-quality performance at a time the team needed it most. I would be the first to say that he deserves a massive share of the credit for what happened in that game and that series. The last day at Leeds and his 8–43 was one of the most extraordinary things I was ever lucky enough to witness close up.

So I think about Bob a lot, never more so than when I am in a hut that I have in my garden. It contains a few bottles of wine, among which I know would be a few of his favourites, like a South Australian Riesling or a New Zealand Chardonnay. I will crack one open sometimes, and it will be one of those many occasions when I wonder, 'What would Bob think about this?'

EDITOR'S PREFACE

In the old days Wednesdays were half-day closing. So it was to prove to be on Wednesday, 4 December 2019, at Parkside Hospital, by Wimbledon Common, where at just after 2 p.m. my brother, Bob Willis, moved from one life to the next.

A group of close friends and family had assembled that morning to join Bob's wife, Lauren, as she kept vigil at his bedside. That had been the pattern for almost a week, but this time the smiles of the nursing and support staff were a little more anxious, a little briefer. Did they know it was the day that Bob would leave us? I think they probably did.

On that last busy morning the ever-present group of Lauren, Bob's daughter, Katie, and I were joined by Lauren's mother and Lauren's best friend, Mitzi, over from Australia. Soon to arrive were two of Bob's greatest mates: the former England fast bowlers David Brown, his mentor at Warwickshire, and J.K. Lever from Essex and all points east. Beefy Botham had visited a few days earlier and Paul (Walter) Allott was due down from Manchester by about midday. (What was it about fast bowlers? It seemed that all of Bob's very closest friends had earned a crust the hard way, not a spinner or batsman in sight – although Botham and Allott might not like their efforts with the bat to be dismissed so lightly.)

Bob was drifting in and out of consciousness by this stage, with the gentle strains of some of his favourite Bob Dylan songs heavily scenting the background. Many tears were shed that day and it was remarkable to see large, experienced, world-worn men sobbing uncontrollably as they made their way out of the hospital and back to their cars.

Would Walter Allott make it in time? A train delay, a problem with a taxi up the hill from Putney . . . but then just five minutes before Bob left us Walter arrived and squeezed Bob's hand. Bob squeezed back and that was that.

After some very sad final farewells we retreated to Bob and Lauren's flat at Mortlake. Corks were pulled, tears were wiped and Mitzi composed half a dozen lines for a press release. It was agreed that as Bob had worked for Sky television for more than twenty years, they should have the news first, so it was duly despatched to Sky Sports, just before 4 p.m.

We watched the television expectantly as the news flash was passed to Vicky Gomersall, who was on the news desk with Jim White that quiet and peaceful afternoon. She began to read it out on air but only made it halfway through before succumbing to tears as she realised what she was reading. Jim White took over and was also clearly very affected by the announcement.

Now at least the world knew, and its reaction was extraordinary. All our phones seemed to ring non-stop for the next few hours. Bob's death was high up on the evening news broadcasts; clips were played; seemingly everybody he had ever met or played with was ready to give a quote – all badly shaken, all very distraught.

The newspapers the following morning were filled with lengthy obituaries – four back pages in the *Daily Mail*, front-page headlines in the broadsheets – tributes flowing in from around the world. Nobody realised quite how many people he had touched, how many people were genuinely fond of him and how many lives he had entertained for so many years.

So, how did this book come about? Back in 2019 Roddy Bloomfield, the doyen of sports publishers in the UK and a friend of Bob's, had been considering working with him on a new autobiography – before Bob became too ill to continue with the project. Seeing the enormous outpouring of grief and affection towards Bob simply confirmed Roddy's conviction that a book in his memory would be a fitting tribute.

Meetings were arranged and one of Bob's closest friends in the media, *Daily Mail* sportswriter Mike Dickson, was approached to provide some biographical chapters. In addition there would be tributes from a host of personalities who had known Bob well, as well as chapters celebrating his finest hour at Headingley in 1981 and a number of other key matches, a selection of Bob's own writing and on-air sayings, and a collection of some of the many tributes and messages that appeared in the press and on social media. Photographs would be selected by Lauren to complete a genuine testament to the memory of one of England's most compelling sporting characters.

Everybody involved in the project is very keen for the book that has resulted to do well and hopes that it will interest readers not just in England, but also in Australia, where Bob had many close friends; in India, a country he much admired; and in many other parts of the cricketing world.

The book is not a commercial venture for the Willis family, however. Bob's cancer was diagnosed late and had already spread to his bones. Lauren is passionate about the importance of improving early testing of the disease and funding research in this crucial area. She and Katie will be donating the full advance payment and royalties on this book, less expenses, to Prostate Cancer UK.

David Willis

Part I

ROBERT GEORGE DYLAN WILLIS

A Life

by Mike Dickson

1
FOREVER YOUNG

The stark and beautiful melody of Bob Dylan's 'Not Dark Yet' filled the chapel when, just before Christmas, a collection of family and friends came together to say farewell to Bob Willis. It was, of course, no surprise that Dylan had been selected as a soundtrack to mark the sombre occasion. Everyone knew how much his music meant to the man people had gathered to remember.

'Shadows are falling and I've been here all day / It's too hot to sleep, time is running away' are the opening lines to one of the songs highest up the Willis playlist. 'Don't even hear a murmur of a prayer / It's not dark yet, but it's getting there' is how this particular Dylan masterpiece concludes.

The decision – as a teenager – to add the Dylan forename was only one indication that England's celebrated fast bowler was a man of many parts. In common with a lot of the most interesting professional athletes, he did not grow up anticipating that he would find fame as an international sportsman.

Certainly he could not have expected that his passing, on 4 December 2019, would elicit such a tsunami of coverage in the media. The outpouring was one of genuine affection and respect, and no little shock for the vast majority, who were unaware his illness had been at such an advanced stage. Bob's final few overs were bowled up the hill and into a strong wind, but he never complained.

The service reflected on a life less ordinary. Bob's brother David, wearing a blue summer jacket that had belonged to his sibling and was one of his favourites, spoke about all that he had packed into seventy years. Paul Allott, not just a friend but a fellow commentator and one-time England team-mate, addressed more specifically his professional achievements.

Bob's time on this earth was one roughly divided into two parts – the first being the portion that featured remarkable feats on the field of play, the second working in business and then the media. It reflects the old adage that anyone who plays professional sport dies twice: initially when their time is up as an athlete, and later when their life meets the end that everyone is destined for.

The many tributes that were paid in the wake of Bob's death had certain themes running through them. There was the obvious passion for the sport at which he made his living, and also the fact that he was a man with an enormous hinterland, whose interests extended way beyond England's summer sporting obsession. The cover of the service sheet was further evidence. It featured a joyous picture of him standing to take the applause of the Centre Court during one of his visits to Wimbledon's Royal Box, tennis being one of the other sports he enjoyed. The playing of Wagner at the service, alongside Dylan, had been another nod to his wide-ranging musical tastes.

Perhaps there was one aspect that permeated through the many kind words said about him more than any other. That was the difference between some public perceptions and the reality. As he happily admitted himself, whilst he was racking up 90 Tests, 64 one-day internationals and 308 first-class appearances with Surrey and Warwickshire, he found it hard to actually enjoy the game. The struggle to achieve success meant so much that it was difficult to 'stop and smell the roses'. The image generated by a slightly stern external demeanour may have been reinforced, subsequently, by becoming the most trenchant analyst of cricket in the media.

Those who met him, or knew him, quickly understood that what he was really like was very different. The generosity of spirit, humour and humanity soon shone through upon acquaintance.

Mark Butcher, former England opener and latterly a broadcasting colleague, went on what might be considered a fairly typical journey in his relationship with Bob. 'As a player, before I had any real knowledge of him as a man, he was kind of terrifying,' recalled Butcher while talking to Cricinfo. He first had an inkling of what to expect when, while still a player, he swapped a joke with Bob at a hotel in Chittagong, on tour in Bangladesh. 'As things progressed, Bob was the funniest, warmest, most generous and interesting bloke that I have worked with. The public perception might have been of a miserable old sod . . . but it couldn't be further from the truth.'

Butcher was only one of many who would enjoy Bob's wry observations about the human condition and his wide-ranging knowledge of all sorts of subjects. His views on wine, for example, were about as strong, and well-informed, as his views on cricket. He was a good cook who appreciated food. He liked the theatre and the cinema. He was a keen follower and player of other sports, notably football, tennis and golf. He was perhaps not the most elegant practitioner of the last two, which will not come as a huge surprise to the millions familiar with that unorthodox gallop to the crease before delivering a cricket ball at high speed.

But then Bob did not grow up in an era when talent was honed through early county age-group teams, progressing on to academies. There was no hothouse in which, from a young age, he was prepared for the institutionalised life of a modern professional.

This contributed to him defying simplistic description, his character being one of fascinating contradictions. He was a serious person, but one who did not take himself too seriously at all. In his cricketing life he had a rebellious streak, while at key forks in the road he often sided with the establishment. He could come across as forbidding, but was the most approachable of high-profile figures. He was England's proud and fierce Ashes warrior, who loved Australia.

In short, the most interesting of men, fast and fearless.

2
NO TIME TO THINK

When it came to remembering Bob Willis, it was notable how many people reminisced about how, while playing in the garden, they used to copy his highly distinctive bowling action. If imitation is the sincerest form of flattery, he should have been pleased. That helter-skelter, veering run, the frantic arms and legs, the idiosyncratic pump of the wrist – it clearly left an indelible impression.

It will come as no surprise that this was honed not by some sophisticated instruction, but through years of extremely competitive games of cricket at home and at the local recreation ground with older brother David. School and club, too, but the Willis method was certainly not one that would be found in any coaching manual.

David explains that it was a question of maximising what he had, and that it came together over time. At one stage his run-up was a more straight diagonal charge to the crease, but it evolved. In contrast to the modern era of constant video analysis, he never saw himself bowl until watching some highlights on the television.

There was a big growth spurt around late puberty that propelled Bob to his height of 6 ft 6 in, and only then did the thought arise that he might turn out to have plenty of potential. 'He was a very big unit and it took a long run for him to get the momentum to reach the crease at pace,' reflects David. 'He had very little upper-body strength and so relied on speed at the crease and a fast arm action. You could see bits of it coming together when we played together as children, but it was something that evolved gradually.

'Someone like John Snow was much smoother and had much more upper-body strength. Bob just ran in at the stumps and tried to arrive at the crease at maximum pace. He was all rhythm, and if the rhythm wasn't there he just couldn't bowl.'

This illuminates why no-balls were an enduring problem through his career – a record 939 of them were bowled for England – not that such things were any consideration in his formative years.

Bob was born in Sunderland, where his father, Ted, was a sub-editor on the *Sunderland Echo*. Though journalism was not a profession that Bob always sympathised with during his playing career, it nonetheless had provided some insight for future reference. His parents had actually met in Canada, where Ted was stationed with the RAF during the war. Mother Anne was English, but had been living there at the time.

The stay in the north-east was brief, as they only remained there for a few months after his birth, before a job switch took the family a little further south. He and siblings David and Ann moved with their parents to Manchester after his father found work on *The Guardian*. Lancashire also proved a temporary stop, just about long enough for Bob to develop an affinity with Manchester City.

After five years his father successfully applied for a position on the BBC newsdesk in London, and they installed themselves in the Surrey commuter town of Cobham, now perhaps best known as the base of millionaire Chelsea footballers. The

Willis family abode did not involve a mansion with wrought-iron gates, however. They lived in a three-bedroom semi in Bray Road, and while it was a childhood short on luxuries, they did not go without any essentials.

Fortuitously, it was also close to Stoke D'Abernon cricket club, which became a focal point of summer activity for the sports-mad Willis brothers and their father. Soon Bob was shadowing the club's scorer during games at the weekend, although the growing obsession with cricket went even further than that. When Test matches were on, the two brothers struck on the idea of setting up a blackboard adjacent to the platform at the local station. They would scribble out the updated score from the radio, for the benefit of commuters coming off the train.

Although not particularly motivated by academic work, the youngest Willis sibling evidently had some natural brainpower. To his surprise, and the delight of his parents, he became the only pupil from his primary-school year group of 105 to pass the eleven-plus exam and gain a place at Guildford's prestigious Royal Grammar School. The expense of uniforms and the like was considerable, but his admission was a source of family pride.

It is fair to say that Bob did not view his days at RGS, overall, with a great deal of affection, but most of the time he was grateful for the cricketing opportunities it offered. For him the massive change came when he hit the ever-awkward age of fourteen. Within barely eighteen months he went from 5 ft 6 in to 6 ft 4 in, and his speed as a bowler increased accordingly.

Regarded as an all-rounder, he found himself playing up a year in the school age-group cricket teams, which was a mixed blessing. His cricket was developing fast, but it also brought with it a degree of jealousy from his contemporaries, marking him as something of an outsider. He began to feel more comfortable in the company of pupils above his year, and his size meant that he was quickly asked to play for the Old Boys' team at both cricket and football. Thereby began, at an early age, a lifelong fondness for what he considered to be proper beer.

The sense of feeling out of place was exacerbated by being held back a year after flunking his O levels. This was not an easy time all round, as his brother recalls: 'My mother moved her own mother over from Canada to live with us without much consultation,' says David. 'It caused a lot of tension in the house, and for a period of months we moved out, living apart from our father. We got through it and came back together as a family, but it was unsettling for everyone and didn't come at a great time, with Bob and me in our teens.'

There was also the issue of having to play rugby, which led Bob to hold a long-term aversion to the sport. Never quite understanding the attraction of the physicality involved in the oval-ball game, and being of lanky build, he hated having to play in the scrum among contemporaries with whom he felt no affinity. Nor did he get on with the coaches, some of whom he considered to border on the sadistic.

This did, however, have some benefit when it came to his beloved cricket. Come the summer months – and the opportunity to get a small, hard leather ball in his hands – he was motivated to exact retribution against some of those who had made his life miserable in the winter. The sense of teenage rebellion extended to refusing to wear a cap atop his burgeoning mop of hair, and the addition of Dylan to his forenames by deed poll was a similar gesture.

'I was a thoroughly disagreeable young man,' he summarised in his 1985 autobiography, *Lasting the Pace*. Detentions and academic struggles were a constant feature, but the beacon of hope was cricket. Around the school circuit that RGS participated in he was gaining a reputation for being fearsomely quick. This came at the expense of his batting, as he was increasingly pigeonholed. On the upside, the self-esteem gained by putting the fear of God into young opposition was a bulwark against the other difficulties experienced at school.

A call-up for the Surrey Schools team was to come as he wrestled with A levels, and with it a first experience of what were to be many cricket tours. This came in the shape of a Surrey Young Cricketers' trip down to the West Country. Thoughts of a professional career were still distant, and he set his sights on joining brother David at university. Yet when his last exams yielded just one A-level pass, that particular avenue was shut down. The job market beckoned for the self-described stroppy youngster, whose main talent was launching a cricket ball at unlikely pace.

It was now the summer of 1968, with flower power in its pomp and a somewhat resentful graduate of the Royal Grammar School on the loose, searching for his purpose. At least his social life had improved through constantly playing cricket with Cobham Avorians club, where he was learning the joys of post-match festivities and the art of drinking.

While his parents were keen for him to get a sensible job,

glimmers of a more exciting future were starting to appear. Several accomplished performances for the county's Young Cricketers' side led, that August, to an invitation to play for Surrey's second team on a mini-tour of matches that would take in Worcestershire and Glamorgan. Bob's main memory of this was of getting fleeced in the pub games of spoof he felt obliged to participate in, soon losing the fiver his father had slipped into his hand for out-of-pocket expenses. He bowled decently without making a huge splash. It was nonetheless enough for him to quietly believe that making a living from the game might be within reach.

Reality hit with a thud at the onset of winter. A string of failed job applications saw the fledgling professional bowler having to settle for life as a petrol-pump attendant five miles away, via bike, in Effingham.

The dark months were to be happily broken up by selection to join a Surrey and Middlesex youth side on a tour of Pakistan over Christmas. For all the privations, and some homesickness during the festive period, Bob looked back on this trip with affection because of the esprit de corps it engendered. While they were overmatched on the field and had to stay at such places as an army camp in Peshawar, he enjoyed it more than any other subsequent trip to the country. One fellow traveller, Graham Barlow, went on to be an England colleague.

That constant source of fascination, the Willis action, was now embedded in his muscle memory, and it came under the spotlight upon his return to the UK and winter nets with Surrey. The coach, Arthur McIntyre, felt that something more ortho-dox was required and tried to reshape it. The results bordered on the comic, with Bob all over the place and several times bowling into the side netting and even the next lane. It was quickly decided to leave well alone, and McIntyre had clearly seen something he liked. In March 1969 Bob was pulled aside after one dreary indoor session at Crystal Palace and offered a season's trial with Surrey, paying £12.50 per week.

Any initial euphoria about becoming a contracted professional cricketer did not last long into the summer of 1969. For a start his parents, when confronted with the reality, were less enamoured than ever with the idea. Bob's innocent expectations were also quickly dashed as he failed to even make the second team at the start of the season, suffering the humiliation of being used as a makeshift scorer. One evening in May he came home in tears and flung his cricket bag down in the kitchen, feeling ready to give up and settle for a more conventional life. The next morning he came down to find his father had cleaned his kit and packed it neatly, with the instruction that if he was to make a proper go of cricket he needed to look the part.

Ted Willis was not a man who would use ten words when one would do, and while he had reservations about his son's choice of career he was quietly supportive. 'Fundamentally he and Bob had a good relationship,' says David. 'They were temperamentally quite alike – shy in quite a lot of ways, but with a dry sense of humour.'

The paternal intervention was crucial on this occasion. The young Willis gradually settled in at Surrey and in July was asked to play for the first team in a one-off game against Scotland. Bob took 3–13 in the first innings, putting him in a strong position when a break presented itself the following month. Improbable as it may seem now, Bob's good friend and fellow Surrey paceman Jim Cumbes had been summoned back early to attend pre-season with his winter employers, Tranmere Rovers, where he was a goalkeeper. This, coupled with Test call-ups, had left the first team short for two away matches, versus Yorkshire at the atmospheric seaside venue of Scarborough's North Marine Road, and then against Nottinghamshire at Trent Bridge.

Having hitched a lift and spent the journey north crammed into the back seat of team-mate Younis Ahmed's Hillman Imp, Bob played a modest part in a narrow victory. He bowled Barrie Leadbeater, after taking the new ball, to record his initial first-class victim. It was when they moved down to Nottingham that he properly announced himself, late on the first day of the match. By the close the home team were 26–4, with the rookie opening bowler having claimed all four wickets. Again the elation was short-lived as the following day he took some punishment, with Garry Sobers almost hitting him for six back over his head off the first ball. Still, he emerged with figures of 5–78, and a few more Surrey appearances were clocked up by the end of the summer.

In those days there was no wintering away for young players, even one who had now been offered a contract for the coming season. Reality hit again in the form of job hunting, which led to a stint working in the billing department of Harrods, commuting in from Cobham every day. While he did not find settling up the personal accounts of the store's well-heeled customers exactly scintillating, he came to look back on his time working in such mundane jobs as grounding. He also enjoyed the substantial discount employees could use for their own shopping, while in the evenings he developed his hobby of going to concerts, both contemporary and classical.

This humble if happy enough routine was livened up by playing as a goalkeeper in the lower rungs of semi-professional football, for Guildford City Reserves. Contrary to his cricketing experiences, he found the other players took it more seriously than him, which was not entirely to his liking. It was also a winter when Geoff Howarth, the New Zealand batsman and Surrey team-mate, lodged with the Willis family, and they became firm friends. They could not have known that one day they would captain against one another in a Test series.

While he was very much a Surrey lad, Bob's relationship with the county was never an entirely straightforward one, and the summer of 1970 saw his full introduction to the political highways and byways of the professional game. It was something of an eye-opener in terms of all the dressing-room wrangles he would encounter, until the end of his playing days and beyond.

The county was stocked with good players, yet this was not a particularly happy era in its history. The first team was riven with splits and had a reputation around the circuit for being surly. The home pitches, at the time, were hard work for the quicker bowlers and there was an air of suspicion felt towards the younger players by those more senior. By now accustomed to the social side of the game, Bob often found himself going out for a drink with the opposition after a day's work rather than his team-mates, who would usually opt to disperse home. (One of the few exceptions was Robin Jackman, with whom he was sometimes competing for a place in the attack.) The

situation was not helped by the feudal attitude of the committee, who had an almost non-existent relationship with those
inside the dressing room.

Despite an atmosphere that was not exactly conducive to
enjoyment, Bob's career was starting to motor. Although he
ended the season in the second team, he had come close to
establishing himself as a regular first-teamer, and notched up
14 first-class appearances, taking 40 wickets at 28 apiece. At
the very least he knew he now belonged at that level, and the
self-doubt which had plagued him the previous season was a
thing of the past.

Another winter loomed of making ends meet while longing
for summer. This time the source of employment came from
Surrey, who were looking for coaches to work with children
down at their indoor Crystal Palace base. Sensing that it was
time to spread his wings, Bob moved into a one-bedroom flat
in Streatham with one of the older boys he had befriended at
Guildford RGS, Martin Tyler. As with Howarth, it was a case
of two young men living together who would later make much
bigger names for themselves, in Tyler's case becoming one of
English football's best-known TV commentators. Both would
confirm that the young Surrey player was the more domesti-
cated of the two.

The primarily cricket half of the flatshare was also enjoying
his football again. Bob had been approached by Corinthian
Casuals, the venerable amateur team who competed with semi-
professionals, and he happily accepted the offer to become their
goalkeeper. There was some surprise when he was informed
that his debut would be in the first qualifying round of the FA
Cup, away to Hornchurch. Leading 2–0 with ten minutes to

go, they contrived to lose 3–2, and that was with the new goalie saving a late penalty. They often struggled against more thoroughly prepared teams, but the post-match enjoyment more than made up for it. Eventually they actually won a match, after thirteen successive defeats.

It was a contented and carefree existence, with Bob going in every day to Crystal Palace to coach, expecting the routine to continue until the days started getting longer and warmer.

That is, until one morning in mid-November, when he was summoned from the nets to take a call in the office. He thought it would be a schoolmaster wishing to make some group-coaching arrangement. Instead, an unfamiliar voice came down the line: 'It's Billy Griffith from the MCC. Alan Ward has been injured and is coming home. We would like you to go to Australia.'

3

THE TIMES THEY
ARE A-CHANGIN'

The fateful phone call from Lord's hit Bob like a freight train. Before he could tackle any of the logistical issues, he had to try and assimilate what had happened. A year previously he had been working as a clerk in Harrods, after a modest introductory season to county cricket. Six months prior to that he had been close to despair during a difficult first few weeks as a professional.

Progress had been made, but still his name had only been vaguely mentioned on the margins of debates about who might be taken to Australia before the squad was announced. He assumed that someone like his far more experienced, and more guileful, Surrey team-mate Geoff Arnold would assuredly be ahead of him in the selectors' thoughts. What transpired was that Ray Illingworth, captain of the team that was already there and preparing in Queensland, had asked around for recommendations. The main qualification he sought was sheer pace.

As Illingworth was to recount to Cricinfo: 'I used to talk to John Edrich and Geoff Boycott quite a bit about things and I asked them: "Where do we go from here?" John told me to go for this young lad, 6 ft 6 in, sharp and able to bowl it in the right areas. I remember asking: "Are you sure, John?" And the reply was: "I don't think he will let you down." So I went on John's say-so.'

Bob was given thirty-six hours to get ready, and in those days there was, of course, no coterie of backroom staff to smooth the process. A new cricket case had to be purchased, as did a suit for the functions the players were required to attend. Then there was a series of jabs before heading to Heathrow for a complicated journey. Bob estimated that there were at least six stops en route to Brisbane, the most exotic being Beirut.

His sense of disorientation upon arrival was added to by being surrounded by a new set of team-mates, most of whom he had never met. Some of them were childhood heroes, like John Snow. In the singular, poetry-loving Sussex fast bowler he quickly found a kindred spirit, while wicketkeeper Bob Taylor was a welcoming room-mate.

An early discovery was the sheer heat in which he was expected to perform, which was nothing like anything he had previously experienced. Another was Australian beer. Being a disciple of bitter since his days as a teenage club cricketer, he made the schoolboy error of thinking that the comparatively insipid-tasting Australian version was automatically lower in alcohol content. Summoned to the first of the many local functions that were customary for touring sides back then, he tucked into the tinnies, only to find that this was emphatically not the case – and got embarrassingly plastered.

He was not required for the Brisbane Test, a high-scoring draw, after which the team made the long journey across to Perth. The record shows that Bob made his first-class debut for MCC on 5 December against Western Australia, taking four wickets in a drawn match, including that of Rodney Marsh, the newly capped Test wicketkeeper.

Like the first, the second Test was a stalemate draw, notable only for the growing controversy over the tourists' inclination to bowl an excess of bouncers, often delivered by Snow. This, in turn, led to Bob's discovery that it was not just in the county game that politics played a major part; far from it. There was friction developing between the dressing room and the management, who made it clear they were unhappy about England's approach in the opening two matches of the series. The relationship between Illingworth and tour manager David Clark came close to breaking down after Clark made public comments along those lines.

Christmas was spent in Tasmania before the New Year Test in Melbourne was washed out, leading to more political ructions. An extra Test was scheduled by the management and presented to the players as a fait accompli, without reference to Illingworth. Another row developed before a further £100 was added to the tour fee, and the party moved on to New South Wales.

It was here that Bob got his break, although only through the misfortune of someone else. Playing an up-country match, Lancashire's Ken Shuttleworth badly strained a groin muscle, ruling him out of the fourth Ashes match at Sydney. Bob was informed the night before the Test began that he was playing. A predictably sleepless night – insomnia was something that would plague Bob his whole life – ensued.

He need not have immediately worried as he sat out the opening day waiting to bat, before going in on the second morning, on a hat-trick, to face the spin of John Gleeson. What was to come was a precursor to plenty of overlooked contributions at number eleven. Plonking a long defensive stride forwards, he survived and went on to hold up an end and add 41 with Peter Lever for the last wicket, dour determination proving a more powerful weapon than elegance. It was not a game in which Bob played a huge part elsewhere, taking a solitary wicket when Ashley Mallett gloved one down the leg side to Alan Knott. Geoff Boycott made 142 on a difficult pitch and Snow took the wickets as the tourists romped home by 299 runs.

By the time they got back to Melbourne for match number five Bob had already been on tour for more than two months – and that after arriving three weeks late. It is another reminder of how modern itineraries have changed. Retaining his place, he took 3–73 in the first innings, including the wickets of captain Bill Lawry and Greg Chappell.

Melbourne proved an unmemorable draw, and the sixth Test in Adelaide also ended in stalemate. But there were three more Willis wickets and, while he had not set the world alight, the somewhat left-field decision to summon the rookie from Crystal Palace was proving a sound one.

It was mid-February of 1971 by the time the seventh and final Test was played, back at Sydney. If what had gone before had sometimes entered the realms of tedium, that was all about to change. The issue of England's aggressive bowling had been simmering for months, and now it was about to explode as the home side tried to save the series. Skipper Bill Lawry, who Bob had dismissed again in Adelaide, was dropped for the match, ushering in the reign of the abrasive Ian Chappell. Boycott was injured and England were down to the bare bones of a squad.

This was to be a fourth Test for Bob, and poignantly his father, Ted, was there. Ted's constant if understated support had been rewarded: his son was shaping up to be an England regular. A whip-round among BBC colleagues had enabled him to fly down to watch the last match of the series.

It was to be tightly contested throughout. England were bowled out for 184 in their first innings and Australia built a lead through the efforts of Greg Chappell, who started to run out of partners. Intent on removing the tail-enders, Snow bowled a shortish ball, which Terry Jenner ducked into, and the blow on the head required him to go to hospital. While Jenner was later to admit it was his own fault, umpire Lou Rowan issued a warning for intimidatory bowling. Long leg was probably not the best place for Snow to be fielding, and when he next walked down there he was met with a hail of bottles and beer cans. After a hiatus for the field to be cleaned up Snow resumed his position on the boundary, only for a spectator to lean over the fence, grab his arm and try and wrestle him into the crowd.

Snow managed to wriggle free, and by this time Bob was sauntering down to offer some back-up to his colleague, with whom he had become close on the long tour. He was also able to pass on the news that Illingworth was about to take the players off the pitch to allow things to calm down. Watching up in the press box, former Australian captain Bill O' Reilly was not impressed by the younger player's intervention. He memorably wrote in his *Sydney Morning Herald* column: 'What did Willis think he could do to help? He looks like a two-iron with ears.' Bob was forever tickled about that.

Illingworth attempted a restart but then ended up evacuating the field of play: 'We agreed to start and then it all began again, and that is when I took them off,' recalled the captain, who had already been riled by the fact that his team were not given a single lbw in the first six matches. 'Rowan was making it appear as if it was nothing, but the bloke who moved the sightscreen was hit on the back of the head by a bottle and was taken to hospital.'

The standard of umpiring on that tour had already left quite an impression on Bob, and it informed his view thereafter about the chronically poor officiating he often encountered. He considered Australians among the worst of the breed, the decision-making either incompetent or plain biased. Early on in that tour, for example, he had what he considered a cast-iron appeal turned down. On walking back to his mark he politely asked the umpire how the ball could have been missing the stumps and received the reply: 'Well, I've got to get my eye in too, you know.'

When the proceedings at Sydney got going again, the contest continued to be close, and Australia were left needing 223 to win. Potential disaster struck when Snow was put out of action after colliding with the boundary fence, heaping more responsibility on the young Willis. With the whole elongated series at stake, it fell to the inexperienced Surrey quick and Lancastrian Peter Lever to make up for the loss of their main strike bowler. Bob would come to reflect that, although he took only 1–32 from his nine overs on the fourth afternoon, it was one of the spells in his career of which he was most proud. By the close Australia were reduced to 123–5, and the next morning a masterstroke from Illingworth, to resume with himself and

Derek Underwood bowling, saw them lose their last five wickets for 37 runs. A 2–0 series win in Australia, never something to be underestimated, had been secured even though the two most effective players – Snow and Boycott – were out of commission by the end.

Bob had a disdain for champagne that lasted all his life, but he made an exception in the celebrations that day. Rod Marsh, one of the Australian players who was to become a friend, joined him for a drink in the dressing room. What meant the most, however, was being able to seek out his father and invite him to the inner sanctum, where they were able to jointly toast an incredible winter.

Yet still the tour was not over. The party moved on to New Zealand for two largely forgettable Tests, with Bob missing out to the restored Shuttleworth in the first, before coming back for the second. He was not to know that, after playing his part for the previous four months, it would be more than two years before he would once again pull on an England sweater.

By the time they touched down at Heathrow it was the middle of March, with only two weeks off before pre-season began back at The Oval. While the squad was garlanded upon its return, there was to be no hero's welcome at Surrey, despite the fact that he was now the proud owner of five England caps.

Pressingly, there was the need to negotiate a contract for the 1971 season, which had been put on hold. He was shocked to be offered only £750, feeling that his new status deserved something considerably better. It did not help that the county already had four other bowlers vying to take the new ball – Geoff

Arnold, David Sydenham, Stewart Storey and Robin Jackman. And nor, it transpired, was it helpful that he was simply exhausted, unsurprisingly, from the mental and physical exertions of the winter just gone. There was bound to be a hangover from such a dramatic turn of events since November, and it showed in his lethargy at the start of the preparations for the summer. Bob had a strong feeling that there was a sense of schadenfreude around the Oval dressing room as he struggled to regain energy and rhythm.

His lacklustre form ruled out the immediate retention of his England spot. From being one of England's Ashes heroes he quickly found himself relegated to the Surrey second team, and persona non grata among the club hierarchy. What really broke his relationship with the county was a meeting with the secretary, Geoffrey Howard, early in the season to discuss his future.

Elder brother David was a source of advice and support, and he remembers what particularly incensed Bob. It was to result in him leaving the county with which he had previously felt such an affinity.

'At the meeting Bob said his piece and suggested to Howard that he would be better off moving elsewhere if he wanted to regain his England place,' says David. 'Howard told Bob to be patient and said that "your time will come". Bob had registered his concerns and the meeting ended. A couple of hours later Bob's work at The Oval finished for the day and he made his way back to Vauxhall to catch the train home. He picked up a copy of the *Evening Standard*, only to spot the headline "WILLIS DEMANDS FIRST-TEAM CAP – EXCLUSIVE."

'He then read an embellished report of what was meant to be a private and confidential meeting. He was incandescent with rage, which was rare but quite a sight. Bob insisted that the question of his first-team cap had never been mentioned when they talked. He was so angry he resolved to leave Surrey and seek another county, no matter what the cost. Some of his team-mates attempted to dissuade him from leaving, but his mind was made up.'

After a couple of months his appetite for the game returned. Although a recall to the England team remained far off, the second half of the season saw him regain his place in the Surrey first team. He played six matches as they forged their way to their first County Championship triumph since 1958.

Micky Stewart and Ken Barrington were among those who visited his flat to try and assure him that his future lay at The Oval. The feeling seemed to be that the happier spirit prevailing at Surrey, engendered by on-field success, would be enough for the parties to reconcile.

Like many top sportspeople, Bob possessed the stubborn streak of a mule and he was not for turning. He also had a remarkably frank conversation with his friend Jackman about the situation, in which he concluded that one of them would have to go and that, as the less established player, it was only right that it should be him.

At that time the profile of county cricket was such that the questions over his future constituted big news, something akin to what major football-transfer gossip might attract today. The levels of interest were added to by the fact that it was relatively rare for significant players to switch counties, with most moving elsewhere only because they had been discarded.

Bob informing Surrey that he was leaving sparked a scramble for his services, with twelve counties in the hunt. One offer, from Glamorgan, was particularly inventive, as it included the guarantee of a goalkeeping winter contract on the playing staff of Swansea City. But the two most attractive approaches came from the wealthiest counties of the day, Warwickshire and Lancashire.

Several things swung it for Warwickshire, with one being, naturally enough, that they were offering three times the money that was on the table from Surrey. They had a formidable clutch of West Indians floating around – Deryck Murray, Rohan Kanhai, Lance Gibbs and Alvin Kallicharran – and were favourites to wrest the County Championship away from The Oval the next season. Bob was also flattered by the chairman and captain travelling down to London to try and persuade him. While he admitted his initial perception of Birmingham was that it was a 'concrete jungle of a place', it had in its favour the fact that his old mate Jim Cumbes, now doubling up for West Bromwich Albion and Worcestershire, would be living close by.

The deal was done quickly enough for him to become a Warwickshire player in 1972, but there were complications. In the early 1970s changing counties was regarded as unseemly in some quarters. In fact, the Test and County Cricket Board had a whole subcommittee to deal with what was considered a contentious area, sitting in judgement on each case.

By late September 1971 Bob was on the dole, having had to sign on at the season's end, barely six months after coming back from the triumphant Ashes tour. The TCCB ended up ruling that he would have to miss the first two months of the 1972 season as penance for leaving his county of origin. The player himself was not happy, but A.C. Smith, the establishment-minded Warwickshire captain, persuaded him that acceptance was for the best, and that he should quietly sit it out.

This enforced spell on the sidelines proved surprisingly agreeable. He played for a welcoming Warwickshire second team and found an immediate social circle in Harborne, built around Cumbes and his West Bromwich team-mates.

By the time July came around, the strange fact was that he had featured in far more second-team than first-class cricket since his return from the Ashes fifteen months previously. But he then played the last nine matches as Warwickshire duly won the County Championship. After being made twelfth man for the last Ashes Test of the summer, back at The Oval, Bob fully expected a summons for the winter tour to India and Pakistan. The call never came.

In those days there was no text message or phone contact ahead of squad announcements, just an agonising wait listening to the radio as the BBC announced the party. Especially agonising when your surname begins with a 'W'. The non-selection was hugely deflating and sparked another frantic search for winter employment. This came in the shape of an offer to coach youngsters in South Africa for several months, although not to play for a team. The wait for a return to the England set-up was becoming a yawning interlude. It was to be an enduring pattern in his career – the advance of several steps forward, followed by several in the opposite direction.

4

HURRICANE

When Bob got back into the England side late in the summer of 1973 it was apparent that a new era was dawning for Test cricket. And it was one that helped him press his claims for a regular place. The trend was moving towards the employment of aggressive fast bowlers, using tactics that were often intimidatory. Given that helmets had not been invented, this was no time to be a faint-hearted batsman.

Australia had come across the firebrands Jeff Thomson and Dennis Lillee, while the West Indies were about to discover an arsenal of quicks who could meet fire with fire. England were going to need all the artillery they could muster.

Now happily ensconced in Birmingham, finding it a far more enjoyable city than he had initially feared, Bob had settled in well at Warwickshire. The winter had been relaxing and he was fully charged up for the challenges ahead. While his county team, denuded of its West Indian stars, was struggling by recent high standards, his own form was highly encouraging. In June, he claimed two hat-tricks within a week: one against Yorkshire in the old Sunday league and another against Cambridge University.

En route to an overall haul of 58 first-class wickets in the season, he received, at long last, a recall to the England team. A three-Test series was taking place against the West Indies, with the last one at Lord's. When he stepped back into the international arena on 23 August, it had been almost two and a half years since his last cap, in Auckland.

In a wider context, the match was a herald of what was to come, with the home side going down to a heavy defeat by an innings. The tourists racked up a gargantuan 652–8, but in opening the bowling he was one of the few players to emerge with any credit. Bob dismissed the top four batsmen, the impressive quartet of Roy Fredericks, Deryck Murray, Rohan Kanhai and Clive Lloyd, in returning figures of 4–118.

An international debut in one-day cricket quickly followed (although it was several years before he became a regular in the short form). A dramatic game it was too, in early September at Headingley, for what was the West Indies' first ever limited-overs international. Having taken 2–29, he and Derek Underwood then guided England to a one-wicket victory with three balls to spare, Bob unbeaten on five.

Change was in the air for England, with Ray Illingworth relieved of the Test captaincy, being replaced by Scotsman Mike Denness. This time, when the touring party was announced for the coming winter trip to the Caribbean, there was little doubt that the maturing Warwickshire fast bowler would be included. Duly picked, Bob made a short trip to South Africa to fulfil the last of his coaching commitments there, then set off with his spirits high.

Not for the first or last time, however, the dream proved better than the reality. In fact Bob always found – right through to his broadcasting days – that, for all its glorious weather, the West Indies was a distant third in terms of places he liked to visit, behind Australia and New Zealand. A summary of his view was that it was a better place for a two-week holiday than a three-month cricket tour.

While there were ructions within the England camp on the trip, he also discovered an underlying sense of animosity from the opposition that extended beyond the boundary. At an early social function which both teams were required to attend, he made an attempt to fraternise with his Warwickshire colleagues Kanhai, Murray and spinner Lance Gibbs. Instead of being greeted warmly, he found them disarmingly standoffish. 'Perhaps I was naive but it took me by surprise,' he later recalled. 'I'd had no problem with any of them in the Warwickshire dressing room, but got the feeling it was about a bit more than cricket. I was particularly surprised by the attitude of Lance, who was a lovely bloke and someone I had got on particularly well with in Birmingham.'

He was also getting a reminder of what he had encountered in Australia, namely that internal politics were rarely far below the surface when it came to the England dressing room. The management seemed remote and high-handed, while there were issues over the captaincy of Denness. A self-effacing man and not a natural communicator, he had to contend with the resentment felt by Geoff Boycott at being overlooked for the vice-captaincy, let alone the skipper's job. There was also another extremely strong character in the side, Tony Greig.

Bob was never to have an easy relationship with the Greatest Living Yorkshireman. He respected Boycott enormously as a player and thinker about the game, but was less keen on the self-focused ways that came, Bob acknowledged, as part of the package. Greig he warmed to more, and also had immense respect for, but over the years they would sometimes find themselves on opposite sides of an argument.

A fractious team meeting followed an opening Test defeat at Port-of-Spain. An inquest was going on into the bowling performance when Bob failed to endear himself to some colleagues by piping up, 'What about the batting?' It is an age-old dividing line in any cricket team when things aren't going well.

He was actually in some turmoil at the time about the technicalities of his famous bowling method. Since the latter stages of the previous season he had experimented with a shortened run-up, which had initially shown signs of promise. Now he was finding it hard to discover any kind of rhythm, which was always the key to whether he bowled well or not. He was also aware, at the back of his mind, that he was not fit enough.

The second Test was saved by a monumental second-innings 262 from Warwickshire colleague Dennis Amiss, which was crucially prolonged by another number-eleven cameo at the other end, Bob surviving unbeaten for 41 balls. The tourists' batsmen also dug in to save the third Test, although, for the second successive time, the West Indies reached just shy of 600 and they only needed to bat once. Having taken a total of just five wickets in the opening three matches, the highlight of which was upending the great Garry Sobers at Bridgetown, Bob was dropped. He was reduced to the role of spectator as England somehow emerged from the five-Test series with a 1–1 draw, holding out until the last match, which was won by 26 runs, thanks largely to 13 wickets from Greig.

Any satisfaction at this remarkable turnaround in team fortunes was clouded for Bob by his limited contribution and the technical problems he was experiencing. Still prone to play the rebel, he let his frustration boil over on the way home when the party stopped off to play an inconsequential friendly against Bermuda. Despite the opposition being no better than decent club standard, he unleashed a series of bouncers against the unsuspecting amateurs in the morning session. A furious Donald Carr, the tour manager, met him on the way into lunch and a stand-up row ensued which, awkwardly, brought the pavilion to a standstill.

Such a headstrong attitude was duly noted in the tour report, and it was not a particularly happy Willis who returned to Warwickshire. While he would admit to a degree of lingering immaturity at this stage of his career, the more fundamental problem was that he was not doing enough to guard his towering frame against the physical rigours of fast bowling. This was to become a developing theme, hampering efforts to establish himself as a regular in England colours.

A decent start to the summer of 1974 saw him picked for the first Test against the visiting Indians, and his return went well enough against a team in the throes of its familiar struggles when playing away from home. Bob took 4–64 in the first innings and added to his burgeoning reputation as a stubborn number eleven by making a then Test-best 24, in a last-wicket stand of 63 with Keith Fletcher. It was a comfortable victory, notable only for being the last England match played by Geoffrey Boycott before he put himself into international self-isolation for three years.

This should have been a summer in which to rack up more caps, but a side strain kept Bob out of the next Test. As the team kept on winning in his absence, he had to content himself with the routine of county cricket, coupled with spells recovering from minor ailments. A sustained run of fitness saw him recalled for the final Test of the English season, versus Pakistan at The Oval. Opening the bowling with former county teammate Geoff Arnold on a dead wicket was a thankless task, and it turned into a predictable high-scoring draw.

It had been enough, however, to secure a place on England's winter tour, which would see the attempted defence of the Ashes he had played an unexpected part in winning four years previously. This time there was to be no dramatic summons from winter coaching sessions at Crystal Palace, and not even an especially tortured wait as the names of the squad were read out on the BBC.

For someone not naturally inclined towards unbridled optimism, this was another trip that Bob set off on with high expectations, only for what eventuated to prove somewhat more uncomfortable. The same old pattern.

It would go down as one of the most brutal Ashes series played, thanks to the no-holds-barred captaincy style of Ian Chappell and the full emergence of Jeff Thomson as the strike partner of Dennis Lillee. Denness was still England captain, and after the successes of the summer he enjoyed more natural authority among his men than he had the previous winter. This was to be sorely tested, however, to the point where he felt the need to drop himself before the series was out.

The England players got their first sight of Thomson in a warm-up game against Queensland and were not overly impressed. That turned out to be a severe misjudgement, as did the expectation that the fire of Lillee might have been doused by recurring injuries. Any hopes of a relatively easy ride were dashed in the first Test at Brisbane, where the city's mayor, Clem Jones, had taken over curator duties and prepared an unpredictable pitch after several days of heavy rain. This proved borderline frightening for England's batsmen, although it was not unhelpful for the Willis method. He took seven wickets in the match and, it should be added, stood firm for 55 balls unbeaten in his tail-ender role. Thomson, meanwhile, was using a barrage of short balls, delivered with that distinctive sling-shot action that was so hard to pick. He announced himself with nine wickets as England perished by 166 runs.

Bob's low opinion of Australian umpires didn't improve during this tour. On his first visit in 1970–71 a major issue had been the likelihood of hell freezing over before the tourists would be given an lbw decision. This time he was among those astonished by the lack of restraint exercised by the officials against the aggressive tactics of the hosts. Historians came to judge this match, which left Edrich and Amiss with damaged hands, as the definitive start of the fast-bowling terror.

It was accompanied by continuous sledging, tacitly encouraged by Chappell. That England were quickly in some disarray was emphasised by the sudden call-up of Colin Cowdrey, just shy of his forty-second birthday, for the second match in Perth.

Among the memorable incidents of this meeting, on a pitch that was plain fast rather than unpredictable, was Thomson shattering the box of David Lloyd, later to become Bob's friend and colleague in the Sky commentary team. 'He was in at number three, and there was no question of any quick singles,' recalls Lloyd of when the portly Cowdrey joined him at the crease. 'He came up to me and said: "I say, this is rather fun, isn't it?" I replied: "I've been in funnier situations than this."'

Bob was also struggling to see the amusing side of life as his team slumped to a nine-wicket defeat at the WACA. 'There is no doubt in my mind that fear was a factor in this series,' he recalled in *Lasting the Pace*. 'Batsmen emerged shaken and bewildered as if they had just come out of the trenches after some particularly violent crossfire. It is amazing that the possibility of wearing helmets was never mentioned.'

The series also saw the introduction of the now traditional Boxing Day Test in Melbourne, with 250,000 spectators enjoying a far more competitive contest. It marked the first time that provision was made for England players' wives and children to fly out and join their husbands over the festive period. Bob, still determinedly a bachelor, took a dim view, and although his opinions on the subject softened in later years, he always saw the practice as a potential distraction. Tour manager Alec Bedser, another bachelor, also struggled with the concept and was none too pleased when a newspaper produced a cartoon of him carrying a teddy bear onto the team bus.

Thomson, meanwhile, was now a folk hero among his people, full of swagger and giving interviews suggesting that he enjoyed hurting the Poms. Such was the impression he made that it contributed to the febrile and often drunken behaviour of the crowd, and the match at the MCG was marred by several pitch invasions, to the horror of traditionalists. It was around this time that the legend of the ground's notorious Bay 13 began to develop, the raucous Melburnian retort to Sydney's infamous Hill.

Socially, Bob found that he rather liked Thomson, initially much preferring him to the abrasive Lillee. The Boxing Day match turned into a thrilling draw, the home team ending up eight runs short of victory with two wickets left standing. Bob excelled in the first innings, taking his first five-wicket haul in a Test. Yet again his batting resistance proved invaluable, contributing 28 runs. In later life he rarely referred to this aspect of his game, unbothered by the widely held perception that it was hopeless, and he would refer to it in largely self-deprecating terms. But it was another example of his courage.

Denness was among those caught up in the shell shock of the Australian assault, and he dropped himself for the next game, in Sydney, after repeated batting failures. The reins were handed over to John Edrich but it made little difference, with the series reverting to type and another big Australian win. Keith Fletcher took a sickening blow to the forehead, and when Bob looked back on that game, he said that at one point he feared for the life of fellow tail-ender Arnold when he was at the crease.

By now Bob was suffering badly with the onset of knee problems, after pounding in repeatedly on hard grounds. In the fifth match at Adelaide, with Denness back in charge, Bob was sparingly used and was reduced to hobbling around by the end. Despite the absence of Thomson, who had bizarrely put his shoulder out while serving during a game of tennis, another thumping defeat put the tourists 4–0 down.

Bob had other matters on his mind beyond the latest reverse in a series whose outcome had long been inevitable. Back at the team hotel he needed to haul himself up the stairs by grabbing the banisters to relieve the pain in his knees, and it was clear that his bruising tour was over. It had been a chastening experience on the pitch, although the tour can also be dated as the beginning of his love affair with Australia – umpires notwith-standing – and particularly Adelaide. Having resolved to make an effort to get out and enjoy the country and mix with the locals, he had found it a pleasurable way of unwinding that proved beneficial to his performances. It was in the South Australian capital where he would make some of his closest friends and where, it turned out, a portion of his own ashes would come to be buried.

Bob was back in England by the time the team garnered a little self-respect with a consolation win in the final Test. It was probably no coincidence that Lillee and Thomson were also injured. Despite missing the last match, the list of averages showed Willis as the tourists' joint highest wicket taker, on 17, alongside Underwood, and that was cause enough to be relatively satisfied. There was, however, a send-off in the form of an interview given by Australian captain Chappell which hit a raw nerve.

The subject of England's bowling performance had arisen, and in characteristically blunt fashion Chappell remarked that Willis was quite the threat before lunch, but that by the post-tea period he was easy pickings and not the same bowler. The implication that he lacked fitness and stamina stung, but Bob was not so headstrong as to ignore the possibility that the comment had a foundation of truth.

The immediate priority, however, was to get his knees seen to. He was not to know that, when the necessary procedures came, they would threaten to bring an end to not just his career, but his whole life.

5

PAY IN BLOOD

Danger was lurking around the corner after Bob made his early return to England from Australia in February 1975. Reluctant to go under the knife to try and fix his knees, he made one last attempt to defy the inevitable and play on without resorting to surgery. Workouts during the spring were promising enough for him to play a group-stage match in the old 55-over Benson and Hedges competition in April, in which he was able to complete his allotted spells.

Yet it was to be attempting to climb the stairs, again, which served as the final reminder that he could not ignore the damage caused by years of wear and tear. That night, having sent down 11 overs, he was once more reduced to pulling himself up using his arms on the banisters.

A few days later he was in hospital, having two operations at once, with investigations showing that the pads of tissue behind both kneecaps were badly worn. These passed off uneventfully enough, and after a week of immobilisation he was able to start walking around on crutches. As he lay back in bed, a friend came to visit and they were both enjoying a glass of gin when Bob suddenly felt an excruciating pain in his arm. The duty nurse quickly sensed what was happening, sparking off some frantic, and very scary, activity. She immediately summoned back-up, the room was cleared and a specialist diagnosed that he had suffered a pulmonary embolism, emanating from the calf. As it turned out, the threat had already passed. The terrifying thing was, the doctor explained, that had it gone through his heart less quickly it would have killed him.

This sobering experience was followed by several months of painstaking rehabilitation. Finally, on 17 August 1975, he was able to play a John Player League game against Worcestershire, taking three somewhat expensive wickets. Three first-class appearances were possible afterwards, but it was to be the least productive summer of his career.

A strange, slightly lost winter ensued. This England cricketer, who had so far amassed 16 Test caps, signed on the dole once more. His inactivity was ostensibly to give himself space to get fully fit for the following summer. Yet, as he was to reflect in later years, he allowed himself to lapse into a lazy stupor prior to Christmas, moping around as the months yawned before him. Bad habits, such as drinking more than was healthy for an athlete, set in. It was only with the approach of New Year that he resolved to take advantage of the fact that his knees were now fit for purpose. After a trip to mid-Wales over Christmas he began to start running in earnest.

The off-season finished on an equally unusual note, with a month-long trip to Los Angeles in the company of Alan Knott. The Kent wicketkeeper had been invited to do some private coaching for a group of cricket nuts based in California and was asked to bring someone along with him. Bob was invited and for several weeks found himself billeted among Mormon families. There was little chance for any hedonism, and he checked back in with Warwickshire for the 1976 season suitably fit and refreshed.

*   *   *

That summer was to be the driest on modern record, and it brought with it the challenge of the West Indies. By then they had assembled an arsenal of fast bowlers with even more fire-power than the Australians had. The spearhead was Michael Holding, who was to become one of Bob's closest broadcasting colleagues. Not only did the islanders have a frightening physical capability, they were also fired up by the comments of Tony Greig, who had replaced Denness as captain. Far from making the tourists 'grovel', in his indelicate phrasing from an interview that preceded the tour, England were getting pummelled.

After a heavy defeat in the third Test at Old Trafford, best remembered for the peppering of Brian Close and John Edrich late on the Saturday, Bob was recalled. His return to the side at Headingley on 22 July marked the end of another hiatus in his international career, this one having lasted seventeen months. The result at Leeds was a more respectable defeat, partly thanks to Bob's contribution of eight wickets. That total included two dismissals of the imperious Viv Richards, who appeared to have taken Greig's comments to heart more than anyone.

Bob was best known for his battles against the Australians, but they were not his only epic head-to-head confrontations. His encounters with Richards were particularly fiery, though underpinned by mutual respect. They were recalled in the West Indian great's autobiography, *Sir Vivian*:

> I didn't have too many problems with the English bowlers, even though the media often tried to hype up a war between myself and Bob Willis and then Devon Malcolm. The Bob Willis business blew up in 1973 when the MCC were touring the Caribbean. I faced Bob for the first time on that tour playing for the Leeward Islands, and he bowled five successive bouncers at me. I hit four

of them and I was visibly annoyed when I was out in the end to the fifth bouncer. But I enjoyed the confrontation. He had won that day, so I was determined to catch him on another day, not to let him get me out and to be even more aggressive than usual.

I had a contract to play in England the next year, and every time I played against him I tried to get the better of him. But what the critics failed to realise was that I did it because I rated him so high. People have weird opinions about Willis, but he was one of England's best and most hostile fast bowlers. Everyone thought Bob had a dodgy run-up, but you only have to look at how many wickets he took and how competitive he was to realise what an outstanding quickie he was. He was a bowler who looked to swing the ball in most often. His dot ball was the one that straightened a little bit, and I never knew when it was coming. He could also be hostile and really quick. I have seen him bounce people out, and to do that you have to have good pace; and to take over 300 Test wickets he had to be a bit special. And he was. It may surprise people, but, alongside Dennis Lillee, Bob Willis was the best fast bowler I faced.

That 1976 series, and its 3–0 victory, is now looked upon nostalgically by West Indies fans, with the team fanatically supported by Britons of Caribbean origin. Many years later it became a source of regret to Bob, and others who cared about the game, that this section of the population largely turned its back on cricket, and were lost to football in particular.

Greig, suitably chastened, was retained as captain for the winter tour of India. He was to become a major player in Bob's life in the coming twelve months, for all sorts of reasons.

Bob Willis – 'fast and fearless'.

Bob's parents, Ted and Anne Willis, aka 'Tannoy' and 'Grummidge'.

With his sister, Ann Conroy, and brother, David, at Bob's 65th birthday party in 2014.

With his daughter, Katie, in Adelaide in December 2017.

Grandson Jack gets all the attention at the Ashes Test at Melbourne in 2017.

Teasing wife Lauren Clark in 2015.

David Brown and Bob, Warwickshire's manager and captain, proudly hold the 1980 John Player League trophy – back in safe hands after its unscheduled overnight stay in a Birmingham pub.

'The Ashes come home.' Bob makes a bold fashion statement with Geoff Miller, John Lever, Graham Roope and Derek Randall at The Oval after clinching the 1977 series.

Michael Holding in imperious form on his way to taking 14 wickets at The Oval in 1976. He would later become one of Bob's closest broadcasting colleagues.

Sampling 'the old fast bowler's staple' – Dennis Lillee and Bob visit a brewery midway through the memorable 1981 Ashes series.

A menacing Lillee bowls to Mike Gatting as England struggle after being forced to follow on in the third Test at Headingley in 1981.

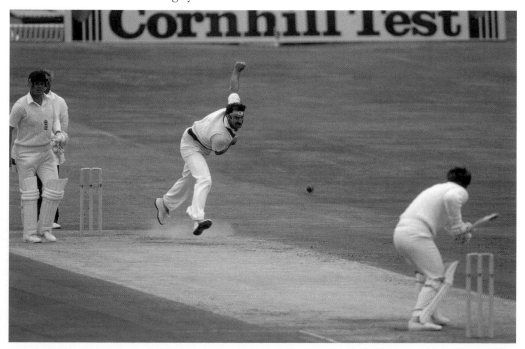

Ian Botham smashes Terry Alderman for six in his match-changing innings of 149 not out in the famous Headingley Test.

Rodney Marsh takes on a short ball from Bob, only to be caught by Graham Dilley just within the boundary rope.

'Beefy', 'Goose' and 'Brears' after beating a Packer-depleted Australia 5–1 in 1978–79. Two and a half years later, they would have their finest hour together against far tougher opposition.

'Why pick on us?' With Bob in the middle of the most devastating spell of his career, Allan Border is forced to take evasive action on the final day at Headingley in 1981.

No time to celebrate – after bowling Ray Bright to finish with figures of 8–43, Bob sprints for the safety of the pavilion.

Still struggling to enjoy the moment, Bob berates the press in a 'somewhat bizarre' interview with the BBC's Peter West after the extraordinary comeback victory.

Two series, two wins – in 1982, his successful first summer as captain, Bob takes the applause for the 2–1 victory over Pakistan that followed a 1–0 win against India.

Bob Willis, MBE – looking suitably honoured with Juliet at Buckingham Palace in 1982 and just about managing to keep his hat on.

Never a fan of champagne, Bob donates his share to a thirsty friend after Botham's match-winning 5–11 against Australia at Edgbaston in 1981 – as manager A.C. Smith diplomatically looks the other way.

Despite the thrashing at the hands of Richards and company, the South African-born all-rounder certainly had the respect of the dressing room, and he liked to lead from the front. The togetherness helped make it arguably the most enjoyable of all the trips Bob embarked on to the subcontinent. This even though it was accompanied by the outbreaks of illness that he rarely managed to avoid in those parts. If anything was going around, he usually got it.

By the time the second Test began on New Year's Day of 1977, England were already 1–0 up. A few eyebrows were raised as they found the conditions in Calcutta surprisingly favourable to pace and swing. If anything, the home team's strength of spin was negated. Opening the bowling with good friend J.K. Lever, Bob took 5–27 in the first innings as they extended the lead to 2–0. The outcome was much the same in the third match at Madras, which Bob reckoned, again surprisingly, to be the fastest wicket he had bowled on. India pulled one back in Bangalore, although Bob's decent form continued with his best Test figures of 6–53 in the first innings.

The series ended 3–1, with the party then reluctantly dragging itself to Sri Lanka for an extra seventeen days, to play a series of friendlies. Even then, the winter was not entirely over, however, for there remained the one-off Centenary Test in Melbourne.

England (still touring under the MCC banner) arrived there in early March, weary and not knowing entirely what to expect. The view of some was that it would be little more than an exhibition-style game, with plenty of social outings on the side.

This proved to be a badly misjudged reading of any contest that involved the two old enemies.

Bob recalled noticing that commercial obligations for the players were being ramped up around the game. At the time few knew exactly where this was heading. It would not be long before he and his colleagues would find out, with all the upheavals that were about to be unleashed by Kerry Packer.

On the field it was deeply competitive, with a Willis bouncer on the opening morning setting the tone. Australian opener Rick McCosker failed to get inside the line of an attempted hook and the ball hit him flush in the mouth, before falling onto his gloves and being diverted onto the stumps. Bob's celebrations quickly turned to concern as he saw the blood – it turned out that McCosker's jaw was broken.

Remarkably the Australian came out to bat in the second innings with his head bandaged and wired up, bravely contributing to a key stand with Rod Marsh that helped the home side to a narrow victory, despite a memorable 174 from Derek Randall. The England bowlers did, however, take it upon themselves to bowl a full length to the stricken McCosker. Bob saw that as a key difference in mentality between the game he had been brought up in and the way it was played in Australia at the time. He did not believe that, had an Englishman come out to bat in such a state, they would have been shown the same deference.

This was also the first time Bob came across a player with whom his fortunes were to become so entwined – Ian Botham. The fledgling 'Beefy' of future legend had made his one-day international debut at the end of the previous summer, although Bob, who had played only three ODIs up until 1977, was not present. Botham was now playing a winter of Grade cricket in Victoria and was brought along to help out around the dressing room, along with Yorkshire's Graham Stevenson. Bob's initial impressions of Botham were not entirely positive, and he was slightly taken aback by what he first thought of as cockiness, which later he came to understand as natural exuberance. He noted how the Somerset youngster was not shy of telling some of the much older players who had been invited to the match, the likes of Percy Fender, how many wickets he would be taking when picked for England in the coming summer.

Of more material long-term significance to the Willis career was a barbecue attended by some of the players after the match, in which he was to have two encounters that were to change his destiny.

The host was a cricket-loving hypnotherapist, Arthur Jackson, who several England players had come across on a previous tour. In conversation, Bob was talking about how sometimes he found the mental side of the game difficult, often feeling crippled with anxiety before and during matches, and unable to relax properly. Jackson invited him back to the house the following morning to try hypnotherapy and, despite some initial cynicism, the experience proved a revelation. Before Bob went back home Jackson made him a half-hour cassette by which he could hypnotise himself. He would send him others in the coming years to maintain the treatment.

Equally significant that night was a less emollient conversation that took place with Greig, tongues having been slightly loosened by the amber nectar. In response to Bob's observations about what a fine bowler Dennis Lillee had become, the captain fired back with unexpected venom. 'You should be able to bowl like that too, but you're always knackered after five overs,' was the gist of it. 'You need to get fitter. It could be the difference between earning peanuts and 70,000 dollars a year.'

Greig clearly knew something which others in the company did not at the time, namely that a scheme, lucrative for players, was brewing which was to rend asunder the international game.

The caustic exchange crystallised in Bob's own mind something of which he was already aware, Ian Chappell having made similar references to it previously. The criticism of his fitness hurt, and this time it prompted something of a Pauline conversion – he decided he was going to do something about it.

Armed with Jackson's cassette, Bob returned to Birmingham with a new resolve and set about establishing a programme based around the thinking of a fitness guru called Ernst van Aaken, who was a great advocate of the benefits of slow long-distance running. Soon his latest disciple was involved in a daily routine that featured lengthy, measured jogs around the suburbs of Birmingham and endless laps of the Edgbaston outfield.

England's influential physio Bernard Thomas did not entirely approve, but the results began to speak for themselves. Bob was to enjoy by far the longest sequence of consecutive England appearances of his career, one that was barely interrupted up to his retirement in 1984.

For Bob, the new regime of hard training and hypnotherapy brought with it the most positive outlook heading into the summer of 1977. Yet while the country celebrated the Silver Jubilee, the cricket parish found itself in a state of convulsion from the middle of May onwards.

That was when the Kerry Packer scheme burst into the open, led by the indomitable Greig, one of Packer's chief lieutenants. Essentially, the Australian media magnate had been seeking the TV rights to cricket in Australia. When he failed to obtain them, he hit on the idea of setting up a breakaway international version of the game to play unofficial series, signing up many of the world's top players.

The whole issue ran in parallel with a much-anticipated Ashes series, in which the Australian tourists would prove to be badly undermined by all the action going on offstage. It quickly emerged that most of Australia's top talent had been recruited, along with the vast majority of the top West Indians, a fair amount of the Pakistan team and a South African contingent grateful for what exposure they could get to cricket's highest level. The initial batch of Englishmen to enlist were Greig, Derek Underwood, John Snow and Alan Knott. Everyone else, including Bob, remained in the dark for the time being.

Greig was swiftly removed as England captain by a perturbed Lord's establishment, to be replaced by the more studious figure of Mike Brearley. This was followed by the return of Geoff Boycott to the fold after his self-imposed exile. Away from all the political shenanigans, it was to be the summer of the three Bs, as it was the series in which Botham leapt into the wider public consciousness for the first time.

Bob and others regretted the sacking of Greig, who remained available for selection. What they soon noticed among the opposition was that this was not the usual fearsome fighting machine of Australia they were up against – especially as Lillee was absent with injury – but a team under siege from its own administrators and media.

The first Test at Lord's saw Bob post a new set of Test-best figures, taking 7–78 in an eventual draw. As the fault lines in the opposition opened up, Australia were then thrashed at Manchester. The next two matches, at Nottingham and Leeds, were dominated by the feats of Boycott. In the former (which saw another five-wicket haul for Bob) he managed to run out local hero Derek Randall before making a hundred. At Headingley he fully established his legend among his fellow Yorkshiremen by making his 100th first-class hundred.

In between times Bob was picked for the three one-day internationals that took place in early July, the first decent run he had been given in the limited-over side. He would go on to rack up a total of 64 caps in the shorter form of the game.

The final Test, at The Oval, turned out to be a rain-affected, inconsequential draw, and it was very much more notable for all that was going on away from the pitch, with clandestine evening meetings afoot. Several more players were approached to seek out their availability for the coming launch of the Packer circus in Australia. Inevitably Bob was among them, especially as another five-wicket haul at his former home ground took his tally to 27 for the series, establishing him as the country's leading fast bowler. His stock had risen markedly since the start of the summer, when he had been left out of the original batch of Packer signings, and even though Bob Woolmer and Derek Randall were also in their sights, he was now the biggest target for the recruiters.

At the time Bob had a reputation, justifiably, for being very much his own man, not inclined to bow to convention. Not an outright rebel, but certainly not an establishment-minded individual, so there was every reason for World Series Cricket to believe that they would get their man. Greig approached him early during the Oval Test to tell him he was on the wanted list. On the second evening he and Randall were asked to attend a meeting with another of Packer's right-hand men, former player and commentating icon Richie Benaud. Bob recalled that he was impressed with Benaud's calm and reasoned sales pitch, which accepted that there were two sides to the argument, as international cricket stood on the verge of splitting.

After some negotiation through his solicitor, an offer guaranteeing £75,000 over five seasons was made to Bob – very considerable for cricket at a time when even the top players hardly lived in the lap of luxury. Greig continued with his efforts at persuasion in the coming weeks, and they had a meeting at a central London hotel. Bob was sorely tempted, although when told that he would be playing for a nebulous 'World XI', he found his enthusiasm for the pure cricketing side waning.

There was also a strong sense of loyalty to Warwickshire, where he now felt very much embedded, and to close friend and skipper David Brown in particular. Weighing against that was the desire for financial security, especially for someone who knew too well how fragile a fast bowler's body can be. Warwickshire made an offer to guarantee him three years' money and there was also a crucial intervention from businessman and MP David Evans, who stepped in to ensure that those who stayed 'loyal' would get a substantial increase in international fees.

'Bob played it quite smartly, and Evans ended up effectively guaranteeing him a decent level of income,' recounts his brother David. After a brief period of reflection the Packer offer was politely declined, and he threw in his lot with the established form of international cricket.

The whole affair was massive news at the time, and the mood was one of polarisation. You were either for or against Packer and, of outspoken inclination, Bob nailed his colours to the Lord's mast, somewhat to the surprise of himself and others. He even called for those who had gone to WSC not to be allowed to play the accepted form of international cricket, which caused long-term damage to his relationship with Greig. The split reached as far as the Warwickshire dressing room, where Dennis Amiss, who he had always liked, was becoming a social outcast among his colleagues after signing up for the new venture.

These were turbulent times, when old friendships frayed, and there were many occasions when Bob had cause to wonder if he had done the right thing. The thought frequently nagged at him on the winter tour that was to come.

6

POLITICAL WORLD

As erstwhile colleagues prepared for their adventure into the brave new world of World Series Cricket, the official England party assembled at Heathrow in late 1977 for a tour of Pakistan. This time Bob's expectations were not high, and he duly recalled it as probably his most dismal trip with the national side. When the subject of modern touring life came up post-retirement, he was inclined to hark back to the long nights spent back then in abysmal accommodation, preparing for cricket matches that were bound to end in draws owing to the lifeless nature of the pitches.

Hyderabad, Sindh, topped his list of the worst places he went to, because the team's digs had little in the way of plumbing, but plenty of foul smells and large swarms of mosquitoes. Away from the big cities, the England team were put up in what were known as Rest Houses. On one stop, in Sahiwal, they slept four to a room and it was so cold the players tried to stay warm by wearing cricket kit in bed at night, with socks used as gloves. For those, like Bob, who had turned down Kerry Packer, thoughts inevitably turned to what the five-star alternative would have been in Australia.

It was little wonder that the players were spoiling for a fight when it emerged that Pakistan planned to import three players from WSC for the final Test in Karachi. The threat of an England strike was only averted when the Pakistan board backed down. There was a concerted cheer from the tour party, now under the temporary captaincy of Geoff Boycott in the injured Brearley's absence, when the plane took off in late January for the second leg of the tour in New Zealand.

After a rout by Richard Hadlee on a terrible pitch in the first Test, the series is best remembered for one incident in the second match at Christchurch, as the touring side tried to force the win. While Boycott had made a decent impression as captain, some in the dressing room felt he was batting too slowly as England pressed on towards a declaration, with the intention of trying to bowl New Zealand out on the last day. Ian Botham went in and proceeded to run the captain out by more than half the length of the pitch, cheerfully telling his team-mates that he had done it deliberately.

Bob, knowing that the young Botham was not a great runner either, always had his doubts. It did the trick, however. The declaration was made, and on the final day Bob bowled one of his most hostile spells as he took 4–14 to help level the series, which ended up drawn.

At this point in his career, Bob was the nearest thing England had found to a strike bowler with the capacity to seriously intimidate batsmen, a quality very much in vogue thanks to the West Indies. His reputation for this was controversially enhanced when Pakistan paid a return visit in the summer of 1978. During the first Test at Edgbaston spinner Iqbal Qasim had come in as a nightwatchman and was providing stubborn resistance after the resumption the following morning. Despite ICC regulations banning bouncers at the lower order, Bob viewed promoted nightwatchmen as fair game and felt that umpires had been slow in enforcing the rules anyway.

He dug in a short ball, which the batsman deflected into his face, drawing enough blood that he ended up being sent to hospital. What especially incensed the media, and some in the crowd, was a refusal on the bowler's part to come to the batsman's aid, with Bob adding insult to injury by stomping back to his mark, rather than offering sympathy. He later explained that his actions were informed by what had happened in the Centenary Test with Rick McCosker. Seeing close up the damage he had done to the Australian's face had shocked him, to the extent that he had become less effective for the rest of the game. He had inwardly resolved that he could not be so compassionate in the future.

Bob maintained that he did not intend to hurt Qasim, although he did admit to one instance when he had tried to harm a batsman, something that was a source of embarrassment. The occasion was back in 1972, in his first season at Warwickshire, when he was playing against Lancashire. Opener Barry Wood had started advancing down the pitch at him, which he took as such an affront that in a fit of pique he deliberately bowled a beamer. Shocked by his own actions, he swore to himself that he would not do it again.

The nearest he would come to something similar was in the final Test of the famous 1981 Ashes series, in which Dennis Lillee was having a successful slog. Bob was being repeatedly no-balled by Dickie Bird and, with the red mist having descended, he intentionally overstepped the crease to deliver a sharply rearing bouncer. The irony was that by this time he had developed a healthy respect for Lillee, who had gone up in his estimation by attending a benefit function of Bob's earlier that summer, despite the Australians having just lost the Edgbaston Test. He also regarded Bird, for all his eccentricities, as the best umpire of the era.

But Bob was, above all, a testosterone-fuelled fast bowler, and he saw the furore that blew up in the wake of the Qasim incident as evidence that English cricket was too soft, and also too quick to side with the underdog.

Both Pakistan and New Zealand were comfortably put to the sword in that summer of 1978. Bob was in his pomp, and in the spring he had been named as one of *Wisden*'s five Cricketers of the Year. Not only did he end up with 25 Test victims over the season, he was also a regular fixture in what was still a limited programme of one-day internationals.

That season also featured a major development away from the world of cricket. During a rained-out day at the Oval Test against New Zealand he had wandered into the Long Bar to meet up with some former team-mates from Corinthian Casuals, and among the company was a young woman whose name was Juliet Smail. They began to see a lot of each other and, by the time he left for what would be a fourth winter trip to Australia, he felt that his resolute bachelor status was now in some doubt.

The strangest dimension of the official Ashes duel in 1978–79 was that it ran in parallel with the second edition of World Series Cricket, with virtually all the world's finest cricketers ending up in Australia at once. As they moved around the vast continent, the two productions vied for the attention of a public who had suddenly been presented with a surfeit of cricket to watch.

The two sets of players hardly ever came across each other, although their paths did cross one evening at Sydney airport when the World XI were waiting for one flight and the official England Test party for another. A few fraternal greetings with old colleagues were exchanged but it was nothing more than coldly cordial. The 'them and us' mentality was, by now, baked in. When Greig invited the England team for a barbecue at his house in Sydney on another date, most of the squad, including Bob, declined.

This is not to say that Bob was a Luddite by nature. He could recognise that Packer had come up with some decent innovations, some of which have stood the test of time. Night cricket under lights worked well in Australia, and the introduction of the white ball was a success. Some of the Channel Nine coverage included short-lived gimmicks, but others represented a necessary updating of broadcasting ideas to attract a new audience.

On the official tour the visitors were considerably less weakened than their hosts, who were barely an Australian Second XI, and England were expected to win fairly comfortably. They did emerge 5–1 victors from the series but it was closer than it looked, with the Australians unearthing a surprisingly potent pair of opening bowlers in Alan Hurst and the quirky Rodney Hogg, who took 41 wickets. And England actually lost the one-day series that ran alongside it.

A huge asterisk will always accompany this peculiar Ashes series, as Wisden alluded to in its review of the tour: 'A lone trumpeter on the sparsely filled Hill at Sydney grimly symbolised Australia's embarrassing defeats, domestic confusions and divided loyalties, by sounding the Last Post as England won the sixth Test inside four days.'

Bob remembered it as an enjoyable trip spent with a group of players who bonded unusually well. By now a card-carrying fitness fanatic, he very much bought into the extra emphasis placed upon the physical preparations, which marked the beginning of a more professional outlook on how touring England teams tuned themselves up. Twenty Test wickets was his satisfactory although unspectacular return, given the opposition.

It was also a visit in which some enduring bonds with the locals were made. One extracurricular trip involved an open day to the Hardy's winery in McLaren Vale, where Bob came across an extrovert young winemaker named Geoff Merrill. The two of them hit it off straight away, and a friendship took root that was to last the rest of his life. Another highlight was a dinner at the famous Doyle's fish restaurant in Sydney, at which the touring Elton John turned up, buying flowers from a seller who walked past to present to the wives in attendance.

The first main assignment for the following summer was the 1979 World Cup. While not the same scale of event as it is now, the competition was to be a source of regret to Bob, particularly for the fact that he never got to appear in a final, even though he played in an era when three successive finals were held at Lord's.

He had not been in the squad for the inaugural World Cup in 1975, but he was guaranteed his place for the 1979 version. England progressed to win a tight semi-final against New

Zealand, but late in his spell Bob turned his knee. Despite frantic efforts to get himself ready, he had to sit out the final. Such was the dominance of the West Indies, he would most likely have ended up with a runner's-up medal anyway, and the islanders went on to lift the trophy.

Further injury disappointment was to follow that summer, as he missed a Test for the first time since 1976. The benefits that had sprung from that fortuitous barbecue back in Melbourne in 1977, the subsequent change in fitness regime, had well and truly paid off. So it was acutely frustrating that he was forced to miss the second Test of four that summer, against India, with a pulled stomach muscle. He was able to come back for the last two, with The Oval witnessing an extraordinary innings of 221 from Sunil Gavaskar that came close to miraculously squaring the series.

As far as world cricket was concerned, the most significant development in that time was an uneasy peace breaking out between the game's establishment and Kerry Packer. A deal was struck and he abandoned his World Series, in return for televising the game in Australia. One upshot was a hastily arranged mini-Ashes series of three matches over the winter of 1979–80.

The 1970s had begun with that dramatic call-up for Bob from obscurity. By the end of the decade he had played in six separate 'series' against the old enemy, if you counted the Centenary Test, five of these being in Australia. Small wonder he developed an appetite for the country: he had spent so much time there.

The itinerary for the 1979–80 trip was a mess, and it was not a visit to Australia that Bob came to regard with much affection. The first Test in Perth did, however, provide him with an anecdote that he would enjoy telling for many years to come. Coming in at number eleven in the final innings, with the game a lost cause, he joined Geoff Boycott, who was unbeaten on 97. Facing the first ball of a Dennis Lillee over, Boycott clipped it away for a probable three that would have taken him to his hundred. But the pair of them had spoken to the effect that the star opener should try and monopolise the strike against Lillee, as Bob fancied his chances against the less lethal Geoff Dymock. After the first two runs were taken, Bob recalled that 'I stuck my hand up like a traffic policeman' to refuse a third. Boycott was unable to score for the rest of the over – and was left agonised on 99 as, off the very next ball from Dymock, Bob nicked a gentle outswinger to first slip.

England had lost by 138 runs and, against an Australian team almost back to full strength, thanks to the return of the World Series players, they went on to lose the series 3–0.

One major plus of the winter had been that the exceptional talent and combativeness of Ian Botham was now in full bloom, and he was reeling off outstanding performances with both bat and ball. When Mike Brearley announced that he had no intention of going on any future tours, the selectors turned to the man of the moment to replace him as captain.

By this time Bob held Botham in the highest esteem, as a player and as a person. However, he immediately saw the perils of making the team's new superstar captain, especially as the next two series were to be home and away against a West Indies outfit at the peak of their powers. Back in Birmingham, he gave a straight-talking interview to a local radio station, stating his opinion that this was not the right time for Botham to be burdened in such a way. Despite the fact that it was clear this was not meant to be a personal criticism of his team-mate, he was fined by the TCCB. The support he had given them over the whole Packer business seemed forgotten.

After returning from Australia, Bob tied the knot with Juliet in a ceremony for closest friends and family at Birmingham Registry Office. The intention was for it to be a small and private affair, away from the glare of any publicity that his profile would inevitably have attracted. This aspect did not go entirely to plan. By chance, the wedding party booked in immediately after them contained in its number a reporter from the *Birmingham Mail*. The following day the happy couple found news of their nuptials splashed all over the local paper, which had scored an unexpected scoop.

Cricketwise, England were to come close to holding their own against the West Indians that summer of 1980. Bob took nine wickets in the opening Test, which was narrowly lost by two wickets, mainly due to dropped catches in the opposition's second innings. He was, however, beginning to struggle with his rhythm, and his morale quickly went downhill after that, as a succession of draws followed.

By the third of them Bob was having issues with his run-up, and he bowled dismally at The Oval. His biggest contribution in that match was what he regarded as his best Test innings, which ensured that England held out for a draw. Coming in at 92–9 to join Peter Willey, he survived 114 balls against Michael Holding,

Colin Croft, Malcolm Marshall and Joel Garner, to take the home team to the safety of 209–9 declared. Unlike with Boycott the previous winter, he was able to stick around long enough to ensure that his partner made it to an unbeaten hundred.

Taking just two wickets in the third and fourth Tests resulted in him being dropped for the final match and, to his acute disappointment, the Centenary Test against Australia that was to follow. The sense of deflation was compounded when all England cricketers who had ever played against Australia were invited to attend the festivities, but he had to miss out as he was sent back to county duty with Warwickshire. One happy upshot was that he was able to contribute to his relatively youthful county side, under his captaincy, claiming one of the season's prime domestic honours, the John Player League title.

The exile did not last long and he was brought back into the fold for the return series in the Caribbean that was to start after Christmas, and as vice-captain as well. His part in the tour proved short-lived. Playing a first warm-up game in St Vincent, in his seventh over of the tour he twisted his left knee on the follow-through. He immediately sensed that his winter, indeed possibly his whole international career, was over. While it was suggested he might stay on as non-playing deputy to Botham, he was sent home to an uncertain future as his thirty-second birthday loomed.

England ended up restricting themselves to a 2–0 defeat, and much worse was to happen off the field. The second Test was cancelled when the government of Guyana refused to give Bob's replacement, Robin Jackman, a visa due to his previous coaching stints in South Africa. More grievous was the sudden death of tour manager Ken Barrington, a massively popular figure in the game who Bob had been especially close to since his days as a youngster at The Oval.

The tragic news from afar tempered any relief felt on Bob's part that his knee problem was not as bad as initially feared. The fast-improving technique of arthroscopy helped remove a piece of ligament from the affected area, and within days he was back on his feet and comfortably able to report for pre-season with Warwickshire. It turned out to facilitate not just the most glorious summer of his career, but a pathway towards the England captaincy.

The events around the third Headingley Test in the 1981 Ashes series are described in a later chapter, but the context of the lead-in centred on the deteriorating state of Botham's captaincy. Bob bowled well enough in the first Test, but a four-wicket win gave the tourists their first triumph at Trent Bridge since 1948.

Lord's was a draw, but represented the eleventh match without a win under the leadership of Botham. Bob's fears had proved well-grounded in terms of his mate's individual performances, which were clearly suffering. Having registered the first 'pair' of his career, the nation's favourite cricketing son decided it was time to relinquish the job. He spoke to Bob about it, and there were no attempts at dissuasion.

Following that second Test, with England in one of their regular spasms of disarray, Bob had worries of his own. He had developed a nasty chest cold during the match that would force him out of Warwickshire's upcoming matches, in which he hoped to prove his fitness. The scene hardly appeared set for his finest hour.

7

WHEN THE DEAL GOES DOWN

Headingley '81 did not exactly change Bob's life, but it propelled him to new heights of recognition in the public consciousness. Ian Botham, who followed up Leeds with more heroics at Edgbaston, achieved a level of national fame almost unimaginable now for a cricketer. He was to own that series, although some felt that the 'Botham's Ashes' tag tended to underplay other contributions.

One who held that opinion was Dennis Lillee. Twenty years on from the great comeback, he and Bob went up to Leeds together to reminisce for the benefit of the *Daily Mail*, and England's former fierce adversary expressed that view. Bob, who had taken 29 wickets in an eventual 3–1 series win, was always phlegmatic on the subject of who got what share of the credit.

Brearley's dramatic return to the captaincy would be brief, given his refusal to embark on overseas tours, and Essex's Keith Fletcher was a popular replacement. Political trouble was brewing yet again, however, even before the England party set off for a six-Test tour of India that winter. This time it was the prospect of a rebel tour to South Africa that was proving a distraction, with the inducements enough to turn the heads of those who wondered how long their Test careers might last. As with Kerry Packer, Bob made no secret that he was tempted. From a moral perspective it was not that he had any time for apartheid – a system he was quoted as saying 'stinks' – but he had a clear view then that politics and sport should not mix. Looking at what went on in other cricket nations, his attitude was 'Let him who is without sin cast the first stone'.

It was also tempting to dream of a lucrative month's work in South Africa while in the midst of what became a difficult tour of the subcontinent. The cricket was dreary, with India intent on holding on to an early 1–0 lead. A distracted Geoff Boycott flew home, while Fletcher, who Bob liked a lot, drew fire for a show of dissent in Bangalore. The party reluctantly flew on to Sri Lanka for what was now a one-off official Test, during which Bob gave an impromptu rocket to the rest of the squad when it looked like they might be left chasing an awkward total to win.

Blushes saved against the fledgling Test nation, the party flew home, and Bob was immediately approached again by South African representatives. It was suggested to him he might captain a rebel side due to leave in the next week. Eventually he decided against it, for reasons that echoed the Packer situation: 'I had become establishment-minded and could still not imagine being sufficiently motivated by international matches which were not what they claimed to be,' he recalled in *Lasting the Pace*.

His assumption was that Fletcher would be reappointed for the approaching 1982 England home series against India. And if the Essex skipper was not retained, then the young David Gower seemed favourite to get the job, especially after he was chosen to lead MCC against the tourists early in the summer. There was also the orthodox wisdom that fast bowlers are simply not suited to being captain. Thus he thought little of it.

He was sitting at home in Birmingham one morning in May when the phone rang. It was the new chairman of selectors, Peter May, and to Bob's near astonishment he was offering him the job of leading England. After the initial shock and delight, and an attempt to ring Fletcher to express his sympathy, the reality sank in. With the South African rebels banned for three years, there would be no Graham Gooch to call on – the player he considered the biggest loss – and a dearth of experience, with Boycott, Derek Underwood and John Emburey among other absentees.

There were always going to be a few hunches followed when it came to selection, and for his first Test as captain, on 10 June at Lord's, debuts were given to the newly qualified Allan Lamb and Cambridge undergraduate Derek Pringle. It turned out to be a very satisfactory start against a decent enough Indian team that featured the likes of Sunil Gavaskar and Kapil Dev. Bob made his equal Test highest score of 28 in the first innings, and then took the lead in bowling them out in the second, claiming 6–101, including a burst of four wickets in four overs. It was a comfortable seven-wicket victory, and an early reminder of the truism that when you are winning, most other things look after themselves.

Among his duties in that match at HQ was presenting the team to the Queen. It was a ritual of Lord's Tests at the time, and would happen after the tea break. After he had gone along the line with Her Majesty, introducing the players, she looked up at the crowd and asked him, 'Why aren't all these people at work?' This elicited a classic Bob-ism as he replied, 'You wouldn't be saying that if this was Ascot, Ma'am.'

With a tendency to get wrapped up in his own performance, as captain he deliberately relied on a few senior pros on the field and this brought the odd grumble from offstage that it resembled captaincy by committee. A 1–0 series win was a fair result, and was followed by 2–1 in the Tests against Pakistan. The one match England lost that summer came when Bob was absent with injury, Gower taking over. Rounded off by winning the one-day matches, the end-of-season report card on the new captain was fairly complimentary.

Yet, as so many of our best cricketers have found, the job of being England cricket captain never stays a comfortable existence for long. Bob's first big examination involved taking a somewhat underpowered England squad on the Ashes tour of 1982–83, selecting from a reduced pool of elite talent because of the rebel tour. That said, there was still some controversy among the selections. Left-armer Phil Edmonds was in the frame, but Bob was never a great fan and did not fancy the man-management challenge he represented, so three off-spinners were taken instead.

Unlike today, on that tour there was nothing like the vast support crew that can sometimes outnumber the actual playing squad, ranging from psychologists to media flunkeys. There was a manager, Doug Insole, his assistant, Norman Gifford, and long-serving physio Bernard Thomas. It would not be regarded as even a skeleton staff in the modern cricketing world.

While Australia scores highly for creature comforts, it is also the most pressurised touring environment, and by the halfway point Bob was starting to make himself sick with worry. At the best of times he inclined towards anxiety, even when just a player.

There was, as he would later come to acknowledge, something of a generation gap at play. Having been blooded at a time when England tourists lived in near penury, suffered privations on away trips and had to make their own entertainment, Bob struggled to understand the attitude of some younger players. He was someone who took defeat personally, and although he liked to party, one piece of his complex make-up was a contradictory puritanical element. He found it hard to comprehend how some players seemed able to shrug off on-field setbacks while they planned the evening's diversions.

Being the underdogs did not serve as a pressure release, either. He felt the stress almost engulfing him as a competitive draw in the opener at Perth was followed by a seven-wicket defeat at the Gabba. As he struggled to sleep, his troubled state of mind was exacerbated when the batsmen persuaded him to insert Australia in the third rubber at Adelaide, much against his instincts. It was a move that backfired badly, as the home team cruised to an eight-wicket victory.

Some honour was restored, however, by a thrilling three-run win in the Boxing Day Test at Melbourne. Australia were in sight of victory in the fourth-innings chase when Bob tossed the ball to Goldenballs himself, Botham. Jeff Thomson then nicked it to slip, where Chris Tavaré fumbled, only for Geoff Miller to scoop up the rebound before it hit the ground.

Bob's reaction was more relief than unadulterated joy. An eventual 2–1 series defeat was no disgrace in the circumstances, but he had found the experience so draining that depression

– the black dog was often lurking around somewhere – was eating into him when they moved on to New Zealand for three one-day internationals. As he recalled in *A Captain's Diary*, a book that relates to the tour, after a second defeat to the Kiwis: 'The buck stops with me, and it was primarily my job to lift [the players] for this game. But I can't do that unless they give some sort of professional response and that, unfortunately, has been sadly absent.'

His captaincy had come under more and more scrutiny in the winter and was criticised for being too reactive. There was little question, however, that he would be reappointed for one last shot at a World Cup, which England was again hosting in the summer of 1983.

The side played well in getting to the semi-finals, and hopes were high that India would be beaten at Old Trafford. The pitch, however, played to India's strengths, and after posting only 213, the host nation fell to a six-wicket defeat. That India went on to upset the West Indies and win the final, and were a better team than initially thought, was of scant consolation.

If the World Cup was to be one regret, then another was that he was never able to help turn Warwickshire into a champion county while he was in his prime. England, in the latter stages of his career, was proving all-absorbing. With little respite, the second half of the summer brought the visit of an underrated New Zealand side led by his old friend, and one-time lodger with his family in Stoke D'Abernon, Geoff Howarth.

England were to win the series 3–1 in relative comfort, with the one wobble coming at Headingley, after two batting collapses from the home side against the unorthodox Lance Cairns. Bob took all five of the Kiwi wickets in the second innings, the fifth and last being the most significant. For when he got past the defences of Jeff Crowe he became only the fourth man to have taken 300 Test wickets, joining Lance Gibbs, Fred Trueman and Dennis Lillee. That list has now extended to 33, which is partly testament to the surge in international fixtures that ensued in coming decades. Given his responsibilities to the team, the much-heralded individual achievement was clouded by the fact that New Zealand had won their first Test match on English soil.

Weary at the end of the summer, he had a private conversation with chief selector Peter May about whether he should carry on. May was seeking to find out whether he still had the appetite for the job, and for Bob it was still there. At the age of thirty-four, however, he was aware that he was entering the twilight, and the first thoughts were creeping in about what he might do when it was all over. Long into retirement, he would come out with a small nugget of wisdom, one that could be applied to anyone playing sport to a rarefied level: 'When you start thinking about what you are going to do when it all ends, you lose that couple of percentage points, and they are the most important percentage points you have.'

He was certainly aware that he might struggle for motivation when it was finished with England, but believed he had earned the right to take charge for another winter overseas. Therefore he assured May that he was happy to carry on in New Zealand and Pakistan.

*　　*　　*

Before long Bob would come to regret the decision to stay on as captain. It was dubbed the 'Sex, Drugs and Rock and Roll' tour by a salivating tabloid media, a reference to what some of the team supposedly got up to in New Zealand. On the playing side, the perennially underrated Kiwis had recently beaten the West Indies and were a serious threat to an England team shorn of several South Africa exiles. England were also hurt by the fact that Ian Botham was going through a dip in form as a bowler.

It all got off to an exotic start with two one-day matches in Fiji to kick off 1984, the idea being to spread the gospel of the game. After some hearty New Year celebrations England had briefly looked in danger of losing the first game.

Worse was to come in New Zealand, both on and off the pitch, and the tour was to go down as a watershed in relations between the media and the players. There had, hitherto, been an unspoken understanding that, given their close proximity, the cricket scribes would afford some leeway to the touring party when it came to their social activities. It was a fact of life, also, that journalists were sometimes a part of evenings when players would let off steam.

Things started to go wrong when, in the first Test at Wellington, England failed to convert a strong early position into victory. Trailing by 244 runs on the first innings, New Zealand were saved by hundreds from Jeremy Coney and a rising young star, Martin Crowe. Matters deteriorated at Christchurch, after what Bob told the media was 'the worst bowling performance I have seen in a Test match'. Batting first, the home side somehow managed to make 307 on a desperately substandard pitch. England's crime had been to bowl far too short, and when it was the tourists' turn to bat, Richard Hadlee showed how it should be done. Bob's team were bowled out for 82 and 93.

The cricketing fallout was bad enough, but then an allegation surfaced that Botham and Allan Lamb had smoked a joint in the dressing room afterwards. This was duly rubbished by all who were there, but it did not help that stories were circulating that rather too much fun was being had on the tour away from the cricket. Partially contributing to this was the high profile, if innocent enough presence, of cricket superfan Elton John. He was touring the country at the time and became a regular social companion for the players.

When an MCC member rang a national newspaper to claim that he had been verbally abused in a bar by Botham and Lamb, who he alleged were the worse for drink, hard-bitten news-hounds began to descend on the tour. Bob, and others, always maintained that the story was a case of mistaken identity. Botham felt as if he was under siege.

'Whenever Elton was around, Beefy went off and spent time with him to get away from the press guys, some of whom were jumping into hotel lifts with players, trying to pick up gossip. It was pretty unpleasant,' Bob subsequently told *Wisden*.

Fellow tourist Vic Marks summed up the atmosphere around the trip in the same piece: 'It was quite a lively, sociable tour but no one was hit, no one was charged, no one ended up in court. The relationships between the two sides were good. I remember John Wright organising a trip in Queenstown, to do some jet-boating.'

The home umpiring also incensed the visiting team. With the hosts 1–0 up, a flat pitch in Auckland for the third and final

Test saw a predictable, high-scoring stalemate. The one-day series was to go England's way, but the damage was done.

It had been the third successive Test series in which Bob had topped England's bowling averages, and at Wellington he had overtaken Fred Trueman's tally of 307 to become the country's leading wicket-taker. The failure of the tour far outweighed any personal satisfaction at those achievements, however, and he was again perplexed by the attitude of some team-mates. At the same time there was an acknowledgement that he had failed to get the best out of them.

A rare dose of glad tidings was the news from back home that daughter Katie had been born safe and well.

The party was now heading for Pakistan, where Bob was struck down with the kind of viral infection that so often afflicted him on the subcontinent. This one was of a different order and it was feared he had hepatitis. After captaining in the three-wicket defeat at Karachi he missed the second Test and was advised to go home during the third.

Back in England, Bob knew what was coming, and word reached him that his exit was being mapped out at Lord's. Plagued by the lingering virus, he was late to file his official tour report. An internal inquiry cleared the touring party of the more lurid allegations, but it was no surprise when the axe fell at the start of the summer.

It would be fair to say that Bob was left with mixed feelings about his stint as captain, this rare experiment of having a fast bowler as skipper. He was in charge for 18 Test matches, won seven, drew five and lost six. While never one to stint on self-criticism, he felt that was a respectable return under the circumstances, having been deprived of those banned for making the rebel tour to South Africa. His Test winning percentage of 38.9 was second only to Brearley's 58.1 among England captains of the 1980s and 1990s. And it could be reasonably argued that Brearley was presented with more favourable circumstances, given his lack of exposure to the West Indies and the bowling resources at his disposal.

Now looking at the end of the 1984 season as the likely finish of his career, Bob felt a slight sense of liberation, ahead of what was to be a brutally tough summer series against a West Indies team at the peak of their powers. Although the virus was continuing to have an effect on his mind and body, there was also the motivation of trying to win something with Warwickshire, who had rarely seen the best of him in the preceding years.

Bob still had three more Tests to play, against the rampant tourists from the Caribbean. His international career was to end with a 90th Test appearance, an unmemorable eight-wicket loss that was to become part of that summer's 5–0 series rout. He took some heavy punishment on the same ground where, three years previously, his feats had been such that they caused a lift in the stock market. When he drove away from Leeds on 16 July it was for the last time as an England player, having taken 325 Test wickets.

The following weekend he was back with Warwickshire for the final of the Benson and Hedges Cup at Lord's. The night before they faced Lancashire he began to feel a fever coming on, and he barely got through the match as his team posted only 139 in being defeated by six wickets. (The game itself is possibly best remembered for the eccentric choice of Man of the Match, made by adjudicator Peter May. It went to the somewhat stunned Lancashire captain John Abrahams, who was given the award despite having dropped a catch, made a duck and not bowled a ball.)

It was to prove Bob's last match as a professional. Graeme Fowler was his final victim, as part of a nine-over spell that went for 19 runs. By the time the team convened across the road at the Westmoreland Hotel to drown their sorrows, he felt so ill he had to ask Juliet to drive him home.

'I spoke to him briefly after that match and I remember him telling me that he thought he was done, but there was no major announcement about his retirement,' recalls close friend Paul Allott, who played in the winning Lancashire team. Bob was never a big one for announcements.

There are few fairytale endings in sport, although when Warwickshire made the NatWest Trophy semi-finals in his absence there was hope he might be well enough to return for the final. Defeat to Kent in the semis, and ongoing medical advice, meant that he was not to appear again for the county, or anyone else. On 11 September 1984 he packed up his kitbag at Edgbaston for the last time, after a career that saw him deliver 83,921 balls for the First XIs he represented.

And at the time of retirement he held, defiantly, the record for not-outs in Test matches – unbeaten on 55 occasions.

8

BEYOND THE HORIZON

The end of Bob Willis, cricketer, in late 1984 was to mark the blowing of an almost exact half-time whistle in his whole life. He was thirty-five years old, married, with a young child, and, after a remarkable playing career, he was examining his options. The one which first presented itself was intriguing, although a potential drawback was that it involved babysitting a young Phil Tufnell, long before he became one of the most recognisable characters in the English game.

An England Under-19 trip was due to depart for the West Indies in early January 1985 and at Lord's they were scouting around for someone suitable to take charge. Bob's immense experience of touring, and relative youth, made him a potential fit for the job of guiding the young tyros, and he was approached. Although he had not held a burning ambition to coach, and the team was likely to be overmatched, it seemed a good opportunity. The England party included what was considered a surfeit of lively characters, notably the garrulous young left-arm spinner from Middlesex. In addition, there was a promising pace bowler, also from north London, in the shape of Phil DeFreitas. One more from that party was to go on and play for the full England side, Yorkshire's Richard Blakey.

The opposition were strong, featuring a young Jimmy Adams and Carl Hooper, but it soon became obvious that another major challenge would be maintaining off-field discipline. In his book *What Now?* Tufnell expresses some sympathy for those trying to keep the teenagers in line.

'It must have been a nightmare for Bob Willis and Bob Cottam, the management team,' said Tufnell. 'For three days I didn't see the right side of seven o'clock in the morning. As a result, the management enforced the quickest curfew in history and, as it turned out, the least effective. If the management fined a player for being out at midnight, we fined each other for being in by then.' Cottam's description of Tufnell and a few of his team-mates as 'bloody headbangers' inspired the relevant chapter heading in the autobiography.

England went down 2–0 in a three-match series of youth Tests across Barbados, St Lucia and Jamaica. Victory had not been anticipated, however, and although exerting control over some of the tearaways had proved tough, the feedback from players was that the actual coaching had been of a high standard.

The first summer Bob had known as a non-cricketer since 1968 awaited on his return, and new ways of making a living had to be explored. The upside was that there was freedom to pursue other interests unhindered, such as going to concerts and indulging his catholic taste in music.

Among the benefits of cricket stardom had been the opportunity to establish friendships with the likes of Eric Clapton and Elton John. Shortly after Bob's return from the West Indies, the latter was in Birmingham to play a concert at the NEC, staying at what was then the best accommodation in town, the top-floor suite at the Holiday Inn. Contact was made and Elton invited Bob and brother David over to the hotel early in the afternoon.

After several hours' (sober) hanging out, Elton came out with an unexpected suggestion: 'Fancy giving me a lift to the gig?' The brothers had parked up in Bob's fairly battered Volvo, but the superstar was not deterred and the three of them piled into the car to make the journey to the venue. The eccentric choice of transport soon proved to be a mistake, as they got caught up in traffic with the thousands of others making their way to the same destination. Realising the danger of a potential delay to the whole concert, a following car that contained the singer's security detail summoned a nearby police vehicle. Only when an escort swung into action did they manage to make headway, cutting a swathe through bemused fellow travellers, who were shocked to see their musical idol sitting in the back of a Volvo behind England's former cricket captain.

Such adventures do not pay the bills, and gainful employment was required. By now Bob had already developed a reasonable knowledge of wine and he decided to dip his toe into the business alongside his brother David by creating a mail-order company, Bob Willis's World of Wine. It was not a huge success; in fact, their efforts were so inept it became something of a family joke.

'I think the idea came about after a couple of pints in the pub, and it showed,' recalls David. 'We got together about twenty types of wine, at not especially attractive prices, and sent maybe 300 flyers out to various addresses and contacts, naively expecting the orders to come flooding in. When I checked at the P.O. Box number we had given out, a grand total of two people had come back wanting to make a purchase. It was a fairly brutal lesson, but we hadn't put much money in, so there was no great loss, and we ended up having a laugh about it.'

That summer did, however, see him take tentative first steps in what was to prove a longer-lived career: broadcasting on cricket. Australia were the tourists in 1985 and there were few more credible voices to assess the visitors than Bob, given that 35 of his 90 Tests had been in the Ashes. Out of the blue he got a call from the BBC asking if he would like to join the team and cover some of the tour.

It was 30 May, the day after the tragic events of the Heysel Stadium football disaster, when he made his debut as a summariser in the television commentary box, for the first one-day international at Old Trafford. Bob would not have described himself as a natural in the role, certainly not in the way that a chosen few ex-players have made a seamless transition to microphone duties. He was slightly shocked at the lack of guidance or coaching that was considered normal at the time, and took some while to get comfortable. His appearances with the Beeb would continue for several years, but were rather sporadic. A bit like a player starting out at Test level, he felt he would have benefited from a more consistent run in the team.

Under the captaincy of David Gower, England won the Test series 3–1, but it had been against an Australian team in transition and undermined by offstage issues involving another rebel tour to South Africa. Beating them was an altogether easier task than the one approaching – a winter tour to the Caribbean. The Test and County Cricket Board were again looking for a management team, including an assistant to tour manager Tony Brown. With his first-hand knowledge of the opposition and ability to offer a younger man's perspective, Bob was offered the job.

On the pure coaching side, he had found the Under-19 trip to the Caribbean slightly more enjoyable than expected. The idea of working with adults on tour, some of whom were close friends, was therefore appealing. He was, however, counselled against taking the job, both by his brother and by Richie Benaud.

'I thought that, given the strength of the West Indies, he would be on a hiding to nothing,' says David. 'The best result they could hope for was 4–0 if it rained and 5–0 if it didn't. Richie, whose views Bob respected, was of a similar opinion and said that a difficult early tour could do long-term damage to any coaching aspirations. Bob had been quite flattered by the approach, and wondered why Richie and I were being so negative about it.'

Unfortunately their fears were not misplaced. The whole trip turned into a catalogue of disasters, both on and off the pitch, and all five Tests were lost. The hosts were as fearsome as expected, with fast bowler Patrick Patterson exemplifying the challenge they brought on some difficult pitches. Even a batsman as brave as Graham Gooch came to look back on the Test in Jamaica and admit: 'It was the first time I had ever got the whiff of danger in my nostrils.'

Objections to the Essex player's past associations with South Africa, and the subsequent threats to bar him from some islands, represented just one of many issues that the tour management had to contend with. Everything combined to make the New Zealand trip in 1984 look almost like a tea party. Much of it was recorded in *Another Bloody Tour*, the bestselling eyewitness book written by Frances Edmonds, wife of Phil, the England spinner.

Bob's past experience had made him wary of the media on tour, and some of the cricket scribes blamed him for excluding them from the various functions laid on in the Caribbean. Frances Edmonds pointed out that the players were supportive of that policy. 'Big Bob demonstrates feelings common to about 99 per cent of the players, and if exclusions either perceived or real are down to him, his actions would no doubt be welcomed by the majority of the team,' she wrote.

The wariness only increased as results spiralled downwards and hard-bitten news reporters descended on the tour. Cricket was then considered such big news that it was fodder for the tabloid circulation war. A former Miss Barbados, Lindy Field, was bought up by one Sunday paper to allege steamy romps after the close of play. David Gower was asked in a press conference if he was having an affair with a team-mate's wife, purely on the basis that he had attended their wedding and been pictured giving the bride a peck on the cheek.

Again the touring party felt under siege and, as anyone who has been on such trips will know, cliques can start to form in the face of adversity. Bob's perceived closeness to Ian Botham, Allan Lamb and Gower saw him characterised as a member of the 'Gang of Four' by some players. As the team was pursued around the islands by a swollen media pack and bloodthirsty West Indian bowlers, the only win of any significance came in a solitary one-day match. Bob returned home having found the whole thing a fairly wretched experience, disappointed once more at some of the lackadaisical attitudes he encountered among his charges. He concluded that the life of a cricket coach was probably not for him.

The summer of 1986 was free of any on-field cricket commitments, although Bob was in demand for visits to hospitality boxes and the like at Test matches. Having experienced that developing side of the sports business close up, he recognised that there had to be commercial opportunities within it. The germ of an idea developed. Still living in Birmingham, he convened a meeting of potentially interested parties at his house: brother David, old cricketing mates Jim Cumbes and Dennis Amiss, his Manchester-based accountant Peter Johnson and Steve Hamer, a friend from footballing days with Corinthian Casuals. Cumbes and Amiss dropped out relatively soon, but the other four decided that there was enough promise in the enterprise to press ahead.

Meanwhile some broadcasting work was still being put his way, by the BBC and Australia's Channel Nine. In the winter of 1986–87 he needed little persuading to head Down Under for several months, working as a tour host for Gulliver's Travels while making some appearances with the domestic broadcasting team covering England's Ashes triumph under the captaincy of Mike Gatting.

By the time he returned to England, solid progress had been made in planning the new business venture. In March the International Luncheon Club and a company called In Style Promotions had been launched. Through the connections of

Hamer, contact was made with Robert Burness, who had married into the Forte family and was managing director of the Café Royal, off Piccadilly.

'We had some meetings with Robert, who felt that the Café Royal at the time was being slightly overshadowed in terms of functions by the big hotels on Park Lane,' recalls David Willis. 'We came to an agreement that he would give us an office and a telephone on the top floor of the premises for a year, to see what we could generate with putting on lunches and the like. If we could make it work then fine, if not then everyone could walk away after twelve months.'

The plan was to hold business lunches with a sporting theme once a month, the group pooling their contacts to try and attract high-profile guests. Sportspeople who had books to publicise, cricketers and visiting teams from overseas were all sources of invitees. In May 1987 Ian Botham became the first guest of honour at the Luncheon Club, although the room, which could seat 450, was barely half full for the fledgling enterprise. Slightly less glamorously, a party from the West Midlands Drainage Company were taken up to the Open golf at Muirfield, as part of developing other activities.

It was not long before they got into their stride, and soon the functions were becoming sold out and a popular fixture on the monthly calendar for the London business and finance community. 'This was a pretty good time to be in the business, with the economy very much on the up and the City buoyant,' says David. 'We found a captive audience who were enthusiastic about entertaining people, and quite prepared to write the afternoon off to go on the toot. There was quite a correction around 1991, but by then we were well established.'

Stories related to the bibulous gatherings began to become legend. There were tales of people taking trains home from Paddington and waking up in Cornwall. Soon the business was taking off sufficiently for Bob to decide that he needed to move down from Birmingham, rather than commuting all the time. That also coincided with a fallout that took place with the committee at Warwickshire, on which he sat.

It had been a very happy association, with both club and Birmingham as a whole, since moving up there in 1971, and he continued to enjoy his return visits to both thereafter. However, there was a dispute over the appointment of a chief executive, which saw Bob at odds with some fellow committee members, and it led to him resigning.

The Willis family headed south in 1988, initially finding a property in Clapham before moving close to Wimbledon Common after a couple of years. The south-west London area was to remain home for the rest of his life.

The move to the south-east did not stop Bob celebrating his fortieth birthday in 1989 back at one of his old haunts, the Bibury Court hotel in Gloucestershire. A little too enthusiastically, it turned out, as before the lunch had properly started Bob was hors de combat, having gone early on the imbibing. His hypnotherapy guru Arthur Jackson was over in England at the time and a guest. There was slight bemusement as the host was soon confined to a bedroom, with Jackson standing sentry outside, refusing to let anyone in. Speculation among friends and family, who carried on with the festivities, was that an unusual combination of hypnosis and alcohol might have been behind Bob's sudden retreat.

The year of him turning forty coincided with an impending revolution in the broadcast world that was to prove enormously significant in his life. British Sky Broadcasting had come into being, through the merger of British Satellite Broadcasting and Sky Television, and in April 1991 Sky Sports was launched.

Bob was among the early recruits, although his move into broadcasting was not an immediate leap, more a matter of gradual steps. The Luncheon Club business was still occupying a lot of his time, and while not everything always went to plan, there was plenty of fun along the way.

An early potential mishap came in the form of an arrangement to host the mighty All Blacks during what was then a rare visit to the UK, in November 1989. These were the days when rugby was beginning the awkward transition from amateurism into the fully professional realm, with New Zealand at the forefront. Before they arrived in London for a match against the Barbarians at Twickenham a deal was done, with supporting documentation, for the team to be guests at the Café Royal. Naturally enough, the event swiftly sold out.

The All Blacks having turned up, Bob went to answer a call of nature in the Gents, and soon become aware of some hulking figures alongside him. It was two of the team, announcing that they were not happy with the money on offer and suggesting that if it was not substantially improved they would not be going into the room. This brought an unexpectedly short-pitched reply from the former fast bowler, who was in no mood to negotiate. Appalled, his reply was along the lines of 'If you don't like it you can get stuffed.' He added that the media would be very interested in the details of their non-appearance. After a brief hiatus the crisis was averted, and the world's greatest rugby team duly trooped into the lunch.

Most events went smoothly, and occasionally they were spectacular. The 1988 'Christmas Ball' saw Eric Clapton turn up incognito, and end up playing on stage with the pre-booked act of Georgie Fame and Andy Fairweather Low, before a rapt audience.

The one office at the Café Royal soon became five. While the All Blacks had proved difficult visitors, they were not the only big name in sport to require some nimble disaster aversion. In 1995 Brian Clough was the star invitee, coming down by train from his home in the Midlands on the morning of the lunch. Unfortunately, en route he became rather too well acquainted with the buffet car and turned up the worse for wear.

'Brian had clearly had a few drinks already,' recalls David. 'For some reason he was trying to kiss all the waiters, and we were frantically telling them not to oblige his frequent requests to fill his glass up. By the time he got up to do his question-and-answer he was barely able to speak, and we had to sit him down after seven or eight minutes. It was not long after the famous Eric Cantona kung fu kick incident at Crystal Palace. When asked what he would do to discipline the offender, Brian responded that he would "cut his balls off". The strange thing was that we had organised another event for Brian in Manchester the following day, so we went up there pretty fearful. But he turned up on time and sober, and was absolutely brilliant with everyone.'

As the 1990s progressed, Bob increasingly mixed his business commitments with working for Gulliver's, while steadily upping his time with Sky. Something would have to give.

In 1997 he and former team-mate Geoff Miller got together to create the England Cricket Club, launching it at the Café Royal. They wanted to fashion an organisation that would offer those who had won at least one Test cap the chance to socialise and raise money for charity. After much research, players were tracked down, invitations sent out and a dinner was held, with around 130 living ex-internationals attending. Another of their ideas was to number each player by the sequence of each England debut made. This was the forerunner of those numbers appearing on the players' shirts. For several years there was also a set day at a certain match where the former players could come together again. The ECC was eventually handed on to the TCCB, although the general concept had a dormant spell until it was later revived by Andrew Strauss.

The England Cricket Club was to be Bob's last major contribution to the wider enterprise established in London's West End. By this time he had made his name as a Marmite type of commentator. Some liked him, some did not, but he was hard to ignore. It had come down to a choice between the business and the broadcasting world, and he chose the latter.

9

DIGNITY

The green shoots of a cricket broadcasting revolution in England could be seen by 1989, with Rupert Murdoch and his lieutenants recognising that there was an appetite for live coverage that was not being catered for. New ground was broken when, for the first time, Sky broadcast an England overseas Test in its entirety – the match in Jamaica against the West Indies in February 1990. Fortuitously, it made an extra impact as Graham Gooch led the tourists to a surprise victory.

Bob was not on the commentary team that winter, but was recruited when Sky acquired the rights for the Refuge Assurance League, which took place every Sunday through the summer of 1990. A roster was assembled that featured Tony Greig, Geoff Boycott, Clive Lloyd, David Bairstow, Bob and professional broadcasters in the shape of Henry Blofeld and Simon Reed.

Now head of commentary for Eurosport, Reed recalls a relatively no-frills operation by today's standards. He immediately noticed the early indications of what was to become Bob's trademark style. 'I wouldn't say he was quite as acerbic as he later became, but he certainly called it as he saw it,' says Reed. 'He was very keen on keeping it real and hated bull. He was never dull. In commentary generally there has been a modern trend of people going slightly over the top in trying to make their mark, but Bob didn't need to do that. In that sense he was ahead of his time. His persona on air was very much the same as what he was like off it. He would say much the same thing in the bar as when he had been broadcasting live. I found him enormously engaging company. I think it might have taken a bit of time for people to realise how intelligent he was.'

The following winter Sky acquired the rights to the 1990–91 Ashes, which was to see a 3–0 victory for Australia. Bob was called up. The start coincided with the merger being announced of Sky and British Sky Broadcasting, and it was the first series to go under the banner of simply 'Sky'. The coverage went smoothly enough, although Bob – who was meant to be used purely as an analyst – used to jokingly recall the unexpected baptism of fire he underwent in the presentation business.

Greig was meant to front the teatime round-up and was splitting his time between working for Channel Nine and the coverage being beamed back to the UK. At Melbourne the boxes of the two broadcasters were at opposite ends of the ground. On one of the days Greig got slightly delayed and then found himself held up in the crowds milling around the MCG. Bob sat there waiting for the main man to arrive, but as the allotted time approached it became clear that Greig was not going to make it. With two minutes' notice he was informed, to his horror, that he would have to hold the fort, presentation-wise. By his own account the result was not pretty, and all concerned were glad that it was the middle of the night back at home, with a minimal audience.

The summer of 1991 saw a slight expansion of Sky's domestic rights, and it was also the time when Bob first hooked up with the man who would become his most enduring on-air partner,

Charles Colvile. Formerly of the BBC and London Weekend Television, Colvile was signed up as Sky Sports formally launched in April. An indication of how things have changed, in this era of 24/7 coverage, is that in the previous month a total of just twenty-seven hours' live sport had been shown on British television.

The 55-over Benson and Hedges Cup was now an additional part of the Sky portfolio, and they had also secured a one-hour highlights package for the home Test matches. This involved Bob and Blofeld sitting in a cubicle commentating on every single ball of the day's play, which would then be cut down into a truncated evening show for satellite viewers.

Meanwhile Colvile was enjoying the start of a near thirty-year partnership.

'My first experience of Bob had been watching him play for Surrey as a schoolboy, and now we were working together,' he remembers. 'One of the first games we did was in May at Derby and it was so cold it was spitting with snow. He went out to cover the toss in this huge overcoat, trying to stop his hands from shaking in the freezing weather.'

The following winter he and Colvile were on duty for the 1992 World Cup in Australia – not on site but anchoring the coverage back in the UK in a temporary studio in west London.

'Our premises for that consisted of two portable cabins bolted together in the Sky car park in Osterley,' says Colvile. 'It was either freezing cold when the lights were off, or roasting hot when we were in vision with the big TV lights just a few feet above our heads. When the early-morning Concorde flew in we couldn't hear ourselves think and the whole place rattled.

'Much of it was obviously in the middle of the night and Bob struggled with the hours. On one celebrated occasion we had to "fill", as an ad break had been taken in Australia, and discuss the play out of vision. I hadn't bothered to look at him when we were told to fill, so asked him, "With two overs to go in their innings, how many more do you think Sri Lanka might get?" Bob had fallen asleep and woke with a start when I asked him the question, blurting out, "78!" My reaction was that this would make the next twelve balls interesting viewing.'

The arrival, as main cricket producer, of John Gayleard, a straight-talking Aussie who had made his name doing the same job with Channel Nine, further ramped up Sky's commitment to the sport. New ideas were tried and this saw the brief appearance of *The Boycott and Willis Tea Party*, a post-match programme which was an early forerunner of *The Verdict*. In 1994 the channel bought the rights to one-day internationals and county cricket, with the BBC retaining the Tests and a domestic one-day trophy, in a £60 million package to run for four years. Early that year Bob was dispatched to the West Indies for England's tour, beginning a long uninterrupted run of winters commentating on the national team.

Free from the pressure of having to worry about his body and perform for his country, he was by and large a contented tourist in this phase of his working life. Having to be wary of the wider media was no longer an issue and he got on well with colleagues, enjoying the social side of travelling, albeit while continuing to be dogged by an inability to sleep as much as he wanted.

His delivery was not to everyone's taste, however, once described by journalist Tim de Lisle as remaining 'on one note, the drone of your neighbour's mower'. While popular with many viewers, Bob's propensity for speaking his mind was also liable to get him into trouble. His unswerving eye would be trained on a variety of targets, from players and umpires, to certain cricket fans.

He was not an admirer of the Barmy Army's football-style chanting at grounds, which he felt could ruin the enjoyment for more traditional supporters. Not that the latter group got off scot-free either. In what he subsequently admitted may have been an unfair generalisation, he described many county members as 'trainspotters and social misfits'. The players were not spared. When Paul Collingwood arrived at the crease, armed with his staunch defensive capabilities, on the New Zealand tour of 2007–08, Bob observed, 'For those of you not asleep already back in the UK, here comes Brigadier Block.'

Even the famous tree inside the boundary at Canterbury got the treatment. After it blew down in 2005, Colvile offered the opinion that this was an awful sight to behold, only to get the retort: 'What's sad about it? They should have taken a chainsaw to it years ago. Now the Kent members want to plant another one there – madness!'

Former Sky executive cricket producer Paul King remembers getting an early taste of Bob's thinking on his first meeting with him, at a restaurant in Colombo, on tour in 2001.

'He asked quite bluntly, "What would I want to be liked by the players for?"' says King. 'Bob was an outstanding technical commentator, although his voice and demeanour divided opinion. My general view was that, as a producer, you would rather have him than a bland alternative, although you knew that he was always going to keep you busy.

'He was a wonderful companion on tour, a fantastic storyteller and a top bloke to share a glass of wine with. He always had time for everyone – from the runners to the director. He understood the TV game. You need a range of voices and he played the part of the arch-critic brilliantly, with impeccable timing. He could get away with it because he had so much credibility.'

Underpinning the trenchant opinions was a deep concern for the welfare of the English game, and cricket in general. And it went well beyond commenting from the sidelines, as he was quite prepared to roll his sleeves up and devote time to the apparatus by which he thought he could change things.

Having left the main Warwickshire committee in the late 1990s, he joined that of Surrey, although it was a relatively short-lived term. The reason was that he and Colvile – who also sat on the Surrey leadership body – got into trouble after an item criticising the sightscreens at Lord's. MCC were unhappy that, in technical contravention of the rules, two members of a county committee were taking a pop at them, so the broadcasting duo stepped down.

Potentially more important, although ultimately fruitless, was his instrumental role in founding the Cricket Reform Group in 2003. He had already given countless hours to sitting on various cricket committees and had found trying to make progress a frustrating business. One of his ideas, for example, was four-day first-class cricket between the counties, but it was hard to get the establishment to listen. This was a time before the broader upswing in England performances had been seen. Through the 1980s and 1990s they had managed to win only 46 out of 211 Test matches.

Bob helped bring together various luminaries, including the likes of Michael Parkinson and Mike Atherton, to try and hasten change in the way the sport was run. Predictably, they met with stiff resistance from the establishment. It did not help that their launch coincided with a thumping nine-wicket victory for England against South Africa at The Oval, which squared what had been an outstanding series.

After eventually admitting defeat, he concluded, 'Long before the CRG I used to spend endless time on TCCB committees. We are stuck with the eighteen-county system. There's a huge reluctance to move forward.'

Late the following year did see a significant change for English cricket, although not necessarily along the lines that his reform group had been driving at. It was announced that Sky would be taking over the broadcasting of the sport almost in its entirety. Channel 4, who had taken over from the BBC in terms of free-to-air coverage, would no longer be involved, although there would be post-play highlights on Channel 5. The trade-off, between much-increased revenues to support the domestic game and loss of mainstream visibility, would be debated for many years to come.

The new deal was the catalyst for some significant shake-ups in Sky personnel. More recent ex-England captains Mike Atherton and Nasser Hussain were elevated to senior roles in the commentary box. While not discarded, Bob was among those obliged to take a step either sideways or backwards. Possibly related, 2005 was also a year of some wider shifts in his life, and his marriage to Juliet broke up.

When it came to the reduction of his profile at Sky, Bob was philosophical enough. At the same time he could not help wonder if the strength of his opinions, and attempts at reforming the game, had counted against him when the deals were done, and if there might have been an element of retribution.

'I know I upset the establishment. I don't know if that affected my commentary career,' he told Colvile in a documentary that Sky made about his life ten years later which was entitled, appropriately, *Well, Charles*. In the course of it, Bob reflected on what had informed his approach to broadcasting from the early days onwards.

'I started off being namby-pamby. I had not long been in the England team but I soon became aware that you can't be all things to all men. I was particularly close to Ian Botham and Allan Lamb, and I made a conscious decision to step away from that. I had never been near the England dressing room until Andrew Strauss invited me in 2015.' (He found talking to the England pacemen an enjoyable experience, and thirty-six hours after sharing a bottle of Rioja with Bob, Stuart Broad went out and took 8–15 against Australia at Trent Bridge.)

Colvile had asked Bob about his broadcasting philosophy: 'My style is honest, some would say acerbic, hopefully humorous as well as honest. Nobody has ever come up to me and said, "How dare you say that about me?", so there seems to have been a ring of truth.'

When pressed on how a young Willis might have taken any flak directed his way from the commentary box, he admitted,

'Pretty badly, because I reacted badly when Fred Trueman on *Test Match Special* said, "I don't know what is going off out there," and that Willis "couldn't bowl a hoop down a hill". No one likes criticism, but in professional sport you find it's part of the job. I suppose I stepped over the line a couple of times. I've had to write a couple of letters of apology to England captains. I'm grumpy when England aren't doing well at cricket. But at the end of the day it's a sport, and it should be enjoyed. We are entertainers and it should be taken that way.'

Having slightly more time on his hands from 2006 onwards had its advantages, notably in being able to pursue his many interests away from cricket. There were more visits to watch Manchester City, an allegiance that owed itself to his brief spell growing up in the area. He became a regular tennis-watcher, and the highlight of frequent visits to summer tournaments were several invitations to the Royal Box at Wimbledon. While never quite mastering golf, he was an enthusiastic player, and a member at Royal Wimbledon. For twenty straight years he attended the Leadership Weekend, an annual pro-am organised in Spain and Portugal by close friend Paul Monk to support GroceryAid, the charity of the food and drink industry. His wide-ranging contributions, which went well beyond playing, helped raise £3 million in that period.

Hiking, quizzing, concerts and the cinema were other passions frequently indulged, while there was a return to the wine business with Botham and Geoff Merrill, producing vintages that went under a label featuring their three surnames. In 2014 he married long-time partner Lauren Clark, a sports television producer, with whom he had happily settled in an apartment on the banks of the Thames in Mortlake. Another dimension was opened up by the arrival of a grandson, Jack, to daughter Katie in 2017. (A second grandson, Robert George, known as Bobby, arrived in May 2020, on what would have been Bob's 71st birthday.)

By that point Bob had long since reinvented his career at Sky in the shape of *The Verdict*, sitting alongside his foil Colvile with another invited guest to consider a day's play, in his inimitable fashion.

'It began after 2006 as a twelve-to-fifteen-minute chat at the close of play,' says Colvile, with whom he had established an easy chemistry. 'Then, for the 2009 Ashes, they decided that they wanted to show the highlights and follow it with a full studio discussion programme, which became *The Verdict*.

'I wouldn't pretend that we immediately got sacks of fan mail, but we knew it was working because when we were out doing something at a match loads of people were coming up to us and making a point of saying how much they enjoyed it.

'Before each show we would discuss in some detail how we were going to do it, and while I knew what Bob's rough thoughts were, I never knew exactly what he was going to come up with. He would go quiet for five minutes before we went on air. I was more the straight man and would perhaps load the gun so he could pull the trigger. Occasionally it would come out the wrong way, but nine times out of ten it was right. There was the odd occasion it would go too far, but Bob's attitude was that this was live broadcasting and sometimes you had to be prepared for that to happen. He was always very professional and serious about it.

'Potentially it could have been quite awkward with some of

the guests we had, because a lot of the time they might have been players who he had rinsed during their careers. But that was never really the case, because he was always so welcoming and encouraging to them when they came into the studio. You could tell that within about thirty seconds their perception of him changed as they could see what he was like. An example was Matt Prior, who he had once nicknamed "Dire Prior". They actually got on like a house on fire when they got to know each other. It worked particularly well with people like Mark Butcher and Rob Key, because they liked an argument, and he responded very well to that.

'There was an element of pantomime villain to it, but underneath it was obvious that he cared deeply about the game and wanted England to do well. For the World Cup final of 2019 he was there with the rest of us, barely able to watch. Same with Ben Stokes' match-winning innings at Headingley. Bob came straight out with the line "Forget about me and Botham in 1981, this was the most extraordinary thing I've ever seen."'

The Verdict was, somewhat curiously, given the summer off in 2017. The replacement offering was not a success, the mistake was acknowledged, and it was quickly revived the year after and rebranded as *The Debate*, in line with a parallel football programme of similar ilk.

By now his regular studio partner was one of a relatively small circle who knew that Bob was contending with health problems, following the diagnosis of prostate cancer. It was proving manageable, but the disease had not been entirely contained at an early stage.

'In 2016 he had sent some of us an email letting us know that he had this issue,' says Colvile. 'He was never one to complain, and we adopted the policy that I would not continually ask him about it when we saw each other. He was keen to keep things private, so the subject rarely came up. He did the whole of the 2019 summer, and after that we were discussing how we would do the following away series in New Zealand.'

As it turned out, the last day of England's Test on 15 September proved to be Bob's valedictory turn of post-match analysis. It was at The Oval, where it had all begun, and the opposition, fittingly, was Australia. He managed one more on-air appearance, determined to accept the invitation to participate in a two-way discussion with Sky Sports News, on 7 October.

As his health deteriorated, a few of his good friends from the other side of the world made the long journey to see him at the end of November. Shortly after they had left he was admitted to hospital in Wimbledon. He passed away during the day that followed England's second and final Test in New Zealand, on 4 December 2019.

During the *Well, Charles* documentary, Bob had been asked what epitaph he might choose for himself. He initially joked 'Bah, Humbug', before settling for 'He always did it his way'. Two months after his passing, and more than a month on from the funeral in London, a second gathering was held at Geoff Merrill's vineyard just outside Adelaide to mark his life. The sun shone, and close family were there, along with Australian friends and a few others, including Ian Botham.

Some of his ashes are laid to rest there, marked by a stone bearing an inscription which ends with beautiful simplicity: 'Cricketer, Wine Lover, Mate.'

Part II

A CELEBRATION

Bob the Cricketer, Bob the Pundit, Bob the Man

10

HEADINGLEY, 1981

Willis's heroics

Mike Brearley, *The Guardian* (2 July 2011)

THE first thing I should say is that the train of events in 1981 was extremely fortuitous. In that third Test at Headingley, for a start, Ian Botham and Graham Dilley, whose second-innings partnership of 117 turned the match, could have been out at any moment. Kim Hughes and the Australians were criticised for bowling too wide to them and it was true, they should have tightened their line. But on any other day they would have edged rather than missed, or edged more thinly, or the ball would have landed differently from one of the thick edges.

And Bob Willis was initially not picked for the match. The selectors were afraid he was not fit and thought this was confirmed by his not playing in the match for Warwickshire the weekend before. We were also concerned about his form (he had lost his strike-bowler status and was bowling far too many no-balls, a sure sign of lack of rhythm). Was he, we feared, over the hill? Then, in the second innings of the match, which end was he to bowl from? Bob had preferred to bowl up the slope, partly to prevent himself over-stepping as a result of running too fast downhill.

It was only on the last day, when we had (over a drink the night before) encouraged him to forget the no-balls, and bowl as fast and straight as he could, and when he had bowled a few overs uphill, that he asked to change ends. I took some convincing. Bob Taylor, I think, was the one who said: 'Give him his head, switch him round.'

Australia were cruising at 56 for one, chasing a mere 130. Then Willis struck, with three wickets, two in the last over before lunch. At 58 for four, we knew for the first time we had a chance. But despite the battering Australia had suffered the day before, despite the shift in balance of morale, still only a slim one. After lunch, John Dyson (century-maker in the first innings) gloved Willis to Taylor, attempting to hook. Rod Marsh was well caught just inside the boundary, hooking. Dennis Lillee and Ray Bright added about 30 in four overs, and seemed to be racing to the target. Mike Gatting ran up to me: 'Tell him to bowl straight at Dennis, it doesn't matter what length,' and sure enough, Lillee spooned a straight, well-pitched-up ball to Gatting at mid on, who dived forward to take his second fine catch of the innings.

Getting us to this place had required (along with Willis's heroics) a terrific supportive spell by Chris Old, who bowled Australia's best batsman, and soon to be the best in the world, Allan Border, and went for a run an over until Bright hit him for two fours to square leg. Finally, Willis removed Bright's middle stump with a perfect yorker. The series was level at 1–1.

DAY BY DAY – A REMARKABLE TEST

Day one – dropped catches and fading hopes

ENGLAND have a trouble that is catching. The disease first afflicted them at Trent Bridge, subsided at Lord's, but flared again in the third Test at Leeds yesterday. Three acceptable chances were bungled and Australia, already leading 1–0 in the series, ended the day in a healthy position at 203–3, with Dyson out just before the close having completed a long, watchful maiden century.

There was not a great deal for Brearley to recall with pleasure on his first day back as England's captain. When he was last in charge his fielders used to catch almost everything that went their way, but no longer. And although there were spells of good bowling from Old and Botham, England's attack collectively was again lacking. In this respect the omission of Emburey could yet prove costly.

Paul Fitzpatrick, *The Guardian*

Day two – Botham with the ball

THE second day of the third Test match, like the second Test at Lord's and also the first day of this one, contained little of the quality or the cut-and-thrust to be expected when England meet Australia – at any rate until Botham, happily, took five wickets after tea. Until they declared at 401 for nine, with twenty minutes left, Australia just plodded along, against much ordinary bowling, helped by a further blackening of England's catching record.

Though nothing like as bad as the one at Trent Bridge, this is not the best of pitches. Australia's batsmen were rapped on the thighs often enough for England's to be sure not to mislay their thigh pads this morning. Besides this, the occasional ball kept low. With their one-match lead in the series Australia were content to take no risks. They batted as though sure enough that a total of around 400 would be an insurance against defeat, as no doubt it will be.

John Woodcock, *The Times*

Day three – cushions and collapses

CRICKET again did injury to itself in the third Test at Leeds when the authorities held themselves up to ridicule. Play between England and Australia was declared impossible at the very moment the field was dry and bathed in evening sunshine. A full house greeted the decision, and another instance of the game's laws being an ass, with a shower of cushions.

Before the bad light, real and so-called, England had been made to follow on 227 runs behind Australia. To a nation expecting that the tide would turn at Headingley, and optimistically hoping that it would bring the Ashes with it, to follow on was a bitter let-down. In their reply England immediately lost Graham Gooch for the second time in the day when Dennis Lillee had him caught in the slips in the first over. It made the worst possible start for a side that still has to bat two days to save itself, on a wicket of increasing eccentricity.

Scyld Berry, *The Observer*

Day four – Botham with the bat

THE amazing Ian Botham had the mourners dancing in the aisles at Headingley last night with the greatest comeback since Lazarus. Botham took up his bat and walked in with England slipping towards defeat in the third Test and the Ashes as good as lost. Three and a half hours later he had transformed a wake into a carnival with an almost miraculous 145 not out – the highest score of even his remarkable Test career.

Australian skipper Kim Hughes was in no doubt: 'That must go down as one of the greatest innings in cricket. He had some luck but deserved it. It was the sort of innings that he might never play again, and I found it very hard to set a field to him. In that mood, he is difficult to stop. The great thing is that he never changes his game, and anyone who tries to change him should be lynched. He is a player who wins games and he is the only one England have got.'

Pat Gibson, *Daily Express*

Day five – the spell of a lifetime

NOT since the golden age of cricket have England won a Test to compare with the one they won by 18 runs against Australia at Headingley yesterday. Only Test cricket could have produced such a fascinating plot as this; no other game could have allowed such an unlikely and outrageous swing of fortune as England experienced. Only a drama that is allowed to unfold over five days could permit such a twist in the plot so wild as to be almost unthinkable.

The Headingley crowd had seen the rebirth of Botham. They now saw Bob Willis peel away the years and give a display of pace bowling culled from his youth, before the days of suspect, creaking knees. No one has tried harder for his country over the years. His performance surpassed anything that he has produced in Test cricket previously. Throughout his spell he found movement, bounce, life and pace; too much pace for eight Australians. No Englishman has ever returned a more impressive set of figures at Headingley – eight for 43, an analysis to give Willis a glow of pride when he is 'old and grey, and nodding by the fire'.

Paul Fitzpatrick, *The Guardian*

EIGHT WICKETS: AS DESCRIBED IN THE BBC TV COMMENTARY

Wicket 1: *Trevor Chappell, 8, caught by Bob Taylor, fending off a short ball.*

RICHIE BENAUD: That really was a difficult delivery. He's gone, and there's not much that could be done about that. Trevor Chappell really had no chance. A very good piece of bowling from Bob Willis. The second wicket goes down at 56.

Wicket 2: *Kim Hughes, 0, caught at third slip by Ian Botham.*

RICHIE BENAUD: What a good catch. Everything is running for Botham. Runs, wickets and catches. And the Australian captain goes for nought. Caught Botham, bowled Willis. Hughes has gone, and it's 58 for three.

Wicket 3: *Graham Yallop, 0, caught at short leg by Mike Gatting.*

RICHIE BENAUD: Ooh, good catch. Super catch, that. Marvellous reflex action there. Yallop has gone without scoring – 58 for four, with Dyson 29 not out. What a marvellous catch and what a great session for England. What a session and what a match. Great piece of fielding that, and it's given England a real chance.

Lunch summary

RICHIE BENAUD: Absolute misery for Australia there – 58 for four – and what joy for England. Three for Willis, two of them in that last over. At lunchtime on this final day, Australia face this daunting task – six wickets in hand, and they still need 72 to win.

Wicket 4: *John Dyson, 34, caught by Bob Taylor, edging an attempted hook.*

CHRISTOPHER MARTIN-JENKINS: He's got a touch on it and he's gone. Going for the hook, which he had played so well in the previous over. But Bob Willis's extra pace getting him. And look at that look of suppressed excitement on Mike Brearley and other England fielders. Willis's fourth wicket, 68 for six.

Wicket 5: *Rodney Marsh, 4, caught, hooking, by Graham Dilley at deep fine leg.*

CHRISTOPHER MARTIN-JENKINS: In the air, Dilley's underneath it, and he's caught it! A very, very good catch indeed in the circumstances. He didn't have much room to play with. Another foot and he would have been over the boundary. Willis has taken his fifth wicket. Sooner or later, Rodney Marsh had to go for the big hit, and England are holding their catches just at the time when they need to. 74 for seven, Australia.

Wicket 6: *Geoff Lawson, 1, caught, edging to Bob Taylor.*

CHRISTOPHER MARTIN-JENKINS: Yes, he's got a touch and he's gone. Willis has taken his sixth wicket. Lawson out for one, and England on the brink of an absolutely sensational victory, which is going to go down as one of the most amazing Test victories of all time, if it happens.

Wicket 7: *Dennis Lillee, 17, caught by Mike Gatting at mid on.*

RICHIE BENAUD: Oh, what a good catch. And Lillee has miscued it to mid on. Gatting didn't sight it to start with, couldn't pick it up in the background, then got it, and it needed a dive forward to take a great catch. 110 for nine. And the first one Willis got up into Lillee's half produced the wicket.

Wicket 8: *Ray Bright, 19, middle stump knocked out by a yorker.*

RICHIE BENAUD: Bowled him. It's all over. And it is one of the most fantastic victories ever known in Test cricket history. Bob Willis, eight wickets, a fabulous performance. England have won this match after one of the most astonishing fightbacks you could ever see.

Post-match summary

RICHIE BENAUD: And what a remarkable scorecard that is. 111: England regard that as the devil's number. Well, there was no devil's number about it today. Australia beaten and England winning by 18 runs. Only John Dyson, 34, Wood, 10, Bright, 19, and Lillee, 17, reaching double figures. And the man who made it all possible for England – a really sensational performance, this – 15.1 overs, three maidens, eight for 43. It's his best ever Test match performance, Bob Willis, and I don't think I've ever seen him bowl better. He bowled like a man inspired out there today. It was almost as though he was in another world. This game has to go down in just a handful of really great Test matches I've seen as a player and a commentator. A marvellous match . . .

MEMORIES OF THE MATCH

The last day at Headingley, 1981

Bob Willis (2019)

July 21, 1981 will be forever etched into my memory, although not for the reasons I ever expected it to be. I woke that morning believing it would be the day that saw my last few sessions as an England cricketer, not the day that came to define my career more than any other.

I was lucky to be playing at all in what became known as one of the most dramatic Test matches of modern times, and I knew it. It was the third encounter of the series, and had been preceded by a win for the Australians at Trent Bridge and then a boring draw at Lord's, most notable for the pair registered by Ian Botham that had seen him stripped of the captaincy, which had then been handed to Mike Brearley. I had suffered from a heavy bout of flu during the Lord's game and had pulled out of Warwickshire's Championship match between the two Tests, against Surrey at The Oval.

The plan was to make sure I was fully fit for Leeds, but on the Saturday morning I took a call in the Oval pavilion from the chairman of selectors, Alec Bedser. He was ringing to break the news that I was not going to be playing at Headingley anyway. 'But Alec, I only pulled out of the game so I could be properly rested for the next Test. I will be fine by then,' I protested. His response was that Brearley was only interested in players who were absolutely guaranteed of being 100 per cent fit. He then asked if there was any cricket I could play to prove my fitness before the team met up on the Wednesday, so I told him I would go back up to Birmingham to play in a one-day game for the Second XI on the Monday.

Alec went back to Brears to tell him the situation and in the meantime rang the secretary of Derbyshire, ordering him to intercept the invitation to play at Headingley that had been sent to Mike Hendrick (that was how it was done back then: the selectors met on Friday night, picked the team and then posted an invitation to play to the individual's county). At Derbyshire they quietly nabbed the envelope that arrived and, having shown I was fit in the Seconds, off I went to Headingley. Even then, I later found out, it was a close call between myself and John Emburey for the final place in the bowling attack.

On the Saturday night, after day three of the Test, best remembered for an angry crowd throwing cushions on the ground because of an early finish due to supposed bad light, England were already following on, and the players had gone up to Ian Botham's house in Epworth for a barbecue, to which the Australians were also invited. After they disgorged from their team bus, plenty of food and drink was consumed amid an affable atmosphere. I was one of a couple of players who stayed the night. At midday on the Sunday, the old-fashioned rest day, Ian and I went to the pub for a couple more beers before I made my way back down to Leeds to prepare for what looked like a certain early finish on the Monday.

As it turned out, we were still batting at the end of day four, myself as the number eleven and Ian on 145 not out after an extraordinary knock. Australian captain Kim Hughes had made the mistake of not bowling their spinner, Ray Bright, and persisting with the pace and seam attack. Ian had begun by slogging and looked pretty sketchy, but then he started to play magnificently as he got support from Graham Dilley and Chris Old. Had Bright come on earlier, I am sure Ian would have offered a catch sooner or later. At the close, I was simply trying to block up an end and keep him company.

The first thing we had to do that Monday night was check back in to our Leeds hotel, the Dragonara, which is now a Hilton. Everyone had brought their belongings to the ground in anticipation of an early finish. After that it was off to our regular haunt, The Junction in Otley, where we had a relatively quiet evening, some of us assessing our futures over a couple of beers. There was a consensus that what had happened, miracle though it already was, was likely to prove only a temporary postponement of our demise as international cricketers. Defeat would mean that we were 2–0 down with three to play in the series, and the likes of myself, Peter Willey, Bob Taylor and

Chris Old might expect to be pensioned off. We had not won for twelve Tests and it felt like we were in the tumbril, trundling over the cobbles of the Place de la Concorde to face the guillotine.

We were right to be concerned. It was notable just how much the side changed in that series, even after we began winning and had the Australians on the run. There was none of the more generous and stable modern policy of giving someone around five Tests to see if they are made of the right stuff. It is remarkable to reflect how many people were dropped after we had turned it around. Graham Dilley did not play in the next Test, at Edgbaston; Chris Old, Peter Willey and Bob Taylor were omitted for the fifth, at Old Trafford; while Graham Gooch and David Gower did not make the last one, at The Oval. Only myself, Ian Botham, Mike Gatting and Geoff Boycott were ever-presents in the series, and we used three different wicketkeepers.

In my case, as a thirty-two-year-old fast bowler, it seemed like the end was nigh. Yet while I was never one to be over-burdened with optimism, I was aware on the Tuesday morning that the Australian camp was not an overwhelmingly happy one, which offered a sliver of hope. Although they were all Western Australians, I knew that Dennis Lillee and Rod Marsh, in particular, were not impressed with Kim Hughes as skipper. It is a truism of cricket that disunity can be the driver of batting collapses under pressure, and they will have been as surprised as we were that the match had gone into a fifth day at all.

I got out almost straight away in the morning, leaving Australia with 130 to win. Beefy quickly removed Graeme Wood but looked a bit jaded after what he had done with the bat. He and Dill opened the bowling but the latter went for 11 in two overs, which was unaffordable. I came on at the football end, first change, and didn't take a wicket in five overs. I said to Brears, tongue in cheek, that I was too old to be bowling up the hill and suggested he give me a chance coming down the hill, even though I hadn't taken any wickets in the first innings.

Throughout my career I had a problem with no-balls, and I had even been dropped the previous summer from two Tests simply for not being able to bowl enough legitimate deliveries. Mike said to forget about that, reminded me that the wicket was starting to misbehave and ordered me to just run in and bowl fast and straight.

This seemed to flick a switch and, charging in with a clear head, I bowled the most important 11-ball spell of my life, which yielded three wickets. In that span I got Trevor Chappell, had Hughes taken by Beefy in the slips and removed Graham Yallop through a nasty lifter that was snapped up by Mike Gatting at short leg. The motivation to save my England career was proving a powerful one.

By lunchtime it was 58–4 and the other figure that loomed large in this match, the odds of 500–1 offered on Saturday against us winning, was starting to look like the bet of the century. It was only then that you could sense a transfer of the pressure from one dressing room to the other. We had a forty-minute break and I sat in the corner alone, chewing on a cheese and tomato sandwich. I was not in the so-called 'trance' at that point but nor was I very communicative.

After we went back out Chris Old got the crucial wicket of Allan Border and, with them still only halfway to the target, the wobble was fully on. Soon I had first-innings centurion John Dyson caught behind, hooking off the gloves, and Rod Marsh was well caught by Dilley on the fine-leg boundary. By this stage I had got in this zone and didn't want to be distracted by celebrations or asked about the field. This was where Brearley was such a good man-manager. He said, 'I will look after the field; you just keep doing what you are doing.'

I kept marching back to my mark, trying to shrug off the fielders after wickets were taken, and did not want to waste energy by being demonstrative. In 1977 I had undergone hypnotherapy via a doctor I met at a barbecue in Australia, Arthur Jackson, and he had taught me to visualise success on the field. He would send me hypnotherapy tapes about relaxing and trying to cure my insomnia. If I was aware of focusing on anything at this point, it was on what Arthur had taught me about how to achieve success.

When Geoff Lawson nicked off behind, they were 75–8 and the crowd's blood was up. It is sometimes said that there were a lot of spectators at Headingley that day, but the truth is there were plenty of gaps in the stands, even though about 250,000 people have told me they were in attendance. However many were there, they were making a racket, although you could sense some anxiety returning when Lillee and Bright came together. They were no mugs with the bat, and Terry Alderman was the only real rabbit in their order.

There was a brief flurry of fours as Dennis began stepping back and angling anything vaguely short over the slips, to get Australia into three figures and closer to the line. So I concentrated on pitching it up and he lifted the ball in a tantalising arc towards mid on, where Gatt ran in and took a fine catch, grabbing it as if it was the last cheese and pickle roll in the buffet. With Alderman in and 20 still needed, I knew we were going do it, although hardly in the dramatic fashion that eventuated, demolishing Bright's middle stump with the score on 111.

Now the main job was to sprint off the ground safely, and the only bit of that I remember is Goochy grabbing me. We ran up to that sideways-on pavilion the ground featured back then, where my finest hour was to be followed by one of my most embarrassing ones. This was the somewhat bizarre interview on the balcony with the BBC's Peter West in the course of which, among other things, I berated the cricket media.

I cannot use the excuse that the adrenaline was still coursing through me, because by then I had been in the bath, come round a little and changed into my standard-issue Duncan Fearnley sweater. We had been given a towelling from the press for losing in the West Indies in the winter, and then there had been the onslaught about Beefy and the running of the side. I was resentful about how he had been treated. The team's relationship with the media had become very strained, which was a strange situation for me because I instinctively liked the media underneath it all – partly through my father's job as a journalist – and early in my career I had got on with them very well.

Everything had been building up inside and now the sluice gates opened. I said a few humorous things, or at least I thought they were humorous, about being too old to bowl up the hill, but then I started going on about the state of British journalism. It seems almost funny now. I could not enjoy the moment, and that was typical of me at the time. The sad thing is we never celebrated as a team either. Brearley had to do a press conference, followed by Beefy and then me. By the time I got back to the dressing room virtually the whole team had gone. It was a bit weird, but everyone had dispersed to all points of the compass, rushing away to play in the NatWest Trophy second round the next day.

Warwickshire went on to lose to Sussex in our NatWest match and the assumption was that I had been up all night imbibing. But I basically had one can of beer with Beefy, who also had a cigar on the go. It was not until I was driving back to Birmingham and put on the Radio 4 news at five o'clock that I began to appreciate the magnitude of what had happened. The lead headline was this amazing victory and only then did it start to sink in, because everything had been so flat at the ground by the end.

I got home early in the evening, had some supper and watched the TV: that was the extent of the festivities. I had to be at Edgbaston at 9 a.m. the next morning to sort out the Warwickshire team. There was no 'We'll enjoy the moment together tonight', as would happen now.

I had my 8–43, but this series rightly became known as 'Botham's Ashes'. Mike Brearley was also to take plenty of plaudits, and I agreed with the sentiment once expressed by Australian Rodney Hogg, who described him as having 'a degree in people'. It should be said, however, that it is easier to captain when you have the likes of myself and Botham at our peak. It has always been the way that bowlers can make captains. A good example is Ricky Ponting, a very average skipper in my view (though a superb batsman), who had

Glenn McGrath and Shane Warne to call upon. But Brears was brilliant at handling fellow players, and the only one he struggled with was Phil Edmonds. I was to find exactly the same thing in trying to deal with the difficult side of Edmonds's nature. At that moment, however, after the glory of Headingley, I had no idea that the resurrection of my career would also lead to me becoming captain myself and having to cope with such challenges.

This previously unpublished piece was written by Bob in 2019.

Unbe-bloody-lievable!

Ian Botham, *My Autobiography* (1994)

Our hopes of adding 50 or so the following morning disappeared when Bob Willis was caught by Allan Border off Alderman after we had added only five to the total. I finished unbeaten on 149 and we had a lead of 129 which, although nowhere near enough for us to harbour real ambitions of winning, at least meant we were still in the match.

Then Bob – who, don't forget, very nearly didn't make it on to the field at all – stormed in at pace to produce one of the greatest bowling performances ever seen.

He was fully aware of the situation; during the week before the match he had discussed with me and a few other close colleagues the possibility that this might be his last appearance for England. There were a few young bowlers knocking on the door and, after having to pull out of the [1980–81] West Indies tour, he had admitted, 'I never thought I'd play cricket again, let alone Test cricket.'

No wonder he ran in that day like a man possessed, and as though his life depended on it. He knew that his career probably did.

Here again we profited from a spot of Brearley psychology. He held Bob back at first for two reasons. Firstly, he reasoned that as Picca [Dilley] and I were on a roll, why not keep the dice spinning? Secondly, he thought it might help to wind Bob up. I had Graeme Wood caught behind by Bob Taylor at 13 for one and we were on our way. Then John Dyson, who had made an excellent hundred in the first innings, and Trevor Chappell pushed the Aussies to 56 without further loss. Now Brears switched Willis from bowling uphill, which he had not enjoyed, to downhill, which he certainly did. The result was the most magnificent spell of sustained hostile bowling it has ever been my privilege to witness. First a bouncer to Trevor Chappell took the glove and went to Bob Taylor behind the stumps; then two runs later, in the last over before lunch, I held on to one at slip off Kim Hughes. Three balls later it was 58 for four when Graham Yallop was caught at short square leg by Mike Gatting.

You could tell that something had happened to the Aussies. As we came out after lunch we looked across the balcony and saw the expression on their faces: talk about rabbits caught in the headlights! By now the pitch had made batting a lottery and our adrenalin was pumping. Chilly [Old] bowled Border to make it 65 for five, Bob tricked Dyson into mishooking (68 for six), Marsh top-edged him to Dilley to make it 74 for seven, and then Geoff Lawson was caught behind for one, making the score 75 for eight.

Now it was our turn to get the jitters as this amazing match took on yet another twist. They still needed only 55 to win and although that should have been too many bearing in mind the state of the pitch, somehow Lillee and Bright managed to put on 35 in four overs. Taking a leaf out of our book by going for broke, Bright got stuck into Chilly, hitting him for 10 in one over.

It was all getting a bit frantic; but then came the moment that made all the difference. Bob bowled a ball to Lillee as near to the blockhole as he could manage. DK tried to go for the big hit but only managed to spoon the ball up in the air. It looked safe at first because Gatting, positioned quite deep at mid on to cope with the slog, had an awful lot of ground to cover and, as we all know, even at his fittest Gatt was always likely to come second to Linford Christie. The ball couldn't have been in the air for more than a couple of seconds but it felt like a lifetime. Everyone just froze on the spot, except Gatt, of course. From somewhere Gatt found the pace he needed, sprinted in, dived and held the catch inches above the ground. It was like watching the winning goal in the FA Cup final.

Although we still had one more wicket to take, I think that was the instant we knew the match was ours. We were even able to cope with Chilly dropping two sharp chances at third slip.

Then came one of the most memorable moments in cricket. Bob, who had never run in with more passion and commitment or sheer self-belief, sent down a perfect yorker and Bright's stumps were scattered to kingdom come – unbe-bloody-lievable!

Coming as it did a week before the wedding of Prince Charles and Lady Diana Spencer, our achievement gave the cricket public and the whole nation an excuse to start partying somewhat earlier than expected.

Courage and determination help Willis stand Test of time

John Woodcock, *The Times* (22 July 1981)

WHEN Bob Willis was forced to return home from Trinidad on 20 February this year, two months before the end of the England tour of West Indies, there can have been few people who did not think he had played his last Test match. Even if the damaged cartilage from which he was suffering were to be repaired, there seemed little chance of it allowing him to bowl for England again.

He first had trouble with his knees in the middle 1970s, when for two years he was under the surgeon and out of the England side. Even as long ago as that his career was in jeopardy, especially in view of his great height and the fact that, lacking the rhythm and action of a born fast bowler, he imposes an unnatural strain upon his frame.

But Willis is no ordinary cricketer. He first came into the public eye when chosen, somewhat surprisingly, to fly out to Australia in November 1970 as a replacement for the injured Alan Ward.

By the end of the tour he had developed from an unbroken colt into a confident young man who had forced himself into Ray Illingworth's Ashes-winning Test side. His bowling was coming on and in the Tests in which he played he held one of the best catches at slip I have ever seen.

Having, when the winter started, been keeping goal for Guildford City, he was in good diving form.

He was, on that tour, irreverently amusing at the Christmas party given by the press to the players.

In 1971 he was to leave Surrey, when they were slow to give him a county cap, for Warwickshire, a gamble at the time but one that has paid him handsomely.

Willis's forthright personality and strong views were reflected in the attack he made yesterday (on BBC television) on those cricket writers who specialise in 'small-minded quotes'. He is a close friend and admirer of Brearley's, and, of course, of Botham's. He was, however, fined recently by the TCCB for saying publicly that he thought the England captaincy was undermining Botham's cricket.

Willis has now taken 214 wickets in 60 Test matches. Among Englishmen only Trueman, Underwood, Statham and Bedser have taken more. Yesterday's heroic achievement comes in his benefit year and less than four months after having a floating piece of cartilage removed from his left knee. Today he will be bowling again, for Warwickshire against Sussex at Edgbaston.

At thirty-two his comeback is almost as remarkable as England's.

The undoubted Man of the Match

Dennis Lillee, *Menace: The Autobiography* (2003)

The wicket was doing a bit at the time and they were still not in front. Fast bowler Graham Dilley and Ian Botham were at the crease, with only Chris Old and Bob Willis to follow. I ask you, what could happen?

I'll tell you what happened. Botham went on to score 149, Dilley 56, Old 29 and even Willis, who scored only two, helped Botham put on 37 for the last wicket to give England a fragile lead of 129. Big deal.

A great innings from Both? Let me tell you it was a bloody lucky innings. We dropped him countless times, nicks went over the top and there was lots of playing and missing. I get sick and tired of people saying it was one of the greatest innings of all time. Even Ian agrees it was not and admits there was an awful lot of luck. He had nothing to lose and just threw the kitchen sink at everything we tossed at him. According to the record books, Botham scored 45 runs off the 24 balls he received from me and I expected to get him with virtually every ball I bowled. He just went for it and it came off. Good luck to him. He chanced his arm and it worked. But great? No.

What was great was Bob Willis's bowling in our second innings. That was the greatest one-off sustained effort I ever saw from a fast bowler in the entire time I played cricket, with the crowd roaring him on. To me, it was Willis's match, despite the superhero thing about Botham. I'd like to point out the next two innings he played, and the way he bowled, made it clear this was Botham's Ashes series, but not as a result of that one innings. So the next time someone comes up to me and says, 'Wasn't Ian's innings at Headingley great?' and I say, 'No,' perhaps people will understand me a little better.

The undoubted Man of the Match was Bob Willis. He was at his best with final figures of 8–43 off 15.1 overs and, remember, we were 56–1 at one stage, chasing that total of 130. I reckon I would still have got 500–1 at Ladbroke's on an England win then.

Willis the indestructible is the saviour of the summer

Frank Keating, *The Guardian* (22 July 1981)

THINGS like this are always better when you know they could not have happened to a nicer chap. Simply, Bob Willis, winter's has-been, has resurrected the summer, saved a whole series. With a little help from his friend Ian, mind you.

Bright-eyed and bushy-haired, long-legged and wonky-kneed; we have never once seen him charge in off his mark, have we, without those high-stepping knees working up the head of steam as stampingly methodical and relentless as those prancing iron bars attached to the flywheel of that first puffing Rocket that was flogged from Stockton to Darlington.

The Willis family hail from up that way. He was born in Sunderland but his journalist father ended up in Surrey. Bob was brought up in Cobham, stockbroker, mock Tudor, mock-life belt.

I had occasion to spend a couple of Christmases in Cobham a few years ago. One festive afternoon we went for a walk across the old Recreation Ground in downtown Stoke d'Abernon. That very afternoon I was aware that under some blazing tropical sun Bob's two great Cornish-pasty boots were slapping themselves down on some foreign field for England. Talk about heart and sole.

We digested our mince pies and dug our new-gloved hands deeper into overcoat pockets as frost rolled in and I fancied I heard those two great feet clattering in over the frost-hard turf of England, grunting and gritting as well . . .

The Rec was where Willis learnt his cricket after his day at grammar school. And then he gangled home to play his whining Bob Dylan records and moonily dream of things like eight for 43 for England that was to come 60 Test matches later.

Early in February, we lined up to say goodbye to Bob before breakfast in the Trinidad Hilton Hotel. The legs had given up again and everyone knew that this was the very end.

Kaput. Finis. Good luck, mate. Don't stick around the county slog too long.

Yesterday I was minding my own business watching a pleasant enough county game in the West, up in the bar above the pavilion and behind plate-glass window. Small match in Bristol, not many there.

Suddenly – honest – tennis balls, satchels, luncheon bags, bags and school caps went into the air from the tiny knot of schoolboys huddled down at third man. England had done it! No, said someone in the bar, Willis has done it.

A man possessed

Allan Border, *An Autobiography* (1986)

We were still on good terms with ourselves, one up in the series with two Tests gone. The next was at Leeds, and to say the wheels fell off is to considerably understate what happened.

I still can't believe it. I can't believe that we could declare at 9–401, bowl England out for 174, have them 7–135 in the follow-on ... and still lose the bloody game. I don't have to remind you what Botham did to us in their second innings: an unbeaten, blistering 149 to lift England to 356.

Despite it, we were odds-on to win the match and take a 2–0 lead in the series. When the England innings ended early on the fifth day, our target was 130. The ball was seaming, but if Botham could make 149 on his own, we'd collectively bowl over 130. No problems. And there weren't too many problems early. We lost Wood with the score at 13, but John Dyson and Trevor Chappell took us along to 56 without further damage. There was no indication of the shocking chain of events which was about to follow.

Bob Willis started it by getting Trevor with a rearing delivery. Our demise was under way. Trevor's wicket was Willis's inspiration and he careered through our line-up like a man possessed. Kim Hughes and Graham Yallop both fell for a duck. It was certainly Willis's day. He had been a lion-hearted performer for England for a lot of years and this was his moment of glory. He richly deserved it. I just wished he'd saved the most devastating performance of his career for some other team. Why pick on us?

ENGLAND v AUSTRALIA

Played at Headingley, Leeds, on 16, 17, 18, 20, 21 July 1981

Toss:	Australia
Umpires:	DGL Evans & BJ Meyer
Man of the Match:	IT Botham
Result:	**England won by 18 runs**

Close of play:
Day 1: Aus (1) 203–3 (Hughes 24*, Bright 1*, 82 overs)
Day 2: Eng (1) 7–0 (Gooch 2*, Boycott 0*, 2 overs)
Day 3: Eng (2) 6–1 (Boycott 0*, Brearley 4*, 4.2 overs)
Day 4: Eng (2) 351–9 (Botham 145*, Willis 1*, 85 overs)

AUSTRALIA

J Dyson	b Dilley	102	(2)	c Taylor b Willis	34
GM Wood	lbw b Botham	34	(1)	c Taylor b Botham	10
TM Chappell	c Taylor b Willey	27		c Taylor b Willis	8
KJ Hughes*	c and b Botham	89		c Botham b Willis	0
RJ Bright	b Dilley	7	(8)	b Willis	19
GN Yallop	c Taylor b Botham	58	(5)	c Gatting b Willis	0
AR Border	lbw b Botham	8	(6)	b Old	0
RW Marsh†	b Botham	28	(7)	c Dilley b Willis	4
GF Lawson	c Taylor b Botham	13		c Taylor b Willis	1
DK Lillee	not out	3		c Gatting b Willis	17
TM Alderman	not out	0		not out	0
Extras	(b 4, lb 13, w 3, nb 12)	32		(lb 3, w 1, nb 14)	18
Total	(for 9 wkts dec) (155.2 overs)	**401**		(36.1 overs)	**111**

ENGLAND

GA Gooch	lbw b Alderman	2	c Alderman b Lillee	0
G Boycott	b Lawson	12	lbw b Alderman	46
JM Brearley*	c Marsh b Alderman	10	c Alderman b Lillee	14
DI Gower	c Marsh b Lawson	24	c Border b Alderman	9
MW Gatting	lbw b Lillee	15	lbw b Alderman	1
P Willey	b Lawson	8	c Dyson b Lillee	33
IT Botham	c Marsh b Lillee	50	not out	149
RW Taylor†	c Marsh b Lillee	5	c Bright b Alderman	1
GR Dilley	c and b Lillee	13	b Alderman	56
CM Old	c Border b Alderman	0	b Lawson	29
RGD Willis	not out	1	c Border b Alderman	2
Extras	(b 6, lb 11, w 6, nb 11)	34	(b 5, lb 3, w 3, nb 5)	16
Total	(50.5 overs)	**174**	(87.3 overs)	**356**

England	O	M	R	W	O	M	R	W
Willis	30	8	72	0	15.1	3	43	8
Old	43	14	91	0	9	1	21	1
Dilley	27	4	78	2	2	0	11	0
Botham	39.2	11	95	6	7	3	14	1
Willey	13	2	31	1	3	1	4	0
Boycott	3	2	2	0				

Australia	O	M	R	W	O	M	R	W
Lillee	18.5	7	49	4	25	6	94	3
Alderman	19	4	59	3	35.3	6	135	6
Lawson	13	3	32	3	23	4	96	1
Bright					4	0	15	0

Fall of Wickets:

	Aus	Eng	Eng	Aus
1st	55	12	0	13
2nd	149	40	18	56
3rd	196	42	37	58
4th	220	84	41	58
5th	332	87	105	65
6th	354	112	133	68
7th	357	148	135	74
8th	396	166	252	75
9th	401	167	319	110
10th	–	174	356	111

11

IF NOT FOR YOU: TRIBUTES AND MEMORIES

A partner to remember

Paul Allott, *Wisden*

There are some things that you cannot be late for. Getting to see Bob for the final time was simply a matter of life or death, and I nearly missed him.

Bob was a champion of public transport. He loved trains, buses and particularly the Tube. He knew every bus route, every underground line, each station, stop by stop. Heck, he even knew the damned timetables. He was a better reference point than the TfL website! How ironic, then, that the delayed South Western Railway service to Putney gave us just seven minutes for one final hand squeeze in a hugely emotional farewell.

The fact that we nearly missed each other would have tickled his sense of humour. I can only ever remember him being late once and that was two weeks later, at his funeral, when the hearse got stuck in the traffic in Barnes. He should have gone by bus.

Our friendship was an enduring one. From the latter part of his playing days, through more than twenty-five years of broadcasting, travelling and holidaying together, we remained the very best of pals.

It began at Old Trafford in 1981 during the marvellous Ashes series that ultimately defined Bob's bowling. I was a naive opening bowler, freshly selected and in awe of the others in that dressing room, most of whom I held as heroes, never mind team-mates. Brearley, Boycott, Botham, Knott and, of course, Willis, who was well established as England's premier fast bowler by then.

I thought of Bob as somewhat stern and unapproachable, and in truth a little frightening. How quickly this was dispelled as he insisted on being the first to buy me a beer in The Romper after practice, welcoming me with a smile and immediate camaraderie as his prospective new-ball partner. A lifelong friendship had begun before we'd even bowled a ball together. Looking back, I think my preconceptions probably stemmed from a deep-seated respect for Bob and a sense of not wanting to let him down.

In that fifth Test, we batted together first and quite improbably put on 56 for the tenth wicket, before Bob tried to hit Lillee back over his head. Never a good idea! However, our partnership with the bat may have inspired Brearley to keep us in tandem with the new ball. As a novice, having scored a maiden fifty and with my home crowd behind me, there was little time for nerves or apprehension on my part. We took four wickets in seven balls between us. Bob ripped out three in an over and I got my maiden Test wicket with the first of the next.

We didn't play many Tests together, but he was instrumental in my success in my first and in his last, when I bowled at my best at Headingley in July 1984.

Bob always cared about cricket and he had a mission, largely unfulfilled in the end, to make the game in England more efficient. He wanted to introduce a slimmed-down county structure that could be more easily managed and understood, with greater appeal to players and public. It was a plan that began, as far as I was concerned, on the boundary edge in Nagpur in 1981–82 during a four-month England tour – my first, his tenth. Sheets of foolscap were consumed with a four-day county schedule, separated from one-day cricket, that allowed rest and practice, with some Test matches as stand-alone fixtures to concentrate the players' and spectators' attention. He was ahead of his time by at least twenty years.

Later Bob was a founder of the Cricket Reform Group, which championed the case for restructuring the game. We even had an audience with an intrigued and sympathetic Duncan Fletcher in Bulawayo in 2004–05. But, in the end, even Bob had to admit that there were too many conflicting interests at work for radical change to be accepted.

From the start we also shared a love of beer, the old fast bowler's staple. He was an honorary member of CAMRA, and later he educated me in the wines of the world. Dylan and Wagner almost exclusively sustained his musical tastes. Dylan I loved, but he had mercy on me with Wagner.

Golf proved to be a frustration, not through want of trying but through inconsistency. I suppose that applies to us all! He was a great partner, because you never quite knew what you were going to get next. He could play four holes of sublime strokes and then, for no apparent reason, he would five-putt from nowhere. One thing you could always rely on, though, was his hugely competitive spirit and a good glass of wine at the end of the round.

Our travels at home and abroad gave us the very best experiences, some with an unexpected twist. On one commentary tour of New Zealand, after months of meticulous planning of our route around the wine lands of Central Otago, Marlborough, Martinborough and Hawke's Bay, Bob decided within a day of landing in Auckland that he would be teetotal for the entire trip. He suffered badly from insomnia and thought that six weeks off the booze might restore his sleep pattern. That approach had never worked at home and needless to say it didn't in New Zealand either. It did, of course, provide me with a driver on our travels, but more than anything it demonstrated his strength of will and the stubborn streak that had made him so successful and sustained him through his playing career.

After simultaneous operations on both knees and a withering assessment of his general fitness from Tony Greig, following the Centenary Test in March 1977, Bob embarked on a training regime of slow-paced running that both rejuvenated and prolonged his bowling. He advocated this training method for all aspiring quick bowlers and remained convinced to the end that the modern bowler spends too much time in the gym rather than pounding the track.

Not too long ago, when we were commentating at Taunton, he marked out his run, all forty-three paces of it, and when he got to the end of it, a yard or two inside the boundary, he looked back at the stumps in the distance, turned to me and said, 'I must have been bloody mad!'

If there was one thing he could have changed about his bowling, however, it was not his high-stepping, idiosyncratic run-up, which became the most mimicked in the game, or his rather awkward, angular bowling action. What really irked him was his penchant for bowling no-balls. He delivered more in Test cricket than any other bowler, 939 of them, which added over 45 miles to the Willis clock and probably deprived him of 20 wickets. No wonder he thought himself mad. (In those days, no-balls didn't count against the bowler. If they had, Sky Sports statistician Benedict Bermange reckons his Test bowling average would have risen from 25 to 28.)

I often wondered just how viciously he would have admonished himself for this in his Sky TV guise as the Hanging Judge on *The Verdict*. He made the programme required viewing and he was rarely wrong in his harsh but fair criticism of the modern player, but he might have been tempted to overstep the mark when judging his own misdemeanour. Bob's apoplexy at England's Test match frailties was all too evident in his carefully constructed TV persona – which was in fact the very antithesis of the caring, funny, shy and determined character that he was in life. Deep down, he enjoyed nothing better than watching the team succeed, and what's more the players knew that too, even the ones who had to watch from behind the sofa.

Bob was undoubtedly a great bowler, one of England's finest ever. When he got to 300 Test wickets, only three had got there before him: Fred Trueman, Lance Gibbs and Dennis Lillee. He was at his best when he bowled fast, angling the ball into the right-handed batsman and getting steep bounce from a length. Over thirteen years he was the scourge of opening batsmen, relying on pace and skill to undermine his opponents. Throughout most of his bowling efforts he seemed entranced, most famously, of course, at Headingley in 1981. He let the ball do all the talking.

He had a wonderful sense of self-deprecating humour, too, that masked a long battle with depression. You would never have known of these struggles had you not been close. On tour once, when commentating in Australia, we went to pick up our accreditation in Melbourne, only to find no pass under the name 'Bob Willis'. There was one for 'Bruce Willis', though, which he wore uncomplainingly and with a smile for the next couple of months.

Bob would be the last person to think of himself as an 'all-action hero' – but, on reflection, that described him perfectly.

This piece first appeared, in edited form, in the 2020 edition of Wisden Cricketers' Almanack *and is reproduced here with the kind permission of Wisden.*

A sense of mischief

David Brown

Bob Willis must have had as many friends in the game as anybody. You only have to see the tributes to appreciate how popular he was, even with the Australians. Like them, he could be pretty abrasive – although he never resorted to sledging – but at the end of a day's play, when everybody had been having a hard dig at each other, he would have a beer with them in the dressing room. Bob was very much like that: on the field is one thing and off it is another.

I first came across Bob when he joined Warwickshire in 1972. At first, we weren't sure what to expect of our new signing. The captain, A.C. Smith, told us that as well as being a high-class Test bowler, Bob was going to revive our Sunday league cricket. He said he was the sort of bowler who would keep hitting people on the chest and he'd be very difficult to score off. Having bowled on the Edgbaston pitch for many years, I thought, 'It's going to be a miracle if he can do that here. He's more likely to hit people on the ankle than the chest.'

When I first saw his bowling action, I couldn't help wondering how long he would last. In one of his early games for us, Basil D'Oliveira took him for quite a few runs, and one or two of us looked at each other, eyebrows raised. But we went on to win the County Championship that season and he proved to be a very important cog in our success. We were already a very good side – we'd been in contention for the title for a year or two – but Bob made an important difference. He would turn out to be one of England's greatest, of course.

The way his legs and knees and feet used to go in different directions while bowling was quite extraordinary, though. Some years later we were joined at Warwickshire by Gladstone Small, who had a wonderful silky action and made fast bowling look easy. Bob and I both found it extremely hard work, and as we watched him enviously, we simply had to acknowledge that we weren't able to do it that way.

The effort and application Bob put in over the years was phenomenal. When he had his operations, in 1975, I went to see him in hospital. I took one look at the state of his knees and thought it would be a miracle if he ever really fired again – but he became stronger and fitter and better than ever. He wouldn't mind me saying that he was not a natural athlete, but he got himself very fit through sheer perseverance and determination.

When he took over as captain at Warwickshire in 1980, and I was manager, he introduced a new fitness regime that came as quite a shock to most of the playing staff. But it paid off and we soon had some of the fittest lads anywhere at the time. We won the John Player League that season, which was down to the fielding and being able to bowl to a tight, restricted field – as well as one or two explosive batsmen.

He didn't always set such a good example, though. We clinched that John Player League title at Leicester, and after starting our celebrations at Grace Road we drove back to Birmingham and ended up at one of our regular pubs, the Prince of Wales. By this stage Bob was in full cry, whereas I was driving. My daughter had come to support us and I was keen to get her home to the farm, but first I had to try to persuade Bob that it was time for him to leave too. He was having none of it, of course, and I remember chasing him out into the street, where he started playing the fool, dodging behind parked cars and then popping out, before running somewhere else and popping out again.

By the time Bob eventually gave in and started to make his way home, I was in such a state that I just bundled my daughter into the car and we shot off. It was a great relief to climb into bed, until I woke in the middle of the night and thought, 'Oh no, what have I done?' I realised that the last time I'd seen the precious, hard-won John Player trophy was on the bar in the Prince of Wales. Thank goodness that the landlady, who knew us pretty well, had seen what was happening and had looked after it for us. But I would never have forgotten it in the first place if it hadn't been for trying to get Willis out of the pub for his own good.

As everybody knows, Bob was a fierce competitor. He didn't tolerate people who didn't make the effort to live up to the expectations he had of them, but he was incredibly kind and helpful to those who did. He was a very loyal man, that's for certain, and we had a huge amount of fun together, socialising, sharing rooms, travelling to games. There was one occasion early on when a group of us visited a restaurant in Yorkshire famous for its Barnsley chops. They were monstrous pieces of meat, but I managed to scoff mine and then polish off another that someone had half-eaten. From then on, courtesy of Bob, my nickname was 'Barnsley'.

When we travelled together we found it very difficult to get from A to B without making a detour, particularly if we'd heard about a good pub. This was taken to an extreme one weekend when we were due to play Glamorgan – Saturday, then Monday and Tuesday, with a Sunday league game in the middle. Soon after we arrived in Cardiff, the day's play was called off because of heavy rain, so Bob and I decided to take the opportunity to visit Bibury Court, a hotel near Cirencester owned by Bob's friends. I had been driven to Cardiff by captain Alan Smith and he kindly lent us his car.

The plan was to stay the night and travel back early the next morning for the Sunday league match, but it rained all night and it was still pouring down when I rang the groundsman after breakfast. He told us that the chances of starting weren't good, so we decided not to rush back, but kept ringing for updates until he confirmed that the game had finally been called off.

Over a very convivial Sunday lunch at Bibury Court, I mentioned that my wife was probably at that moment standing in the rain watching the daughter of some friends of ours show-jumping at Abingdon, which is not a million miles from Bibury. Bob decided that we should drive over to cheer them up, so off we headed – even further away from Cardiff. We were having supper with them when Bob suggested, 'Oh, it's not a bad trip from here in the morning, you know. We could leave early and be back in plenty of time for the start of play. It's filthy, it's pouring with rain – we'll stay here!'

On Monday we were feeling pleased with ourselves for getting all the way back to Cardiff in good time and were gazing at the water on the outfield when a couple of our lads came up to us and said, 'A.C. is looking for you two and he's not very happy.' Not knowing what on earth was wrong, we headed to the dressing room to find that everybody had vanished. Alan Smith stormed in and started tearing a strip off us, calling us selfish this and inconsiderate that. He had needed his car on the Sunday to have supper at Ossie Wheatley's house outside Cardiff. He'd ended up having to pay out for taxis and we were not very popular, to say the least. Happily, we were able to calm the waters fairly soon, but that was as cross as I've ever seen Alan over the years. It wasn't a bright move on our part, but there was no harm done in the end.

I remember Bob offering to help out once when the builders were working on my stud farm. He was keen, but I can say he was definitely better at being a fast bowler than at mixing concrete. That kind of strong-arm work was not his forte. Bob was a fit and durable man, but he was never a strong man, and some of the jobs the builders gave him stretched him to the extreme. Over the years he spent a lot of time with us at the farm. The kids loved him because he had a sense of mischief that appealed to them enormously. I think he enjoyed getting away from the eye of the media and away from cricket.

There were undoubtedly times when he found it difficult to motivate himself for run-of-the-mill county games, but he always tried. Members would complain that he was faster in the Test matches, but the thing is that Bob thrived on adrenaline. When his adrenaline was up he was a different beast. If games drifted along, as quite a few did in those days, he'd find it difficult to rev himself up. But put him in a county match in which you had half a chance and watch him go. That was one reason why he was such a tremendous one-day bowler: the excitement of that form of the game got him going.

You could see the change in a matter of minutes, and woe betide anyone who did anything he didn't agree with when he was like that. But then he was a dogmatic so-and-so at the best of times. Because he was so black and white in his views, it was easy to find yourself in an argument with him. When we shared a room we often fell asleep still arguing fiercely, but then the first one to wake up in the morning would say, 'Do you want a cup of tea?', and the whole thing was passed over. It never affected our friendship at all.

His stubborn streak showed itself again in 1985, when we were sharing a hotel room in Nottingham and watching the famous World Championship snooker final between Dennis Taylor and Steve Davis, the one that went on into the early hours. The game was at a crucial stage when the hotel fire alarm went off. I quickly got up and said, 'Come on, Bob, we've got to make a move,' and he said, 'No, I'm going to stop and watch this.' I tried to persuade him, but he wouldn't budge, so I headed out and, after some waiting around, it turned out to be a false alarm. I got back to the room just in time to see Dennis Taylor brandishing his cue above his head in victory and Willis with a great big grin on his face.

That side of him served him well on television in later years, when he did *The Verdict* and *The Debate*. They were right up his street. It completely changed the way the public saw him. You'd be surprised how many people came up to me and said, 'Oh, I saw your pal on that programme again. He's brilliant, isn't he?' Quite a lot of the colossal outpouring of affection we have seen for Bob can be put down to those programmes. They brought him to the attention of people who perhaps had been aware of him as a great fast bowler but hadn't really thought of him as a character. He seemed to appeal to nearly everybody.

I've heard a lot of people describing Bob as a wine connoisseur. When he and I first drank wine together there was no connoisseurship involved – it was just a matter of grabbing whatever could be found that was vaguely drinkable. Occasionally, a gang of us used to go to a little wine bar in Birmingham – this was when wine bars first came in – and there was a motto behind the bar that struck a chord: 'A day without wine is a day without sunshine.' Bob used to quote that very frequently. I miss him a lot.

What happens on tour

John Lever

Bob was great fun to be with in the changing room. On the trip to India in 1976–77 we just clicked, and we stuck together quite a bit on tour after that. In later years I found it difficult to understand why people thought he was boring on TV, because he's one of the funniest guys I've toured with. We were away for a long time in those days and you needed people to get you out of your hotel room, to enjoy life. Bob certainly did that.

On tour, as the MCC, we had to attend more than our share of social functions, 'flying the flag'. Bob was the instigator of closing ranks as a way to enjoy those evenings without getting too much of an earbashing from the other guests. He'd pull me and the likes of Geoff Miller into a 'laager' – into a circle – and he'd say, 'There's somebody hovering, there's somebody hovering.' At other times we would start talking absolute gibberish until people gave up and walked away. Another tactic was to ask them questions all the time – ridiculous questions. It was our form of entertainment, to keep us sane before we could disappear back to the hotel.

Team spirit was a very important thing for Bob, and the next tour, to Pakistan in 1977–78, was probably the hardest I've been on in that respect. At one point there was a tricky situation when it was announced that the Pakistan players who had joined Kerry Packer were going to come back from Australia to play in the last Test. Bob didn't agree with that at all – and we were adamant that we weren't going to play against them. And then came the riots. So it was a relief when we flew to New Zealand for the second leg of the tour.

I think that's where his real leadership started. The first Test in Wellington, which we lost, was a hangover from those weeks in Pakistan. But it meant that we had to win the next game, in Christchurch, because the last one was in Auckland and that was so flat there was never going to be a result. That was the background to the famous moment in our second innings at Christchurch when we needed quick runs and Geoff Boycott was just batting and batting, so Bob took it upon himself to push Beefy up the order – and we know what happened after that with the run-out. Bob then bowled like a man possessed and won us the match. We duly drew the last Test and came away with a series draw. I think Bob got more respect from quite a few cricketers after that series. It was certainly a landmark for him.

On that New Zealand trip, we also went to see his all-time favourite Bob Dylan in concert. We were in a huge amphitheatre, a long way from the stage, and the noise was fantastic. But out of the thousands of people there watching, there must have been about three or four hundred around us who were more intent on watching Bob singing along, with his big mop of hair going backwards and forwards. He knew every single word. He came away from that rather pleased.

We then went to Australia – which was his favourite place to tour – for two winters on the trot, because of Packer. (I don't think Bob was tempted at all by Packer.) Christmas away from home could be pretty hard, so we used to organise fancy-dress parties, to help get through the day. Manager Doug Insole turned up as Inspector Clouseau and Bob came up with the nickname 'Inspector' as soon as he entered the room. From that day on he was never called anything else. Bob was a nickname maniac. He liked to give everybody a name. I remember him talking about his dad and referring to him as 'Tannoy'. And I was once going out with a young lady who was quite tall and she became 'Stretch' straight away (I went on to marry her – she's Chrissie to everyone else). He never went back to the ordinary name either. He always used the nickname. It was probably his way of remembering people.

Someone else Bob was close to was 'Deadly' Derek Underwood. There was a lot of respect between them. Bob knew that he was one of the best left-armers that we were going to see in our lifetime, and Deadly enjoyed watching this guy running in and running in. It was certainly a sight to behold. It wasn't so good if you were twelfth man, mind you. I can think of a few tours when I had that role and Bob would come off at tea and there wasn't one item of clothing that wasn't sopping wet. As he sat down, it was a matter of peeling off all this wet gear and trying to get it dry for the last period of the day. Getting the shirt off was the trickiest bit. It was the lucky twelfth man's job to do all that. I don't imagine they have to these days.

Today's cricket would have suited Bob far more than what we faced back then: the drudgery of three-day cricket, plus one-day cricket, plus Test matches. I wouldn't say he had a hard-work action but he put everything into it. That long run-up and everything else seemed to take a lot out of him. He would have benefited from rests after games more than most.

It was Bob who got me on the fitness track, though. With the help of Bernard Thomas, the physio, he did a lot of stretching and running, and I got into that habit too. After the first two tours, I used to take the training at Essex, just copying what Bob did. Bob was always saying it's the last session, the third spell of bowling, that really counts. The first spell, you run in and it all works quite nicely. The second one, after lunch, is a little harder. But the last one, after tea, is when so many batsmen are looking to cash in, and that's when you've got to do a job for the team and your fitness is going to count. That stayed with me.

I'm not sure how confident Bob was sometimes, and he would often have trouble sleeping. He used to pop the headphones on and listen to a special tape that reinforced the self-belief that every sportsman's got to have. It seemed to do the trick.

I did some work with him on his no-balls, but I don't think I achieved anything. It was always a problem – even at Headingley in 1981. He wanted to run down the hill, but at the same time he was still a little apprehensive about overstepping. I watched that Test on TV and the thing that sticks in my mind is the look on Bob's face. 'In the zone' they'd call it now. We called it a trance. Nobody could get near him when he was like that. He just wanted to go back to his mark and come in again. You couldn't get a word out of him. All he would do was shout at people if they didn't catch the ball. Or if they didn't throw it in quick enough, there'd be this maniacal scream: *'Get it in!'*

Part of Bob's love for Australia over the years was his friendship with winemaker Geoff Merrill. On one day off, I remember Bob took some of us into a bar with a vast range of wines on offer. We sampled quite a few as he tried to educate us, but we were in a bit of a state by the end of it. It was another way in which Bob helped us get through life on tour.

Being with Bob always helped enormously – everything he did.

A passionate opponent

Rod Marsh

Bob was a good bloke to play against. You always knew you were in for a contest – and at the end of the day, you always knew you were in for a cold beer with him. It was a great way to play cricket.

The 1970–71 Ashes was my first series and it was also Bob's first. He was a bit younger than me, but not much. In those days, we weren't used to seeing people quite that tall. The fast bowlers of that era – John Snow, Dennis Lillee – none of those guys were that big. But then along came Bob. At the time, Bill O'Reilly said he looked like a two-iron with ears, and it's not a bad description. One memory that sticks out from that series is of Bob taking a really good catch to get rid of me in the final Test at Sydney, but I do forgive him.

Our next series together was in 1974–75, in Australia again. I'll never forget Dougie Walters, at the WACA, hitting Bob for six off the last ball of the day to bring up his hundred in the session. Bob had bounced him several times in a row and Dougie reckoned the last ball would be a bouncer too, and it was, and he hooked it for six. Bob had succeeded in getting him to hook in the air; it just went a bit further than he wanted, that's all. Then the next morning Dougie was out to Bob without adding to his score.

For me, batting against Bob was a little different, being a left-hander. I recall him getting me out a couple of times lbw with balls that, from where he bowled, *must* have pitched outside leg stump. So I always say that I would have averaged three or four more had it not been for those bad decisions!

He was always at you, Bob, that was the main thing. When he had his rhythm, he was quite sharp; when he didn't, like all fast bowlers, he was very gettable. You could tell when he was in rhythm because everything seemed to go right with his run-up, but when he wasn't, there was a certain hesitancy about the way he approached the crease and he'd over-pitch or bowl too short. When he was in rhythm, he always seemed to find the right length.

One thing they pride themselves on, the great fast bowlers, is being able to find their rhythm more often than not. When it came to our second innings at Headingley in 1981, my word, he was in rhythm that day. Bob really was switched on. He just tore in. He can never have got to the crease quicker. He probably never bowled much faster in his life. He surely never bowled better.

It was an amazing game of cricket and a highly unlikely victory. The incredible part was that we were one for 50-odd, chasing 130, and we were sitting back feeling pretty relaxed. We knew the pitch wasn't doing tricks, because Ian Botham and Graham Dilley had just put on more than a hundred runs together in the England innings. What happened next was simply a great spell of fast bowling, with some good catches taken. I was caught off Bob's bowling by Dilley on the fence. Had he not been so tall, it might have gone for six, but . . .

When things start to slide like that, it takes a really good performance from someone in your team to stop it, and we just weren't up to it. As much as we'd like to forget it, we can't, because it's just one of those games of cricket you will never forget. So well done, Bob, and England.

We got the better of England in the 1982–83 series, when Bob was captain, but they did win at Melbourne and what a match that was. Thommo and Allan Border put on 70 for the last wicket, only to fall short by three runs. You could hardly believe a Test could go that close to being a tie. Looking back at it now, there were some unbelievably good games of cricket over those two or three years, but we got the rough end of the pineapple on all the close ones. We just weren't good enough to win them.

After we'd stopped playing, I saw quite a bit of Bob when he came out to Australia. He used to spend some time here almost every year, because he has a lot of lifelong friends in Adelaide – and it just happens that there are a lot of good winemakers here as well. Those guys loved Bob – and why wouldn't you?

In 1994–95, when I was with the Australian Cricket Academy, we played a couple of one-day games against the England team and we won both of them, at the North Sydney Oval. Bob was there and he was very disappointed with the England players – mainly because, apart from Angus Fraser and Mike Gatting, they didn't come in and have a drink with our boys afterwards.

England were playing horribly in those days and Bob used to get really cranky when England performed badly, which showed how much he cared. He had passion and that's what you want from Test players. You want them to be passionate about playing for their country – it's special – and Bob never lost that. So he hated getting beaten, but that didn't stop him from putting on a brave front and having a drink with the opposition, which is the way it should be.

In my era we were taught to do that. If the opposition had fielded all day, it was the batting side's duty to take a couple of bottles of beer and go and sit next to someone and have a chat. It was incredible how many on-field problems were solved in the dressing room afterwards by simply having a beer and talking about it, and I venture to say that the game of cricket now would be different if they still did that. I'm sure Bob got angry when he didn't bowl well and people knocked him around the park – I know all our bowlers did – but as soon as it was all done and dusted you went and drank a beer and had a good laugh about it.

It might not have been obvious from the outside, but Bob was great fun. I remember organising a reunion tour in 1987–88 for those who had played in the Centenary Test ten years before. I got every England player but Alan Knott (Bob Taylor took his place) and all the Australian players, and we played in Perth, Adelaide and Brisbane – and it was a *very* social tour for the England guys. At first Bob was worried about his knees – we all worried about our knees – but he ended up having a great time.

The rebel with a cause

Martin Tyler

It was Monday, 16 November 1970. Robert George Dylan Willis went off to work, coaching cricket at the Crystal Palace National Recreation Centre. 'Don't suppose I'll see you tonight,' I said. 'You'll be in Australia, haha!'

Bob and I had moved into a first-floor flat in Thornton Avenue, Streatham, in South London, a couple of months earlier. It was a friendship born out of a passion for sport at RGS Guildford at the time when passing the eleven-plus examination got you a free grammar school education. We were like that buddy movie *The Odd Couple*. Bob was neat and tidy. I was not. Bob listened to Mahler. I was a pop music freak from the sixties. He was a slave to everything Dylan. I only loved the tracks with a strong melody, like 'Lay Lady Lay' and 'Positively 4th Street'.

There was plenty of fun nonetheless and that particular early-morning gag was born out of a visit a few days earlier from Alex Bannister, a highly regarded cricket correspondent at the time. There had been an injury on the Ashes tour to one of the fast bowlers, Alan Ward. The theme of the subsequent article in the *Daily Mail* was that England should 'Send for Willis'.

Bob had put on a tracksuit and gone through some fitness routines for the newspaper's photographer, but those pictures only succeeded in emphasising his youthfulness – the lean, callow frame of a cricketing prospect, no doubt, but one with very little experience of the first-class game. He had turned twenty-one during the 1970 season, in which he had played just 11 County Championship games for Surrey, taking 28 wickets with what *Wisden* called his 'odd method'.

Within a couple of hours a mundane Monday became manic. Bob called me at my job, at a market research company in Holborn.

'I go on Thursday!'

He asked me to put aside my disbelief and bunk off work to monitor the phone calls which were bombarding our flat while he spent the day on a tour of media duty which finished with an appearance on ITV's *News at Ten* that evening.

With no mobiles, of course, the landline was the only way to feed the frenzy of Fleet Street. I had a narrow-lined foolscap pad. By the time Bob finally got home, there were four sides of messages for the young man of the moment.

We had a small black and white television on which we had already watched a lot of sport. Within weeks Bob himself was on that screen, not only playing for England but really contributing to bringing the Ashes back home. For both of us it was an extraordinary experience.

There was an inevitable reaction to the physical and mental stresses of the tour when he returned to the flat and county cricket. Surrey would win the County Championship in 1971, but Bob needed time and understanding. His winter triumphs, however, carried no weight with the old-school Surrey hierarchy. Five Test caps but no county cap. The wages barely increased; a problem I was suffering from too.

Even Micky Stewart, Surrey's captain and one of the finest men I have ever known, was short on sympathy. One evening he popped round to the flat and asked me, 'What's up with Bob? He's got no energy. What's he eating? He should be having steak!' I replied that the best we could afford was rissoles from the local butcher at fourpence each – and that was old money! Micky just shook his head and departed, and Bob was soon doing the same – from Surrey.

The rebellious streak I had seen when our paths first crossed at school resurfaced. That same rebellious streak which had driven him to add 'Dylan' officially, not just as a nickname, now had him looking for greater appreciation elsewhere. Our phone was hot again, this time with calls from other counties. Lancashire, I remember, offered the most, but he plumped for Warwickshire. The very personable footballer-cricketer Jim Cumbes was a big influence. It was not easy to transfer counties then, but Bob was so determined that a short ban was no deterrent.

The flat-sharing also came to an end, of course, but the Surrey connection continued as Kiwi Geoff Howarth took his place, though I nicked Bob's room, bigger and better! If anyone writes a book about great moments of reflected glory, I offer the Lord's Test match of 1983 when my two past flatmates went out to toss the coin as captains of their respective countries. Between them, they had smuggled me into the top tier of the hallowed pavilion at the home of cricket. As they walked back from the middle, together they gave me a quick wave, a secret signal. I could not have been prouder of my two great friends.

How remarkable, too, you might think, that Bob and I ended up as fellow broadcasters at Sky Sports. Bob, though, had the background. His dad, Ted, was an exceptional news editor at BBC Radio. Indeed, when I used to go round to Bob's house after school and his dad was at home, the rule of law was never to speak at the top of the hour. Ted listened intently to every word of the bulletin. Bob from a very early age knew the value of a 'story'.

I have to mention his football prowess too. When we moved into the flat, I was already playing Isthmian League football with Corinthian Casuals. Bob had been connected with Guildford City, then of the semi-professional Southern League, but he was happy to train more locally in London. At 6 ft 6 in he was ahead of his time as a tall goalkeeper. What was the exception then is now almost the rule. He soon got into the first team and saved a penalty on his debut.

But cricket was his real calling, and it was so special to be around an exceptional man and sportsman when his journey started properly, the day when his country first called – Monday, 16 November 1970.

Bob Willis, MBE

The Right Hon Sir John Major KG CH

The point about cricketers is that – to their admirers – they are forever young, even when they have reached advanced years. We remember them, and *wish* to remember them, in their prime. So it is with Bob Willis.

I first saw Bob play cricket at The Oval during the seasons he spent with Surrey, competing for a first-team place against the club's established opening bowlers, Geoff Arnold and Robin Jackman.

Good as Arnold and Jackman were, it was easy to imagine – even during Bob's earliest days in the Second XI – that he would become something very special.

Even as a young man, he was an imposing sight: nearly 6 ft 6 in of beanpole, with a crazed hairstyle – modelled on Einstein – careering to the wicket from a lengthy run. His technique was his own, and largely remained so.

Bob had an idiosyncratic long run-up to the wicket, which began halfway to the boundary, and curved inwards as he approached the stumps.

I can still picture him vividly: he began with his right hand gripping the ball, which he held cocked behind his right thigh, legs bounding as he approached the wicket – at which point his right arm whirred over like the arms of a windmill in gusty weather. It was an imposing sight to witness from the boundary and, with his rapid pace and bounce, must have been seriously intimidating for any batsman a mere pitch-length away.

He was proud to play for England, and rejected the Kerry Packer shilling. This argues self-confidence yet, throughout his career, Bob lacked sufficient self-belief in his ability. He lacked bombast, too. To suggest to him that he was an iconic figure was to invite a wry smile and a sardonic response.

I always found him to be a little shy, understated, and slow to put himself forward. His humour was dry – even droll – with a gift for self-mockery. His one-liners could be sharply apt, and rarely affected by sentiment – but they were never spiteful or unkind. He was also a shrewd judge of character.

It was all of these gifts that made him such an honest commentator when his playing career was over: he communicated what he saw, what he truly thought and – whether that incited his praise or his criticism – the listeners gained an insight that they might otherwise have missed.

As a cricketer, Bob was courageous. Fast bowling put a great strain on his knees – inevitably so – as his left boot thudded into the turf with every ball he bowled. He accepted philosophically the discomfort and injuries, and the resultant operations to both knees – after which he moved from the surgeon's table to crutches; to physiotherapy; to repair – and did so with willpower and dogged persistence. It was his own determination – indeed, sheer bloody-mindedness – that returned him to top-class cricket.

I never found Bob to be boastful or resentful of others. Whenever we met, we spoke mostly of cricket and sometimes (but less so) of public affairs. Almost always he would talk admiringly of other cricketers – only very rarely would I hear him be critical. But, always, he would fend off any discussion about his own career. About that, he remained resolutely matter-of-fact.

I sometimes wish that Bob had been less laconic, and more proud of his achievements. When he finally retired from cricket, he had taken more wickets than any other English Test bowler, and moreover – Botham apart – did so without any established fast-bowling partner. There was no one of his pace to share the opening attack: no Statham, no Trueman, no Anderson, no Broad. Bob was often alone in directing his firepower against Test opponents.

This modest but immensely talented man would be surprised to know how fondly he will be remembered, and for how long. Surely, for as long as cricket is played, Bob Willis will be remembered as one of England's greatest ever bowlers.

Leave nothing out there

Mark Nicholas, ESPN Cricinfo

It is with the heaviest heart that these fingers hit the keypad. Bob Willis has gone, just like that, gone. He had been suffering from an aggressive form of prostate cancer for some time, not that other folk would have known. That was Bobby for you, no fuss. It seemed as if the fight could be won, but no, even the indomitable Willis spirit was mown down. The loss is gut-wrenching. Those close to him are a mess – disbelieving, discombobulated, heartbroken. Robert George Dylan Willis was very special.

That Sky television persona was the game face. Away from the call of 'lights, camera, action', he was the kindest man: charming, polite, funny and not in the least bit judgemental, unless standards were breached. Then he could fire both barrels. Oh boy, could he fire.

Bob first appeared in my life when the England selectors sent for him in Australia during Ray Illingworth's successful 1970–71 tour. Alan Ward had broken down and pace was needed. It was a brave call by the selectors, for there was little pedigree to go on, but it turned out to be one of England's best. As, of course, did Bobby.

I was a young boy with a crush on John Snow – Bob's own gold standard – and precious little of that series passed me by, thanks in the main to a tiny wireless radio that brought commentary from the Great Southern Land to a small boarding school in southern England. Each night I smuggled this splendid trinket of technology to bed, nestled it beneath my pillow and positioned the long, retractable aerial between the iron bedhead railings in order to find an acceptable signal. The slightest move compromised this, so I lay still, transfixed as Lawry was beaten, Redpath held and Chappell trapped. To the sound of Alan McGilvray, Bob took four wickets in the final Test, in Sydney, as England completed a 2–0 series win. Oh my days!

On occasions I was lucky – or unlucky, depending on your take – to play for Hampshire against Bob, but, gamely as he ran in for Warwickshire during the evening of his career, he was not a patch on the bowler who blew the Australians away. Of course, he was all arms and legs, but it never appeared to the opponent as a shambles, more a clear and present threat. Sure, Snow was smooth, economical, rhythmical, while Willis was, well, Willis, but somehow you knew that he knew that you knew that he had you covered.

The *pièce de résistance* came at Headingley in 1981. There is nothing I can add to the many thousands of words that have celebrated that incredible performance on the most extraordinary of days, other than to say that Bob had those figures of eight for 43 in his soul. Somewhere, sometime R.G.D. Willis was going to do something utterly compelling, ridiculous even, as if it were written. He cared so deeply for the game – almost to the point of aching – and the destruction of Australia on 21 July 1981 was both a return for his investment in sweat and blood and a calling card for his future as pre-eminent observer, coach and critic. It is infuriating that his intelligent ideas for the game's future were never absorbed, considered or acted upon. Twice he put forward detailed reforms of the English cricket system and twice his words fell on deaf ears.

Those of us lucky to know him well have golden memories of friendship, a gift that comes in many guises. With Bobby, friendship came in an unconditional, organic form and with a leaning towards kindness. Examples of it have been everywhere this last couple of days but none better illustrates his legacy than the journey made by two fine men of Adelaide, one a wine-maker, the other from the motor industry, who travelled to sit by his bed last week and share the final chapter. They, like Sir Ian Botham who telephoned with the news, are beset by grief.

Bob knew right and wrong like few others and when I sought his advice at the early stage of my stuttering career, he invited me to dinner at a favourite Indian restaurant. In summary, his message was: 'Be true to yourself, trust yourself, leave nothing out there and let others do the worrying.'

Thus, it was a privilege to join Sky in 1995 and be able to work with him. We lived nearby and invariably travelled by car together – I was always at the wheel, Bob never drove – creating a road-trip narrative to our life that covered anything and everything but always, by the time we hit the North Circular on the way home, came back to our respective affections for Bob Dylan and Bruce Springsteen. While filtering left to the A40 and into town, the cursing of political leaders and pusillanimous cricket administrators was drowned out by 'Visions of Johanna' or 'Thunder Road'.

He could be very funny, a point often missed by TV viewers who failed to pick up the wit in the barb and the relevance in the fun. He was a fine broadcaster and his role in *The Debate*, Sky's Test match review show, became cult.

When I left Sky for Channel 4, he never once judged the new kids on the block, only encouraged. Neither did he talk behind our back, preferring to applaud when something was well done and otherwise keep his counsel. I valued that more than words can say. First up for Bob was warmth and kindness, like a beacon in the often selfish world of professional sport.

Meantime, I shall think of his smile and remember our wonderful lunch in London this last autumn, bathed as it was by sunshine and with the best of friends from cricket and his other lives.

Yes, the memories will linger of a brilliant cricketer and an even more brilliant and inspirational man. I will leave the final word to his own greatest inspiration – the other Bob, Dylan.

> May you grow up to be righteous,
> May you grow up to be true,
> May you always know the truth
> And see the lights surrounding you.
> May you always be courageous,
> Stand upright and be strong,
> May you stay forever young . . .

And, apart from the grey hair (!), that was Bobby. He knew the truth, he lent us his wisdom and he lived his life with the heart of a lion.

This piece originally appeared on ESPN Cricinfo on 6 December 2019.

Getting to know Bob

Michael Holding

I first played against Bob in 1976, but I didn't have a lot of interaction with him in that series because it was my first tour of England and I was also ill for part of it. I didn't know many people anyway, because I hadn't played any county cricket. So I think the first time I got to know him a bit more would have been in the 1980 series, when he and Ian Botham were close and Beefy was a friend of Viv Richards. By 1984 I knew him a lot better, and that led to an incident in the Headingley Test match that still brings a smile.

It was Friday the 13th, I remember, and I was batting and getting a few runs against Bob. As we went off the field at the end of a session, I ran up to him and tapped him on the back to get his attention. Now, Bob had bowled quite a few bouncers at me, so I don't know what the spectators might have been expecting – they probably thought I was going to have a few angry words with him – but what I actually said was, 'Oh, Bob, don't worry, it's my day today: I've had four winners on a yankee as well!' And he burst out laughing. He knew I liked to dabble in the horses, you see. When I got to the dressing room I couldn't help wondering what the people in the stands must have made of it all.

Bob and I built much more of a relationship when we were at Sky. I started there full-time in 1998, but before that I worked with Bob and the Sky team on the England tour of the West Indies in 1993–94 – though strictly speaking it wasn't a Sky production, as it was TWI who had the rights for cricket in the Caribbean back then. That was the series when Brian Lara got all those runs in Antigua. Bob was on commentary when Lara broke the world record for the first time.

The first overseas tour I did for Sky was a very important one for me. It was England's tour of South Africa in 1999–2000. Bob, Paul Allott, David Lloyd, Beefy – they were all there, and there was a lot of rain, which meant we ended up playing a lot of cards. Paul Allott, who plays bridge well, taught the rest of us, and that helped build the camaraderie.

Away from the pitch and the commentary box, Bob was a lot of fun. When you went for dinner with him, you really got to know the man and the kind person that he was. He liked to encourage a good team spirit and, in his commentating days, he would often invite a lot of his workmates, including production crew, around to his house in Wimbledon for an evening during an Oval Test. I have also been out with Bob on quite a few occasions when he's started singing his Dylan songs, and that was a side of him that did not often come across to the public.

On commentary, Bob was very reserved; it was almost as if he was holding back. But he showed a lot more of the real Bob when he switched to doing *The Verdict* and *The Debate*. He relaxed and people got to see his personality, which was definitely a good thing. Perhaps one of the reasons he was sometimes not so relaxed was that he always dedicated a lot of effort and time to his work and he could get frustrated with others who didn't do the same. He definitely got irritated with cricket's administrators, who in his eyes didn't always look after the sport well. He wasn't afraid to express his opinion in that regard – even when he was a player.

Watching his great bowling performance on the last day of the Ashes Test at Headingley in 1981, I recognised the trance he was in. He tended to do that at times – he would just have this look in his eyes as if he saw nothing else but what he wanted to see. But what struck me most was the interview with Peter West on the BBC afterwards when he complained about the press. I think that really shocked a lot of people. They didn't expect a player to be so bold and to speak out so vociferously. But he was always that way. If he thought the game was being damaged by wrong attitudes or wrong actions, he would say so, and you had to admire him for that.

Another side of Bob that had a lasting effect on me was revealed during that 1999–2000 series. As well as all the card-playing, the Sky team often used to go out to eat together as a group, partly because of the security situation in South Africa at the time. In those days I didn't really drink, I only had the occasional beer, and it was Bob who did his best to educate me about wine. He began by giving me a Sauvignon Blanc to try – not Bob's personal favourite, to say the least – and it tasted fine to me, so he said if you like it you should start out on that type of wine. But I never moved on! I have kept on drinking Sauvignon Blanc to this day and I love it.

On that tour Bob and David Gower were the wine connoisseurs, but Ian Botham has grown into it a bit more now. With the winemaker Geoff Merrill in Adelaide, he and Bob produced a wine they called 'BMW' – Botham, Merrill and Willis – but then the real BMW car company spoilt it all when they got in touch to stop them using their name.

Bob and Beefy were close for such a long time. They were inseparable on that tour of the Caribbean in 1993–94 when I first worked with them. Everywhere I went, especially in my native Jamaica, Beefy and Bob were with me. And from what I know about Beefy, he doesn't get very close to people easily, particularly after his problems with the press in his playing days, so he wouldn't have anyone as a confidant unless he could really trust them.

I think that says a lot about Bob. He was a loyal friend. He is sadly missed.

The Bob Willis I knew

Mike Atherton, *The Times*

THERE is no worse welcome home than with the news that a mate has died. I feared the worst when I switched on my mobile phone after the long flight from New Zealand, and sure enough the confirmation came. The only solace was in seeing the genuine outpouring of warmth and affection for one of the great men – and a sometimes misunderstood man at that – of English cricket.

Bob Willis himself might have been surprised at the reaction. His doleful countenance on television and the deliberate way he took on a hard-hitting, sometimes scathing, persona in punditry meant that the general public rarely came to see the Willis I knew: warm, generous, hilarious at times and someone who cared deeply, really deeply and passionately, about English cricket and those within it.

There are cricketers who have been exceptionally popular with the public at large, but less so among their dressing-room colleagues. Willis was the opposite: those who knew him, who played with him, who worked with him would not have a bad word against him. I lost count of the times I would have to defend him to a present player who had borne the brunt of another Willis bouncer on the *The Verdict*, the show on Sky Sports after each day of a Test that he came to make his own.

When the modern players did get to know him, they came around quickly. In the infrequently organised gatherings between England cricketers of different eras, Willis would become a fast bowler again, sympathising with the present crop against the indignities the game forces upon them, whether it be chief-executives' pitches, batsmen, umpires or those who set the schedules. They were all in it together.

It is so long now since his retirement in 1984 that a generation would know him only as a commentator and pundit, rather than a great fast bowler. With Stuart Broad and James

Anderson having gone way past the totals set by Willis and then his long-standing mate, Ian Botham, it is easy to forget just how rare it was for an England fast bowler to pass the 300-wicket mark; easy to forget the hurdles that were presented to a previous generation. Fred Trueman (307) did it first, then Willis (325), then Botham (383), before Broad (485) and Anderson (584) came along to blow those records away.

Without taking anything away from the great careers enjoyed by Broad and Anderson, they would be the first to admit that central contracts have played to their advantage. Unlike Willis and his contemporaries, they have been afforded more time and resources to allow their best overs to be for their country rather than their counties. Only fast bowlers know how physically hard it is to do both.

So, Willis himself was sometimes criticised for not bowling at full tilt for Warwickshire, the county to which he moved from Surrey in 1971, because he was saving his best for England. In this, and his fitness programmes during which he would pound the roads to get mileage into his legs, he was ahead of his time and that allowed him, despite two knee operations in 1975 and countless other physical ailments, to finish his career among the greats.

Wearing the Three Lions and the crown in 90 Tests meant everything to him and I lost count of the number of conversations we had over the years trying to work out how to make English cricket better.

His method was quirky to say the least. When he was a young bowler at Surrey, the Second XI coach, Arthur McIntyre, tried to change his action to something more orthodox but the ball kept hitting the side-netting. He once told me that he'd never seen himself bowl until he played for England on television and, until that point, he'd imagined he had a relatively normal, side-ways-on action, something smooth and rhythmical like Trueman, perhaps, or Brian Statham, or John Snow.

He got the shock of his life when he did finally see how ungainly and awkward it looked. Because of that, there cannot have been a young cricketer of a certain age who did not imitate Willis the fast bowler, either in backyard games or practice: the great Goose – 'Goose' was his dressing-room nickname – flapping and winding his way to the crease, right arm pumping furiously, back and forth, by his side. Even the present players were apt to try – Alastair Cook's solitary Test wicket came via an impersonation of the Willis run-up and delivery during a tame end to a Test against India.

When it clicked, there was damage to be had. Headingley '81 remains one of the abiding memories of my childhood. It was the only Test I attended as a paying spectator before I played for England, although I didn't see any of the glory live, only a John Dyson hundred. As a thirteen-year-old, beginning to have aspirations, the second-innings hundred from Botham, the devastating spell of eight for 43 from Willis, orchestrated by the éminence grise, Mike Brearley, was a sustaining and inspirational memory.

The last few weeks were gruesome, as the cancer spread, but thankfully the end was peaceful. There was a regular flow of friends and family through the door in the final days. John Lever and David Brown, among others, represented the fast bowlers' union, and there were visitors who had flown in from Australia. At the end, there was his wife Lauren, daughter Katie, brother David and another thirsty former bowler, Lancashire's Paul Allott, for company. Bob Dylan's 'Positively 4th Street' was playing in the background.

Although I had been in text contact from New Zealand, the last time I saw him was at the end of the season. A handful of us put on a lunch in his honour at the River Café in south-west London out of consideration for the tough times he'd been going through, and for the next round of chemotherapy that was to come shortly afterwards.

It was a perfect occasion to remember him by: the sun was shining; we had a table on the terrace; the food was sensational; the company was a mix of cricket, media, mates of longstanding, Australians and English. The Ashes had just been shared. The wine flowed. There was lots of laughter.

This piece first appeared in The Times *on 6 December 2019.*

Leading the charge

David Lloyd

'Should we go for a spot of lunch?'

This is proper Willis speak. When you turned up there could be anyone there – Paul Allott, Michael Henderson, Tim Rice, Mike Dickson, Robert Holmes – all good company and all with a tale to tell.

Bob was a great organiser. There was one occasion when he and Allott decided we should go on a steam-train-and-walking trip to north Wales for three days. The Ffestiniog and Welsh Highland railways, to be precise. Overnight at a pub in Caernarfon and then full steam ahead ...

Of course, a first-class compartment had been booked (a few free-standing easy chairs and a table) and Bob had packed a picnic. Wine glasses, seriously good wine and cheese.

A quite jolly chap was also in the carriage and Bob immediately engaged him in conversation.

'Are you holidaying?' he asked.

'No,' the chap replied, 'I'm returning home from London.'

'Have you been on business?' enquired our leader.

'No, I've had to see an accountant,' said our new friend.

'I hope it was nothing serious!' Bob chortled.

'No, it was rather pleasant,' said the chap. 'I've just won the National Lottery!'

'Do come and join us!' said Bob.

And a bloody good time was had!

We found our way to Portmeirion, the 'fantasy' village created by Clough Williams-Ellis from 1925. En route we took a hiking detour, with Allott in charge of Ordnance Survey. As usual Bob, with those long strides, led the charge. Most of the time I had to break into a trot to keep up!

Bob was way in front and went over a stile and disappeared into a field of cows. Allott said we ought to stop and just let him carry on.

'Come along, Walter,' bellowed Bob, 'do keep up!'

'You're going the wrong way, you daft bastard,' returned 'Walter'.

This was our first 'domestic' of the trip, which was debated at length later over a few pints of North Wales's finest ale. I tended to just sit there and umpire as the two of them traded insults.

Then there was the time we went on a Sky golf trip, twelve of us, to PGA Catalunya. Golf during the day, restaurant at night. On our way home from a particularly long evening of great conversation and far too much wine, Bob decided to ring Lauren. He declared to her that he was with a bunch of ****ers. He was getting louder and louder on the phone and the pitch of his voice was getting higher and higher. He ended the conversation with 'ANY NEEEWS?'

The whole van was in hysterics, with everyone repeating, 'ANY NEEEWS?'

The people on that trip work together, play together, and the usual greeting is not 'Hi' or 'Hello' . . . it's 'ANY NEEEWS?'

God, we will miss him.

A batsman's tale

Sir Michael Parkinson

I first met Bob Willis sometime in the 1980s. It was not an altogether auspicious occasion, not for me anyway. In those days I was still turning out on a fairly regular basis for the Vic Lewis Celebrity XI, an assembly of showbiz odds and sods who loved the game and were attracted to making a fool of themselves on the off chance they might end up changing next to one of their cricketing heroes. It was because of Vic Lewis, musician, band leader, captain of his own cricket team and chief selector, that I shared a dressing room with Gordon Greenidge, Wes Hall and best of all, the greatest of them all, Garfield Sobers. He was our special guest team-mate on that unforgettable day when I opened for the Vic Lewis XI against Warwickshire in a match to raise money for charity, which granted me the indulgence of being able to ask my grandchildren, 'Did I ever tell you about the time I played in the same team as Garfield Sobers?'

We won the toss and chose to bat. I took guard and then looked around the field. Bob Willis was a distant figure, a taxi ride away.

The close fielders – and there were many – were a talkative bunch. They sounded like a flock of parakeets. Their main topic was concerned with how long they imagined I would last against Mr Willis, who was raring to go after injury. Anyone who ever saw Bob bowl was intrigued by his action. As he ran towards me, all flailing arms and galloping legs, I considered the possibility he might not be able to stop after delivering the ball until he collided with the sightscreen at my end.

The first ball I received flew past my chin before I had time to see it. I heard the ball smack into the keeper's gloves when I was still in my backlift. There was a murmur of laughter among the close fielders. David Brown, the skipper, was at gully. I looked beseechingly at him, hoping he might remind Bob this was a Sunday romp for charity, not target practice with me as the bullseye. He shrugged and smiled sympathetically.

Bob Willis rampaged in for his second ball, which I almost saw. The third ball, a fast yorker, would have burst through my defence had I been positioned to defend my wicket. As it was, I had very sensibly taken up a position near the square-leg umpire, from which vantage point I was able to witness my stumps reduced to kindling.

Next man in was John Alderton, cricket lover, fair cricketer, fine actor. At that time he was making a movie, so it was important that he arrived on the set on Monday looking like he did when he had left it. As we crossed he asked, 'Is he serious?' I replied, 'I think he is.' Fortunately he escaped unscathed as David Brown quickly replaced Bob with a slow bowler.

When I arrived back in the dressing room my hero was highly amused. 'Enjoy that?' enquired Garfield when he had stopped laughing. When the great man batted, they brought Bob back into the attack and there followed some serious cricket. I seem to remember Garfield scored a century, but that memory could be the result of wishful thinking.

Many years later, in the company of Tim Rice, Michael Henderson, Mark Nicholas, Harold Pinter and Bob, we had one of those special lunches where wine and anecdote came together in memorable fashion. In fact I don't remember much that was said except we laughed a lot. And when I went home I told the kids of the great time I had enjoyed in the very best of company, including and in particular Bob Willis. I remember thinking I wished I had known him better. A singular man.

A bowling captain

Scyld Berry

Bob Willis ran in as if he had his right arm tied behind his back and he was trying to wrestle it free from the piece of rope. Metaphorically, too, he had one arm tied behind his back, and it was by finding a way to overcome these handicaps that he made himself into one of England's finest bowling captains.

He had one arm tied behind his back in two ways. Firstly he was a fast bowler at the wrong time – after the rest day in Test matches had ceased to be observed religiously, and before central contracts were introduced. Fred Trueman, Brian Statham, Harold Larwood ... these great fast bowlers bowled 1000 overs a season but never played a Test match for more than three days in a row. They put their feet up every Sunday.

Playing a Test match over five consecutive days did not occur until the 1980s, when cricket had to become more urgent, less leisurely, in response to World Series Cricket – and it is when bowling fast for the fourth or fifth day in a row that the strain really tells.

So Bob would return to Edgbaston the morning after a five-day Test, and Warwickshire members would moan that he was not steaming in off his full run. They paid his salary too, they would grumble; and it was true, antiquated as the system now seems, that professional cricketers were paid to play for their counties not their country. John Snow was first to cop it in the neck from Sussex, then Bob, then Ian Botham at Somerset. They were expected to bowl fast seven days a week before central contracts were introduced in 1999–2000, which allowed cricketers to save their best for their country. In this context it was a clever campaign by Bob which led Warwickshire to their first Sunday League title in 1980 – a shrewd channelling of available energies.

The second sense in which Bob had one arm tied behind his back was that he was a bowling captain. Captains nowadays just do not bowl. Of England captains, Stuart Broad was the last to have been a pace bowler, and that was a few games as England's T20 skipper. Jeetan Patel did a fine job as one of Bob's successors at Warwickshire, but bowling off-breaks is not taking the new ball. Spinners like Patel, and Ray Illingworth, have been canny enough to lead and contribute as bowlers, notably when the ball was turning on the final day. But leading the attack from the first over, and having to think about everyone else while taking a breather at mid on: rare is the captain who has combined two all-demanding jobs.

So rare indeed that Bob sits alongside Arthur Gilligan and Gubby Allen as the only men to have succeeded as an England captain bowling fast. There were ancients in the 19th century who bowled medium pace, like Lillywhite and Shaw; there have been all-rounders, but they normally bowled pace in their youth before being appointed England captain: once they had reached that stage of life, Bob Wyatt and Wally Hammond, Ted Dexter and Tony Greig, did not bowl flat out for long, if at all. Great overall records though they had, Greig took 24 wickets at 42 each as England captain, and Ian Botham 35 wickets at 33, while averaging 13 with the bat in his 12 Tests as leader.

It is only this trio of Gilligan, Allen and Bob who have bowled fast and captained England successfully for more than the odd game. Gilligan and Gubby were rather more establishment figures than Bob. Gilligan was a Cambridge blue who bowled quick for Sussex and, briefly, England until he was hit over the heart while batting in the 1924 season – and carried on batting until he had reached a century. He had the puff to become a famous radio commentator in later life but never bowled fast again, which made his record in Australia in 1924–25 very modest. Allen solved the problem of not having a central contract by having a job with Debenham's and only playing for Middlesex and England when he felt like it.

'If the cap fits, wear it': but what if the cap does not fit on top of frizzy hair? Bob had to work out his own style as a fast-bowling captain, not being an amateur like Gilligan and Gubby, who were essentially accountable to nobody – not the press, not the players, not the tour manager – until they reported back to

Lord's after a long winter, by which time all incidents had been forgotten or buried in the MCC archives.

Bob's Ashes series in Australia, in 1982–83, was one of the finest feats of its kind: to lose so closely, 2–1, was a terrific result given the resources of the two sides. Australia were awash with fast bowlers, too many to squeeze into their side. England had been depleted by rebels going off to South Africa, which left them without an opening pair of batsmen for a start. It was very creditable to stay in that series, with the hope of retaining the Ashes, until the latter stages in Sydney – one that testifies to the team spirit which Bob, in his own unprecedented way, had engendered.

A record of seven Tests won and five lost is as good as that of most England captains. To have taken 77 wickets at only 21 each, while the captain, should be forever remembered as a superlative achievement.

Bob Willis, music lover

Michael Henderson

In his working life Bob tore in off a long run, to fling thunder-bolts at batsmen. He also came off a long run in his musical life.

Where Bob Dylan was concerned he put down his marker near the sightscreen. He had all the records, and seemed to know the words of every song, whether or not they were worth singing. Even the coasters at his Thames-side flat featured the covers of Dylan long-players. You plonked down your glass of pinot noir on *Nashville Skyline*! It was a rare evening when Dylan was in England if Robert was not present, marking his minstrel of choice as scrupulously as he did England's cricketers on Sky.

'Excellent in Bournemouth,' he would pronounce. 'Not so sharp at Hammersmith. Should have taken his sweater after "Tangled up in Blue".'

He was a Wagnerian, too, and no mistake. A night-and-day, in-all-weathers Wagnerian, not some timid soul who occasionally dipped his toe in the Rhine. Bobby was entranced by the sorceror of Bayreuth, as completely as he was at Headingley in 1981 when he wrote his name in the annals of English sport. 'A perfumed fog,' Thomas Mann called *Tristan und Isolde*. Bob was happy to be trapped in that vapour all night long whenever the curtain went up. Wagner took him into another world, where time could never be measured by the hands of a clock. From *Holländer* to *Parsifal*, he supped deep from the goblet.

His relationship with the Master began in Vienna, weeks after he had retired from first-class cricket in 1984. Offered the choice of a night in a bierkeller or a performance at the State Opera, he took himself off to the stately house on the Ringstrasse. They were performing *Die Meistersinger von Nürnberg* that evening, which weighs in at four and a half hours; nearer six with intervals. In that time even Geoffrey Boycott might make a half century. Bob didn't flinch. By midnight, transported to medieval Franconia by Wagner's serious comedy of art and national identity, he was a made man.

It was quite something to observe him listening to Wagner. However animated he was beforehand, the moment the music began he became so deeply immersed in the drama that he appeared to be under a spell. He was. This music has often been described in terms of magic, which robs listeners of reason. In this famous English cricketer the cranky German composer found one of his most receptive celebrants.

We shared more than twenty Wagner operas on stage, in London, Edinburgh, Adelaide and Paris. In December 1998 a *Ring* cycle at the Festival Theatre in Adelaide, the first to be staged in Australia for a century, coincided – oh wonder of wonders! – with an Ashes Test at the Oval, just across the river Torrens. So it was possible to leave the Oval at stumps, and toddle over the bridge in search of Valhalla.

That was a glorious week. In a city he loved, surrounded by people who loved him, he could feast on cricket's oldest rivalry and the music that touched him most. In the hours left over he shared a few tables in Adelaide's many fine restaurants, with a bottle or two of something pleasing from local vineyards to mark out of ten.

There was another *Ring* cycle in Edinburgh, and half a dozen *Parsifals*. But it is Hans Sachs, the cobbler poet in *Meistersinger*, Bob most clearly resembles. Sachs is the conciliator who brings together the lovers, acknowledges a younger man to be his true successor, and tries to introduce order to a world riven by pettiness and mistrust.

When I see Robert, which I will every week for the rest of my life, like all his other friends, he is at the centre of the gathering. He was a great facilitator, who looked for the good in people and usually found it. He never sought to hog the conversation, or remind others of his deeds on the cricket field. He was a sympathetic listener who knew that others also had lives, and tales to tell. Whenever you introduced him to people who may have known nothing of his life in flannels they were always taken by his modesty. He had that rarest of qualities, grace.

Which is not to say he pulled his punches. When the third bottle was uncorked, and the cheese arrived, Robert could be magnificently withering about the frauds and impostors who sully our national life. He was a fair-minded man, but he never indulged those who failed to show loyalty or adhere to the spirit of the corps. He lived by a code of friendship, generously bestowed, which was entirely reciprocal.

Oh yes, all those glorious afternoons of wine and merriment! Life was 'too short to drink Italian wine'. Not true, but it always raised a laugh. Craft beer was piss. Now that was a call to arms we could all obey. The Manchester City defenders should be placed in detention for persistent misconduct. Yet they won the Premier League in 2012, on a day never to be forgotten. The river walkers at Mortlake, out for a pleasing stroll, heard some wassailing that evening!

David Brown, his captain and confidant at Edgbaston after he had moved to Warwickshire in 1972, was one of his great personal landmarks. Bobby thought the world of D.J. Brown. Ian Botham became a presence in his life in 1977, when he exploded into the national imagination like a firecracker. Theirs was a remarkable alliance, all the more touching for being expressed with so few words. It was one of the great English friendships.

'When Beefy talks about having a glass,' Bob liked to say, 'you can be sure there will be a few bottles on the table!' Both men had earned their fill, many times over. 'Botham and Willis' trips off the tongue like Lennon and McCartney, or Pinky and Perky. Those of us who saw them at close quarters were the lucky ones, though Bobby could never persuade Both that a touch of *Rheingold* would make his life complete!

A life of glory on the field. Days of glittering friendship thereafter, in the restaurants, pubs and concert halls of our land,

and beyond: days that will resonate until the last of us are called home. What a joy it was to share so much with this beautiful soul, whose kindness illuminated the lives of all who were proud to call him a friend.

Not a goose?

A sonnet/acrostic for Bob

Sir Tim Rice

> Remember more than wickets now he's gone,
> Or speed, or run-up of eccentric mode,
> Beginning somewhere way beyond long on,
> Emerging from a distant postal code.
> Remember more than flying stumps and bails
> That troubled every nation's very best,
> Gave him his fame and all that that entails,
> Deserved – but he stood taller than the rest.
> We knew him as a cultured Bob, refined,
> In thrall to Wagner, Dylan, white and red,
> Laconic, warm and witty, spoke his mind.
> Life's verdict: he was true Renaissance bred.
> It's not a goose but eagle that we see,
> Still soaring high with eight for 43.

12

SIX MEMORABLE MATCHES

1. AUSTRALIA – SYDNEY, 1971

In Bob's first Test series, England win the seventh and final Test to secure a 2–0 series victory and regain the Ashes under captain Ray Illingworth.

The view from the press box

DAY two and day three. Off the first ball of the day Lillee was caught at the wicket off Willis, who, in his second over, bowled Greg Chappell round his legs. Willis thus finished with three for 58 and also to his credit was a staggering catch on Saturday morning.

When Marsh picked a ball from Lever off his toes nothing in the world, it seemed, could prevent it from going for four – until Willis appeared through the air to catch it a foot or two off the ground. In full elongation he must cover 10 feet and there was his dive to add to that. Were Willis a professional, rather than an amateur, goalkeeper, this catch would have doubled his value.

John Woodcock, *The Times*

THE final day. A soldier's general led England to victory in the final Test by 62 runs here today and regained the Ashes after twelve years. Ray Illingworth was chaired by his men and carried triumphantly to the dressing room.

Illingworth said afterwards that throughout the tour his players had given him 100 per cent support and that was no idle platitude. He was asked what victory pep talk he gave them before taking the field. He replied: 'I just said, "Come on, let's go," That was all that was necessary.'

Brian Chapman, *The Guardian*

*T*HE *final day.* Ray Illingworth has finally had the last laugh. England were the better side throughout the series. It's as simple as that. The Australians could not match the brilliance of the opening-partnership permutation of any two from Geoff Boycott, Brian Luckhurst and John Edrich.

And of course there was John Snow. This unsmiling man from Sussex was England's trump card. It was snarling Snow at his best, hurling in the legitimate short-lifting delivery, who got Australia's ace batsmen into all sorts of trouble – the only exception being opener Keith Stackpole, who had a splendid hard-hitting series.

Peter Lever improved as the season progressed and my man Bob Willis, whom I wanted in the original party, had a splendid tour after flying out of the English winter. Some of his sensational catches, plus some highly effective bowling late in the tour, more than compensated for his airfare out here. Don't write off either Willis or Lever. Under trying pace conditions, they get full marks.

Keith Miller, *Daily Express*

The view from the dressing room

Bob Willis, *Lasting the Pace* (1985)

On the fourth afternoon, at a psychologically disastrous time for us, John Snow was put out of the game when he collided with the boundary fence, breaking the little finger on his left hand. First Boycott, now Snow. Our two key figures out of action. Were the Ashes about to slip away?

They were not. Peter Lever and I bowled steadily and well to the end of that penultimate day, leaving Australia to begin the final day of the series needing another 100 runs with five wickets standing. It was then that Illingworth made the bravest and best decision of the entire series.

Lever and I, expecting to bowl, were both loosening up when Ray came over to say that he and Derek Underwood would be opening. Ray was often criticised for not bowling himself enough when captain, but now at the most critical time of all, with the success or failure of the tour resting on it, he took the matter into his own hands. The move succeeded. Greg Chappell was stumped early on and the rest folded tamely to give us a victory none of us was likely to forget. It may not have been the smoothest or happiest of tours off the field, but this was undoubtedly a memorable triumph, and for me, an incredible manner in which to set out on the long road with England.

Back in the dressing room, Doug Walters and Rod Marsh were, as ever, quick and sporting in joining us for a drink, while Boycott and Snow sat side by side with their arms in slings. And there was my father, pouring a glass of champagne for me.

Ray Illingworth, *Yorkshire and Back* (1980)

We had a certain amount of misfortune with our bowlers. Alan Ward had to be flown home and then Ken Shuttleworth injured himself and was never the same man who took five for 40 at Brisbane. But Bob Willis came out as a very young replacement for Wardie and did a great job. He had to learn a lot and some of it was not easy. For instance, we had to tell him that while keeping the same line he had to bowl about a yard further up to Stackpole, who was such a good back-foot player, than he had to, say, Greg Chappell. He listened, he learned, he did his stuff and he got us a wicket almost every time he went on to bowl.

John Snow

Like most cricket followers I knew little about Bob until he arrived to join us as a replacement. In fact, my younger sister probably knew more about him, as his mother was a patient at the surgery where she worked. But there had been mutterings on the county cricket circuit about 'a new kid on the Surrey block' from batsmen who had found him a bit of a handful.

Ray Illingworth wanted more firepower and so a young, inexperienced Bob arrived in Australia somewhat dazed at his rapid promotion. With his innate wisdom, he quietly but wholeheartedly picked up the spirit of the team and soon found his niche. Geoffrey Boycott and I both had golden tours, but it was the contributions of the other members of the side at important moments that brought final success. Bob played his part here. In the last gruelling month of the tour, with four Tests plus more wearying days travelling, he took 12 wickets, three important ones in the first innings of the vital last Test.

It was not all serious, however, and Bob's droll sense of humour and cackle of a laugh enlivened many a moment, while his dancing was similar to his bowling action. I can distinctly remember him, head and shoulders above everyone else at a party (no play the following day, I must add), happily flailing away to Johnny Johnson and the Bandwagon's 'Blame it on the Pony Express'.

AUSTRALIA v ENGLAND

Played at Sydney Cricket Ground, Sydney, on 12, 13, 14, 16, 17 February 1971

Toss: Australia
Umpires: TF Brooks & LP Rowan
Result: **England won by 62 runs**

Close of play: Day 1: Aus (1) 13–2 (Marsh 2*, IM Chappell 0*, 6 overs)
Day 2: Aus (1) 235–7 (GS Chappell 62*, Lillee 6*, 57.6 overs)
Day 3: Eng (2) 229–4 (D'Oliveira 37*, Illingworth 25*, 54 overs)
Day 4: Aus (2) 123–5 (GS Chappell 19*, Marsh 12*, 31.4 overs)

ENGLAND

JH Edrich	c GS Chappell b Dell	30	c IM Chappell b O'Keeffe	57
BW Luckhurst	c Redpath b Walters	0	c Lillee b O'Keeffe	59
KWR Fletcher	c Stackpole b O'Keeffe	33	c Stackpole b Eastwood	20
JH Hampshire	c Marsh b Lillee	10	c IM Chappell b O'Keeffe	24
BL D'Oliveira	b Dell	1	c IM Chappell b Lillee	47
R Illingworth*	b Jenner	42	lbw b Lillee	29
APE Knott†	c Stackpole b O'Keeffe	27	b Dell	15
JA Snow	b Jenner	7	c Stackpole b Dell	20
P Lever	c Jenner b O'Keeffe	4	c Redpath b Jenner	17
DL Underwood	not out	8	c Marsh b Dell	0
RGD Willis	b Jenner	11	not out	2
Extras	(b 4, lb 4, w 1, nb 2)	11	(b 3, lb 3, nb 6)	12
Total	(76 overs)	**184**	(100.7 overs)	**302**

AUSTRALIA

KH Eastwood	c Knott b Lever	5	b Snow	0
KR Stackpole	b Snow	6	b Illingworth	67
RW Marsh†	c Willis b Lever	4 (7)	b Underwood	16
IM Chappell*	b Willis	25 (3)	c Knott b Lever	6
IR Redpath	c and b Underwood	59 (4)	c Hampshire b Illingworth	14
KD Walters	st Knott b Underwood	42 (5)	c D'Oliveira b Willis	1
GS Chappell	b Willis	65 (6)	st Knott b Illingworth	30
KJ O'Keeffe	c Knott b Illingworth	3	c sub (K Shuttleworth) b D'Oliveira	12
TJ Jenner	b Lever	30	c Fletcher b Underwood	4
DK Lillee	c Knott b Willis	6	c Hampshire b D'Oliveira	0
AR Dell	not out	3	not out	3
Extras	(lb 5, w 1, nb 10)	16	(b 2, nb 5)	7
Total	(83.6 overs)	**264**	(62.6 overs)	**160**

Australia	O	M	R	W	O	M	R	W
Lillee	13	5	32	1	14	0	43	2
Dell	16	8	32	2	26.7	3	65	3
Walters	4	0	10	1	5	0	18	0
GS Chappell	3	0	9	0				
Jenner	16	3	42	3	21	5	39	1
O'Keeffe	24	8	48	3	26	8	96	3
Eastwood					5	0	21	1
Stackpole					3	1	8	0

England	O	M	R	W	O	M	R	W
Snow	18	2	68	1	2	1	7	1
Lever	14.6	3	43	3	12	2	23	1
D'Oliveira	12	2	24	0	5	1	15	2
Willis	12	1	58	3	9	1	32	1
Underwood	16	3	39	2	13.6	5	28	2
Illingworth	11	3	16	1	20	7	39	3
Fletcher					1	0	9	0

Fall of Wickets:

	Eng	Aus	Eng	Aus
1st	5	11	94	0
2nd	60	13	130	22
3rd	68	32	158	71
4th	69	66	165	82
5th	98	147	234	96
6th	145	162	251	131
7th	156	178	276	142
8th	165	235	298	154
9th	165	239	299	154
10th	184	264	302	160

2. INDIA – CALCUTTA, 1977

On a pitch prepared to suit India's formidable spin-bowling attack, Bob's seven wickets, along with captain Tony Greig's hard-fought century, bring a ten-wicket victory and a 2–0 lead in the series.

The view from the press box

*D*AY *one and day two.* The problems with the pitch really began on Thursday afternoon. When I came to the ground that morning it was not easy to tell from the stand which was the pitch – the square was a uniform green – but through the rest of that day and during Friday the ground staff used wire brushes and a fine mower to remove all signs of grass. When play began yesterday the strip was bleached and colourless, in places the surface was loose, and India's spinners had clearly been given a pitch which was going to help them turn the ball a long way before the end of the match.

Bedi won the toss, which was another important piece of luck for India. This gain was then to some extent neutralised by a wonderful performance by England in the field. They bowled well, especially Willis – whose five for 27 was his best return for England – and Lever, although the latter's figures may not have been as eye-catching as those he had in his first Test in Delhi. With luck, though, he might have had four wickets instead of two and he and the other three bowlers used were backed up by the most impressive fielding and out-cricket I have ever seen from an England side.

Henry Blofeld, *The Guardian*

*D*AY *one and day two.* Bowling India out so cheaply had been greatly to England's credit. Willis finished with five for 27, remarkable figures in anybody's book for a fast bowler in a Test match in India.

I have never seen England more mobile in the field, with Randall, Barlow, Lever, Old and Tolchard to the fore. Old's magnificent left-handed catch at third slip, which got rid of Gavaskar in the first over of the match, set the tone. The bowlers kept their line and length unerringly. Willis, Old and Lever were all equally good.

John Woodcock, *The Times*

*F*INAL *day.* On the 12th day of Christmas Tony Greig led his England players around sunlit Eden Gardens on a triumphant lap of honour that was inconceivable when they left the gloom of the English winter six weeks ago.

Then they were a captain and a team on trial after two years of suffering, pain and defeat at the hands of Australia and the West Indies and the fastest bowlers in the world. Today they are the stars of India, having followed their innings victory at Delhi with a 10-wicket win here to take a 2–0 lead in the series, become the first England side ever to win in Calcutta and the first since Douglas Jardine's in 1933–34 to win two Test matches on the subcontinent.

Pat Gibson, *Daily Express*

The view from the dressing room

Derek Randall, *Rags* (1992)

In the hour before play began I watched in horror as the groundsmen busily scrubbed every blade of grass off the pitch. It would suit their spinners in no time.

Bishan Bedi won the toss and elected to bat. The obvious choice, as scoring any runs in the final innings on that strip was going to be a miracle. India, however, made a terrible start. Chris Old took a tremendous catch off the third ball, bowled by Willis, to dismiss Gavaskar. It was a brilliant delivery and only someone of Gavaskar's skill could have got a bat to it.

Tony Greig, *My Story* (1980)

First day. By the time the first over was complete, any complacency India may have felt must have disappeared. Sunil Gavaskar, fortunate not to touch Bob Willis's fizzing opening ball, was not so lucky with the third and Chris Old took a superb one-handed catch to his left at third slip. 'Sunny' was the man we wanted; his wicket, so early, was a psychological triumph.

The Indians didn't put up much resistance today. We have always suspected that their batting is weak and, here again, our seamers found them out. Willis took three wickets in the day, John Lever two and Chris Old one. They finished at 146 for seven, but it was no time to pat ourselves on the back and relax. To win, we simply had to get them out cheaply twice and avoid any sort of fourth-innings target.

Day two. Last night's togetherness had left everyone bubbling and we came on to the field soccer-style. I was scarcely out of the gate at the head of the team before Randall sprinted past, then Barlow, Willis and Tolchard. It was an exuberant entrance that set off a murmur of expectancy in another vast crowd on another inevitably sunny morning.

Willis bowled like a man possessed and finished them off clinically. They are scared of him, there can be no doubt about that. In appearance he is so different from the Indians – huge in height, fierce in expression, curly hair bouncing round his sharp-featured face. What's more, he is fast. This wicket has nothing for him, but I've never seen him bowl quicker.

Bob has had so many problems in the past that this is like starting again. He has had to make a huge effort to regain fitness and, every morning, he completes a series of exercises in the dressing room. Surprisingly, for one of his humour and character, nerves are a big part of his make-up. He sleeps badly and has suffered more than most out here. Today he made it, though, and I was delighted for him.

It was around tea-time when I got to the wicket, devoid of any thought of heroics. The priority was simply to be there tomorrow morning and my head went down accordingly. The last session was gruelling. Every ball demanded maximum concentration and I felt drained as I climbed the stairs to the dressing room. Willis was waiting at the door and he greeted me with an action that said more than any words could have done. Reaching out as I passed, he grabbed my sweat-sodden arm and squeezed the shirt-sleeve. This was the bowler who had set it all up for us and watched us come so close to throwing it all away. Bob lives every ball of a Test; he has a compulsion to watch, yet he punishes himself by doing so. I knew his gesture was one of appreciation, coupled with the urge to keep going.

Day four. I felt well again this morning and the century duly arrived – occupying, I'm told, all of seven hours. Prasanna dismissed me lbw for 103, but Chris Old went on to score a half-century that was incongruously aggressive and we were finally all out with a lead of 166. I thought we might still need every one.

The wicket was still turning and Underwood was wheeling maiden after maiden. But Sharma and Patel played him safely for a long period and I was left with a decision to make. I decided on Bob Willis, who had been skulking around with the air of someone unfairly out of a job.

Bob tends to vary his run nowadays, but this afternoon he went back almost to the sightscreen. It seemed a perverse action, considering the intense heat out there, but Bob later explained that it gave him a longer break between each ball. I wasn't going to argue.

Two catches by Knotty got rid of Sharma and Solkar, both Willis victims, and we were back on the road.

Final day. We bowled them out for 181, Underwood finishing with three wickets when he might have had seven with a slice of luck. It was reality at last. With only 16 wanted, we could not fail now. Graham Barlow was almost out once or twice, but we got there with all ten wickets intact and I've rarely seen a more exuberant dressing room.

INDIA v ENGLAND

Played at Eden Gardens, Calcutta, on 1, 2, 3, 5, 6 January 1977

Toss: India
Umpires: B Satyaji Rao & HP Sharma
Result: **England won by 10 wickets**

Close of play: Day 1: Ind (1) 146–7 (Kirmani 20*, Prasanna 1*, 69 overs)
Day 2: Eng (1) 136–4 (Tolchard 31*, Greig 19*, 73 overs)
Day 3: Eng (1) 285–6 (Greig 94*, Old 35*, 159 overs)
Day 4: Ind (2) 145–7 (Patel 48*, Prasanna 12*, 55 overs)

INDIA

SM Gavaskar	c Old b Willis	0	b Underwood		18
AD Gaekwad	b Lever	32	c Tolchard b Greig		8
PH Sharma	c Greig b Lever	9	c Knott b Willis		20
GR Viswanath	c Tolchard b Underwood	35	c Lever b Greig		3
BP Patel	hit wicket b Willis	21	lbw b Old		56
ED Solkar	c Greig b Willis	2	c Knott b Willis		3
Madan Lal	c Knott b Old	17	c Brearley b Old		16
SMH Kirmani†	not out	25	b Old		0
EAS Prasanna	b Willis	2	c Brearley b Underwood		13
BS Bedi*	c Lever b Old	1	b Underwood		18
BS Chandrasekhar	b Willis	1	not out		4
Extras	(lb 2, nb 8)	10	(b 2, lb 4, nb 16)		22
Total	(75 overs)	**155**		(70.5 overs)	**181**

ENGLAND

DL Amiss	c Kirmani b Prasanna	35	not out	7
GD Barlow	c Kirmani b Madan Lal	4	not out	7
JM Brearley	c Solkar b Bedi	5		
DW Randall	lbw b Prasanna	37		
RW Tolchard	b Bedi	67		
AW Greig*	lbw b Prasanna	103		
APE Knott†	c Gavaskar b Bedi	2		
CM Old	c Madan Lal b Prasanna	52		
JK Lever	c Gavaskar b Bedi	2		
DL Underwood	c Gavaskar b Bedi	4		
RGD Willis	not out	0		
Extras	(b 5, lb 5)	10	(lb 1, nb 1)	2
Total	(178.4 overs)	**321**	(for 0 wkts) (3.4 overs)	**16**

England	O	M	R	W	O	M	R	W
Willis	20	3	27	5	13	1	32	2
Lever	22	2	57	2	3	0	12	0
Underwood	13	5	24	1	32.5	18	50	3
Old	20	5	37	2	12	4	38	3
Greig					10	0	27	2

India	O	M	R	W	O	M	R	W
Madan Lal	17	4	25	1	1	0	3	0
Solkar	6	1	15	0				
Bedi	64	25	110	5	1.4	0	6	0
Chandrasekhar	33	9	66	0				
Prasanna	57.4	16	93	4	1	0	5	0
Sharma	1	0	2	0				

Fall of Wickets:

	Ind	Eng	Ind	Eng
1st	1	7	31	–
2nd	23	14	33	–
3rd	65	81	36	–
4th	92	90	60	–
5th	99	232	70	–
6th	106	234	97	–
7th	136	298	97	–
8th	147	307	146	–
9th	149	321	171	–
10th	155	321	181	–

3. WEST INDIES – TRENT BRIDGE, 1980

In Ian Botham's first Test as captain, Bob's nine wickets bring England agonisingly close to a rare victory against Clive Lloyd's formidable West Indies team.

The view from the press box

*D*AY *two*. Bob Willis, written off as England's main strike bowler in Australia last winter, proved everybody wrong at Trent Bridge. The 6 ft 6 in pace man, 31 last month, roared in with all his old aggression in the first Test against the West Indies. And that was just the inspiration England needed to reduce them to 270 for seven – just seven runs ahead – by the end of a fiercely contested second day.

Pat Gibson, *Daily Express*

*D*AY *two*. If England's total of 263 was less than a side batting first at Trent Bridge would expect, it might have been worse but for catches dropped by West Indies. Crucially, however, the English bowlers behaved as if they believed it to be defensible, and if it is not a cricketing axiom it ought to be, that any side's total is as good as its bowling proves it. Willis bowled with much of his old fire; perhaps his appointment to the Warwickshire captaincy has proved the revitalising factor.

Bacchus promised a bright innings until Botham caught him at slip off Willis, who almost at once had Richards taken by the wicket-keeper. The extent of Richards's self-disgust was apparent in an angry gesture with the bat as he came into the pavilion.

John Arlott, *The Guardian*

*F*INAL *day*. Well, the first Cornhill Test match did, in the end, have a thrilling finish. Those who were wanting England to win it will say, to their dying day, that they would have done so had they held their catches. As it was, they were beaten, in spite of some heroic bowling by Willis, by two wickets.

At the heart of England's great effort was Willis, whose ten morning overs brought him three for 31. At lunch, taken at 176 for six, the chances were, I thought, that Willis would seize up. Instead, with the first ball afterwards he beat Marshall with a terrific leg-cutter and with the fourth he caused him to play on. From then on Willis must have passed the bat, on average, twice an over. All he could do was to tear at his hair.

John Woodcock, *The Times*

*F*INAL *day.* Bob Willis, his heroic bowling in vain, walked away early from the presentation ceremony close to tears. Willis was the match's martyr and he could take no more.

'I got very upset. I hate losing when we get this close,' he said, before driving away, the first England player to leave. 'I meant no insult to anyone, opponents or sponsors. I just wanted to be alone. And naturally, I'm very pleased with my bowling. It's what I've been working for all season. But I cannot feel happy after this result.'

Pat Gibson, *Daily Express*

The view from the dressing room

Bob Willis, *Lasting the Pace* (1985)

Although Ian was landed with a formidable set of fixtures with which to launch himself in the job, things might have turned out very differently for him had we won, as we should have, the first Test of his captaincy at Trent Bridge. It was a low-scoring game on a sporting wicket on which, in the frenetic final stages, we dropped at least two straightforward catches before Andy Roberts slogged the winning runs for a two-wicket victory. Had we won at Trent Bridge and taken the series, Ian would have been a hero again and, who knows, might still be England captain today. As it was, he did not even last another twelve months.

Ian Botham, *My Autobiography* (1994)

My first Test in charge was a tremendous match. I won the toss and decided we should bat. I went on to prove that I could captain the side without losing my natural aggression by top-scoring in the first innings with 57 as we made 263.

The West Indies replied by making 308, with Viv Richards and Deryck Murray both hitting 64, while I picked up three for 50 and Bob Willis returned four for 82. Second time around we made 252, leaving them a target of 208 in just over eight hours. It was never going to be easy against our attack of Bob Willis, John Lever, Mike Hendrick and myself as the pitch was doing a bit. When Greenidge was caught behind off Bob by Alan Knott with the score at 11, we felt that another breakthrough would be decisive. Unfortunately, Viv Richards tore into the bowling, scoring 48 in 56 minutes to ease the pressure on the rest of the batsmen. Although I got his wicket just before the close, when the last day started the West Indies needed only 99 to win with eight wickets in hand.

The crowd barely reached 1000 but those that bothered to come saw us win, lose, win and ultimately lose the game. As the day wore on, wickets fell regularly and the tension mounted. When the West Indies were 180 for seven, thanks to Bob Willis's five for 65, we felt a win was within our grasp. They were still 23 from victory and despite two dropped slip catches things were going our way. And then disaster struck.

In those days, if you had to pick a fielder to take a catch to win a Test match, the man you would turn to without hesitation was David Gower. Ninety-nine times out of a hundred he would have snapped up Andy Roberts at cover off Bob without even thinking about it. This just happened to be the hundredth time. No one on the field could believe it, least of all David. You can never say that one catch is the difference between winning and losing; but just how important that particular chance had been to both sides became obvious when, after he was run out for 62 by a direct throw from Peter Willey, Des Haynes ran from the field in tears believing his mistake had probably cost the West Indies the game, even though only three runs were required with two wickets remaining. If only he had been right.

ENGLAND v WEST INDIES

Played at Trent Bridge, Nottingham, on 5, 6, 7, 9, 10 June 1980

Toss:	England
Umpires:	DJ Constant & DO Oslear
Man of the Match:	AME Roberts
Result:	**West Indies won by 2 wickets**

Close of play:
Day 1: Eng (1) 243–7 (Knott 6*, Lever 14*, 84 overs)
Day 2: WI (1) 270–7 (Murray 49*, Roberts 3*, 79 overs)
Day 3: Eng (2) 145–2 (Boycott 61*, Woolmer 20*, 58 overs)
Day 4: WI (2) 109–2 (Haynes 29*, Bacchus 19*, 33 overs)

ENGLAND

GA Gooch	c Murray b Roberts	17	run out (Bacchus)		27
G Boycott	c Murray b Garner	36	b Roberts		75
CJ Tavaré	b Garner	13	c Richards b Garner		4
RA Woolmer	c Murray b Roberts	46	c Murray b Roberts		29
DI Gower	c Greenidge b Roberts	20	lbw b Garner		1
IT Botham*	c Richards b Garner	57	c Richards b Roberts		4
P Willey	b Marshall	13	b Marshall		38
APE Knott†	lbw b Roberts	6	lbw b Marshall		7
JK Lever	c Richards b Holding	15	c Murray b Garner		4
RGD Willis	b Roberts	8	b Garner		9
M Hendrick	not out	7	not out		2
Extras	(b 7, lb 11, w 3, nb 4)	25	(b 19, lb 13, w 10, nb 10)		52
Total	(91.5 overs)	**263**		(111.1 overs)	**252**

WEST INDIES

CG Greenidge	c Knott b Hendrick	53	c Knott b Willis		6
DL Haynes	c Gower b Willis	12	run out (Willey)		62
IVA Richards	c Knott b Willis	64	lbw b Botham		48
SFAF Bacchus	c Botham b Willis	30	c Knott b Hendrick		19
AI Kallicharran	b Botham	17	c Knott b Willis		9
DL Murray†	b Willis	64	(7) c Hendrick b Willis		16
CH Lloyd*	c Knott b Lever	9	(6) lbw b Willis		3
MD Marshall	c Tavaré b Gooch	20	b Willis		7
AME Roberts	lbw b Botham	21	not out		22
J Garner	c Lever b Botham	2			
MA Holding	not out	0	(10) not out		0
Extras	(b 1, lb 9, w 2, nb 4)	16	(lb 8, nb 9)		17
Total	(91.1 overs)	**308**	(for 8 wkts)	(68.4 overs)	**209**

West Indies	O	M	R	W	O	M	R	W
Roberts	25	7	72	5	24	6	57	3
Holding	23.5	7	61	1	26	5	65	0
Marshall	19	3	52	1	24	8	44	2
Richards	1	0	9	0				
Garner	23	9	44	3	34.1	20	30	4
Greenidge					3	2	4	0

England	O	M	R	W	O	M	R	W
Willis	20.1	5	82	4	26	4	65	5
Lever	20	2	76	1	8	2	25	0
Hendrick	19	4	69	1	14	5	40	1
Willey	5	3	4	0	2	0	12	0
Botham	20	6	50	3	16.4	6	48	1
Gooch	7	2	11	1	2	1	2	0

Fall of Wickets:

	Eng	WI	Eng	WI
1st	27	19	46	11
2nd	72	107	68	69
3rd	74	151	174	109
4th	114	165	175	125
5th	204	208	180	129
6th	208	227	183	165
7th	228	265	218	180
8th	246	306	237	205
9th	254	308	248	–
10th	263	308	252	–

4. WEST INDIES – THE OVAL, 1980

Against a West Indian attack featuring Marshall, Holding, Croft and Garner, Bob's unbeaten three-hour 24 in the second innings helps Peter Willey reach his century and ensures a draw in the fourth Test.

The view from the press box

FINAL day. England were saved from all but certain defeat in the fourth Test match by a splendid and purposeful last-wicket stand of 117 between Willey and Willis. Willey, whose place was in jeopardy for the second successive Test, produced his best performance for England and not only retained their chance to square the rubber at Headingley but scored a century, saved himself and won the Man of the Match award.

Willey, who had been written off two Tests ago only to save himself in the second innings at Old Trafford, batted soundly and responsibly. Crucially he sheltered Willis from Holding. Willis, for his part, has never batted better. He played Garner carefully, Marshall hopefully and the spinners, Kallicharran and Richards, who tried to buy his wicket, with avoidance of error.

John Arlott, *The Guardian*

FINAL day. Although England saved the fourth Test match comfortably enough in the end, they had some anxious moments on the way. With seven wickets down, and four hours 20 minutes left, and England leading by no more than 178, West Indies had an even chance of winning. As at Old Trafford, though, they finished with an incomplete set of fast bowlers, and as there, too, Willey stood in their way. This time, with prolonged and improbable assistance from Willis,

he reached his first Test hundred.

West Indies were still in with a winning chance when Willis came in. With three hours and a half left for play England led by 197. Willey at the time was 13. More than once, when aiming to play the ball to the on side, he had seen it finish up in the gully. But he was amply rewarded for sticking at it. With Willis as his partner he farmed the bowling; once the danger to England was past he played some splendid strokes, while Willis, in spite of being hit a time or two by Holding and Marshall, kept up his end.

As Willey neared his hundred Willis's record on such occasions came ominously to mind. At Lahore some years ago he was last out when Miller was 99; at Perth last December Boycott was also left with 99 when Willis was caught at slip off Dymock; and at Sydney a week or two later Gower was 98 not out when Willis departed, also to a slip catch, off Lillee. Yesterday, happily, there were no such accidents.

John Woodcock, *The Times*

The view from the dressing room

Ian Botham, *My Autobiography* (1994)

At The Oval our best batting performance of the summer put us in the driving seat as we finished our first innings with 370 on the board. I then claimed my 150th Test wicket, the sweet prize of Viv Richards, who was brilliantly held by Peter Willey in the gully. The West Indies finished 105 behind us and but for a battling 61 from Faoud Bacchus we could have been in an even better position. The advantage, however, quickly swung away from us at that point and in our second innings we plummeted to 18 for four. Peter Willey then got us out of jail with 100 not out in an unbeaten last-wicket stand with Bob Willis worth 117, and that allowed us to declare at 209 for nine. However, time ran out and our chance of winning the series went with it.

Bob Willis, *Lasting the Pace* (1985)

The third [selectorial mistake of the summer of 1980] was their failure to drop me after the third Test at Old Trafford, in which I bowled as badly and ineffectually as I have ever done in all my years with England. I was thoroughly and mercilessly hammered, especially by Richards, and felt utterly hopeless and depressed about it. It was then that Ian's loyalty, which he shows to all his friends and team-mates, came shining through. He took me out for a drink, cheered me up, and made sure I kept my place for the next game. It was more than I deserved, but I have always been grateful.

As things turned out, it was only a one-match stay of execution, for I bowled more rubbish at The Oval, crowning my frustrations by taking two wickets with no-balls. Although I played my part in saving the game with the bat during a long and unlikely partnership with Peter Willey, I was quite properly dropped from the side for the first time in five years.

ENGLAND v WEST INDIES

Played at The Oval on 24, 25, 26, 28, 29 July 1980

Toss:	England
Umpires:	BJ Meyer & DO Oslear
Man of the Match:	P Willey
Result:	**Drawn**

Close of play: Day 1: Eng (1) 236–3 (Boycott 39*, Gatting 18*, 74 overs)
Day 2: WI (1) 45–2 (Richards 14*, Bacchus 5*, 22 overs)
Day 3: No play
Day 4: Eng (2) 20–4 (Rose 11*, Gatting 1*, 17 overs)

ENGLAND

GA Gooch	lbw b Holding	83		lbw b Holding	0
G Boycott	run out (Greenidge)	53		c Murray b Croft	5
BC Rose	b Croft	50		lbw b Garner	41
W Larkins	lbw b Garner	7		b Holding	0
MW Gatting	b Croft	48	(6)	c Murray b Garner	15
P Willey	c Lloyd b Holding	34	(8)	not out	100
APE Knott†	c Lloyd b Marshall	3	(9)	lbw b Holding	3
IT Botham*	lbw b Croft	9	(7)	c Greenidge b Garner	4
JE Emburey	c Holding b Marshall	24	(5)	c Bacchus b Croft	2
GR Dilley	b Garner	1		c sub (CL King) b Holding	1
RGD Willis	not out	1		not out	24
Extras	(b 7, lb 21, w 10, nb 19)	57		(lb 6, w 1, nb 7)	14
Total	(128.3 overs)	**370**		(for 9 wkts dec) (94 overs)	**209**

WEST INDIES

CG Greenidge	lbw b Willis	6
DL Haynes	c Gooch b Dilley	7
IVA Richards	c Willey b Botham	26
SFAF Bacchus	c Knott b Emburey	61
AI Kallicharran	c Rose b Dilley	11
DL Murray†	hit wicket b Dilley	0
MD Marshall	c Rose b Emburey	45
J Garner	c Gatting b Botham	46
MA Holding	lbw b Dilley	22
CEH Croft	not out	0
CH Lloyd*	absent hurt	
Extras	(lb 12, w 1, nb 28)	41
Total	(95.2 overs)	**265**

West Indies	O	M	R	W	O	M	R	W
Holding	28	5	67	2	29	7	79	4
Croft	35	9	97	3	10	6	8	2
Marshall	29.3	6	77	2	23	7	47	0
Garner	33	8	67	2	17	5	24	3
Richards	3	1	5	0	9	3	15	0
Kallicharran					6	1	22	0

England	O	M	R	W
Willis	19	5	58	1
Dilley	23	6	57	4
Botham	18.2	8	47	2
Emburey	23	12	38	2
Gooch	1	0	2	0
Willey	11	5	22	0

Fall of Wickets:

	Eng	WI	Eng
1st	155	15	2
2nd	157	34	10
3rd	182	72	13
4th	269	99	18
5th	303	105	63
6th	312	187	67
7th	336	197	73
8th	343	261	84
9th	368	265	92
10th	370	–	–

5. INDIA – LORD'S, 1982

In his first Test as captain, Bob makes his highest Test score of 28 and takes nine wickets as England enjoy a seven-wicket victory against Sunil Gavaskar's India, despite the valiant efforts of all-rounder Kapil Dev.

The view from the press box

*D*AY *two*. Some time today India are likely to have to follow on in the first Test match. Yesterday, after England's last four wickets had added another 155 runs, India lost most of their main batting for only 45 to Botham, Willis and Pringle.

For England's eighth wicket, Randall and Taylor had added 72, for the tenth, Allott and Willis 70, a record for England against India, beating the 57 put on by John Murray and Robin Hobbs at Edgbaston in 1967. It was not quite Morecambe and Wise. Allott and Willis take their batting more seriously than that, Allott always, Willis when he thinks he will. The last England captain to bat at No 11 was Lord Hawke at Cape Town in 1899.

John Woodcock, *The Times*

*D*AY *two*. Randall, burgeoning visibly, completed his third Test hundred, a good one and his first in England. Taylor thrived and then, in the final act of mortification for the tourists, Allott and Willis collected 70 untroubled runs for the last wicket. Willis's 28 was his highest Test score, the partnership a tenth-wicket Test record for England against India.

In such circumstances India cannot have enjoyed the prospects of batting for the remainder of the afternoon and misgivings were justified. Willis produced pace, bounce and a lot of hostility from the Pavilion End.

Paul Fitzpatrick, *The Guardian*

*D*AY *three*. Willis and Botham dismissed the five outstanding Indian wickets with an energy which, like the grass, was refreshed by the several interruptions for rain. Botham performed that feat which is as much a ritual as rain on the Saturday of the Lord's Test: he took five wickets in an innings for the 19th time.

At the other end, Willis rolled back some of his years to accost the batsmen with some hostile fast bowling about the ribcage. As captain, he had the uncomplicated task of keeping himself and Botham on, the pair accounting for all but two overs of the day.

Scyld Berry, *The Observer*

*D**AY three.* Willis has had an encouraging match so far as batsman, bowler and captain. His solution to the 'chatting' by Edmonds from his suicidal position at short leg showed his authority. On Friday afternoon Willis told Edmonds that he did not mind him geeing up his own players but that he did not want him talking to the Indian batsmen. 'He has since desisted,' he said in his characteristically laconic way.

Paul Fitzpatrick, *The Guardian*

*D**AY four.* The unbelievable events of Headingley last summer must have been flashing through [the England players'] minds when Kapil cut loose with bat and ball. Just as Botham revitalised England after they had followed on in that third Test against Australia, so Kapil Dev attempted to bring India back from the dead.

For his first trick, the 23-year-old Punjabi went close to the fastest century in Test history, smashing 89 in 79 minutes off only 55 balls with 13 fours and a six. Then, having forced England to bat again, he made the 65 needed for victory look anything but a formality by grabbing three wickets in eight balls.

So a match that looked like being almost a walkover for England is not quite finished yet after a compelling fourth day that had already produced two heroes before Kapil made an appearance. Dilip Vengsarkar, the 26-year-old batsman who saved India with a century in a similar situation at Lord's three years ago, went a long way to doing it again. But after batting 5¾ hours for a monumental 157, he was thwarted when England's captain Bob Willis suddenly pulled out yet another inspiring spell of fast bowling that brought him four wickets in 29 balls, and six in the innings.

There were only eight overs left of the 96 to be bowled in the day when England began their task of scoring 65 – but it was time enough for Kapil Dev to give them another shock or three. He bowled Chris Tavaré, had nightwatchman Taylor caught at short leg and then claimed Geoff Cook lbw, to leave England sweating on 23 for three and keeping their fingers crossed that it doesn't rain today.

Pat Gibson, *Daily Express*

*F*INAL *day.* Kapil Dev, Freddie Trueman's choice as Man of the Match, had no more wonders to perform, and England won the first Test against India at Lord's by seven wickets yesterday. Allan Lamb put bat to ball and the inhibitions of England's batsmen of Monday evening had gone. The end came in a suitably brisk manner.

Paul Fitzpatrick, *The Guardian*

The view from the dressing room

Derek Randall, *The Sun Has Got His Hat On* (1984)

To widespread surprise, it was announced that Bob Willis was to take charge. Even Bob had not considered himself a prime candidate for the captaincy but, so far as I was concerned, it was a sensible choice. He had always been a strong, inspiring figure as vice-captain and it seemed only right that he should be given the chance to do the number-one job.

A Lord's Test has an atmosphere all its own. This one seemed particularly special. Two years, two long years out of the Test team had left me hungry for more success. What better stage could I have than the game's headquarters on a June Thursday? I did not have to wait long for the chance to prove myself.

Bob won the toss and chose to bat but we lost three wickets for 37, all to Kapil Dev. The fall of a fourth wicket brought me to the crease with the score on 96 and a repair job to be done before any thoughts of personal attainment could be considered. I was in the 80s by the close that night, and carefully completed my hundred the next morning. It was a sweet feeling to be back, made sweeter still when we went on to win the game comfortably, with two sessions to spare.

ENGLAND v INDIA

Played at Lord's Cricket Ground on 10, 11, 12, 14, 15 June 1982

Toss: England
Umpires: DGL Evans & BJ Meyer
Man of the Match: Kapil Dev
Result: **England won by 7 wickets**

Close of play: Day 1: Eng (1) 278–6 (Randall 84*, Edmonds 59*, 96 overs)
Day 2: Ind (1) 92–5 (Gavaskar 41*, Kapil Dev 28*, 41 overs)
Day 3: Ind (2) 61–2 (Vengsarkar 30*, Shastri 6*, 26 overs)
Day 4: Eng (2) 23–3 (Lamb 6*, Gower 2*, 7.5 overs)

ENGLAND

G Cook	lbw b Kapil Dev	4		lbw b Kapil Dev	10
CJ Tavaré	c Viswanath b Kapil Dev	4		b Kapil Dev	3
AJ Lamb	lbw b Kapil Dev	9	(4)	not out	37
DI Gower	c Viswanath b Kapil Dev	37	(5)	not out	14
IT Botham	c Malhotra b Madan Lal	67			
DW Randall	c Parkar b Kapil Dev	126			
DR Pringle	c Gavaskar b Doshi	7			
PH Edmonds	c Kirmani b Madan Lal	64			
RW Taylor†	c Viswanath b Doshi	31	(3)	c Malhotra b Kapil Dev	1
PJW Allott	not out	41			
RGD Willis*	b Madan Lal	28			
Extras	(b 1, lb 5, nb 9)	15		(lb 2)	2
Total	(148.1 overs)	**433**		(for 3 wkts) (19 overs)	**67**

INDIA

SM Gavaskar*	b Botham	48		c Cook b Willis	24
GA Parkar	lbw b Botham	6		b Willis	1
DB Vengsarkar	lbw b Willis	2		c Allott b Willis	157
GR Viswanath	b Botham	1	(5)	c Taylor b Pringle	3
Yashpal Sharma	lbw b Pringle	4	(6)	b Willis	37
AO Malhotra	lbw b Pringle	5	(7)	c Taylor b Willis	0
Kapil Dev	c Cook b Willis	41	(8)	c Cook b Botham	89
RJ Shastri	c Cook b Willis	4	(4)	b Allott	23
SMH Kirmani†	not out	6		c Gower b Willis	3
Madan Lal	c Tavaré b Botham	6		lbw b Pringle	15
DR Doshi	c Taylor b Botham	0		not out	4
Extras	(lb 1, nb 4)	5		(lb 2, nb 11)	13
Total	(50.4 overs)	**128**		(111.5 overs)	**369**

India	O	M	R	W	O	M	R	W
Kapil Dev	43	8	125	5	10	1	43	3
Madan Lal	28.1	6	99	3	2	1	2	0
Shastri	34	10	73	0	2	0	9	0
Doshi	40	7	120	2	5	3	11	0
Yashpal Sharma	3	2	1	0				

England	O	M	R	W	O	M	R	W
Botham	19.4	3	46	5	31.5	7	103	1
Willis	16	2	41	3	28	3	101	6
Pringle	9	4	16	2	19	4	58	2
Edmonds	2	1	5	0	15	6	39	0
Allott	4	1	15	0	17	3	51	1
Cook					1	0	4	0

Fall of Wickets:

	Eng	Ind	Ind	Eng
1st	5	17	6	11
2nd	18	21	47	13
3rd	37	22	107	18
4th	96	31	110	–
5th	149	45	252	–
6th	166	112	252	–
7th	291	116	254	–
8th	363	116	275	–
9th	363	128	341	–
10th	433	128	369	–

6. AUSTRALIA – MELBOURNE, 1982

Bob achieves his only win against Australia as captain, guiding his team to a thrilling victory by just three runs, despite suffering from the effects of a virus for most of the match.

The view from the press box

DAY three. It is doubtful whether Rex Whitehead's forefinger or Graeme Fowler's big toe will take their places in the Ashes legend. Yet they were the major influences on a compelling third day in the fourth Test, which left Australia needing 292 to win and clinch the series.

Umpire Whitehead's finger intruded sensationally into the proceedings when he gave out England's key batsman David Gower caught behind at a critical stage of their second innings. Gower, hooking at a Geoff Lawson bouncer, obviously failed to make contact with the bat – a fact confirmed by television replays – and looked disbelievingly at Whitehead before making his sorrowful exit, with England in peril at 45 for three.

Then, after Fowler and Allan Lamb had gone a long way towards repairing the damage with a fourth-wicket stand of 83 in 87 minutes, Lancashire left-hander Fowler's toe brought the match to a standstill. He cracked a bone in it when he played a ball from Jeff Thomson on to his foot and, after hobbling around painfully for an over, sent for a runner.

It took him almost ten minutes to get one – because Australian captain Greg Chappell objected to Gower, the obvious choice, on the grounds that he is better between the wickets than Fowler. The rules do not give Chappell that right and eventually Gower took the field. But the delay – which reflected no credit on the captains or the umpires – had broken the batsmen's concentration and allowed the Australian bowlers to regain their composure.

And in the next over, Fowler and Lamb fell in the space of four balls from Rodney Hogg, to put England back in desperate trouble at 129 for five. But adversity brought the best out of England – not for the first time in the 100-year history of the Ashes – with Ian Botham, Derek Pringle and Bob Taylor all producing their best batting of the series as the last five wickets added another 165.

So the stage was set today for a thrilling climax to a match England had to win to stay in the series, while Australia needed only to draw to regain the famous prize.

Pat Gibson, *Daily Express*

*D*AY *four and day five.* England finally settled the fourth Test in Melbourne early today by three runs. It was both equal to the closest result ever and one of the most consistently thrilling of all time.

England had done 99 per cent of the job yesterday when Australia were reduced to 218 for nine, 74 short with only one wicket left. But Border and Thomson first gave Australia half those 74. Then, thanks to a downpour, England were obliged to return on the fifth morning, when for 85 minutes Australia looked as though they could pull off a victory that would not only have given them the Ashes but would have been sensational enough to expiate the memories of their failures in England last year.

England's tactics of trying to offer singles to Border to make sure that Thomson had most of the strike failed abysmally. Thomson dealt confidently with most of the balls he had to face and Border was sharp enough to turn ones into twos.

However, with disaster staring England in the face, Botham discovered a sudden burst of energy and found the edge of Thomson's bat. The catch went to Tavaré in the slips, who dropped it. Mercifully, Miller, next door at first slip, was sharp enough to fall to his right and make the catch. England had won, to stay in the series.

Matthew Engel, *The Guardian*

The view from the dressing room

Bob Willis, *The Captain's Diary* (1983)

We took the new ball as soon as it became available, but still the Aussies continued to inch ever closer to the target. Border was doing well, farming as much of the strike as possible and punishing the loose deliveries, but Thommo was also holding up his end without giving us great grounds for confidence.

'Flash' [Cowans] was plainly tiring after his exertions on the earlier days, and probably we were all suffering from the absence of a rest day in such a high-pressure game. So I turned to 'Beefy', the magical Botham, hoping that the sorcerer had something left up his sleeve. At first, nothing. Down, ever down, the target slipped, until only four runs were needed. Almost 20,000 people had turned up at the end of a tremendously well-supported match and, although they may have seen no more than one delivery, they were now being rewarded and were showing their appreciation while we tried to convince ourselves that defeat could still not happen.

It didn't. With Border on strike, I summoned reserves of energy and bowled my best and tightest over of the day. Border just could not get a single, so Thomson had to face the start of a new over from Ian. The end came with the first delivery, but not without further cause for coronaries. Thomson edged the ball to second slip and Tavaré, normally a safe catcher, fumbled it. History shows, however, that he did manage to knock the ball upwards, over his head, and Geoff Miller ran behind him from first slip to grab the ball.

I remember throwing my arms jubilantly into the air, and then running blindly off. I remember that when I reached the dressing room, the non-players were still bear-hugging Doug Insole, who had probably bitten through another couple of nails during the agony. Most of all, I remember the overwhelming relief that every person in our dressing room showed.

Allan Lamb, *My Autobiography* (1997)

It could have taken one ball to finish the match the next morning, but 18,000 Aussies turned up to watch, many of them with their 'eskies' as though they were there for the day. We stayed with the same tactics, but we couldn't shift Thommo and now they must have been favourites, with only six runs wanted as Willis started an over to AB.

It was a magnificent over, with two runs coming from the first three balls, but then three spot-on block-hole balls meant we could start an over against Thommo. What was extra special about the last Willis yorker was that he'd mis-counted. Having wound up his concentration for what he thought was the last ball of the over, he then turned to decide who would bowl and to what field, only to realise that he'd got another ball to bowl.

I feared the worst, but to his eternal credit, he did it again and now the real drama started. Who else to bowl other than golden-arm Both, so Willis called him up and gave him two slips. Four to win, and Thommo decided that the time had come to win the game. He aimed a square cut, the ball flew to Tavaré at first slip, who couldn't hold it. He knocked it up and behind him, but 'Dusty' Miller nipped round the blind side and took the catch.

All hell broke loose, both on the field and in the television commentary booth, where Channel Nine had gone away for the break between overs and missed the wicket. As for Tav, some of us were nearly off the field when Bob Taylor turned round and saw him, still standing at slip, as white as a ghost, thinking of what so nearly was. What a morning, what a finish, what a day and what a night that was.

Allan Border, *An Autobiography* (1986)

The Melbourne match against England in December 1982 produced one of the most exciting finishes in Test cricket history. To my eternal sorrow, Australia lost. But I am proud to have been involved in that game's breathtaking conclusion.

When Jeff Thomson had joined me at the wicket in the final session of the fourth day ... we were 9–218, chasing 292, and only a super-patriotic spendthrift would have had a dollar on us. It was remarkable, then, that Jeff and I were still together at the end of the fourth day and the target had been whittled away by exactly half: 37 runs to win.

The next ninety minutes produced some of the best, most tension-packed cricket ever. Every time Thommo laid bat to ball, the crowd went wild; every run he scored brought the stands down. As we inched towards our target, I could sense panic taking something of a grip on the England camp. When the partnership had started, the Poms had been full of the joy of living. By stumps, they were showing a little strain. Now they were yelling and screaming at each other.

The strain was really telling on the batsmen, too. Jeff and I screamed obscenities at each other at every false stroke, every near-miss (and there were plenty of those). Even the huge electronic MCG scoreboard (in use for the first time) got into the act, flashing the number of runs needed and replaying every incident. It was frantic cricket, which became even more so as we approached the target.

The end came with the first ball of the 18th over of the morning. We needed three to tie, four to win. It was Ian Botham to Thommo, the ball was short of a length and wide of the off stump. In retrospect, you could say that Jeff should have left it alone. On the other hand, given the right amount of luck, he could have hit it for four and won the game for us. What happened was that Jeff sparred at the ball and got an edge to Chris Tavaré at second slip. It wasn't a particularly difficult chance but Tavaré was obviously affected by the occasion because the ball popped out of his hands. My immediate thought was that it had beaten the field and it would run for four. It didn't. The ball popped over Tavaré's shoulder and was snapped up by Geoff Miller at first slip.

Oh my God! We'd lost. After all that, we'd lost!

AUSTRALIA v ENGLAND

Played at Melbourne Cricket Ground on 26, 27, 28, 29, 30 December 1982

Toss: Australia
Umpires: AR Crafter & RV Whitehead
Man of the Match: NG Cowans
Result: **England won by 3 runs**

Close of play: Day 1:   Eng (1) 284
              Day 2:   Aus (1) 287
              Day 3:   Eng (2) 294
              Day 4:   Aus (2) 255–9 (Border 44*, Thomson 8*, 79 overs)

ENGLAND

Batsman		Runs		Runs
G Cook	c Chappell b Thomson	10	c Yardley b Thomson	26
G Fowler	c Chappell b Hogg	4	b Hogg	65
CJ Tavaré	c Yardley b Thomson	89	b Hogg	0
DI Gower	c Marsh b Hogg	18	c Marsh b Lawson	3
AJ Lamb	c Dyson b Yardley	83	c Marsh b Hogg	26
IT Botham	c Wessels b Yardley	27	c Chappell b Thomson	46
G Miller	c Border b Yardley	10	lbw b Lawson	14
DR Pringle	c Wessels b Hogg	9	c Marsh b Lawson	42
RW Taylor†	c Marsh b Yardley	1	lbw b Thomson	37
RGD Willis*	not out	6	not out	8
NG Cowans	c Lawson b Hogg	3	b Lawson	10
Extras	(b 3, lb 6, w 3, nb 12)	24	(b 2, lb 9, nb 6)	17
Total	(81.3 overs)	**284**	(80.4 overs)	**294**

AUSTRALIA

Batsman		Runs			Runs
KC Wessels	b Willis	47	(2)	b Cowans	14
J Dyson	lbw b Cowans	21	(1)	c Tavaré b Botham	31
GS Chappell*	c Lamb b Cowans	0		c sub (IJ Gould) b Cowans	2
KJ Hughes	b Willis	66		c Taylor b Miller	48
AR Border	b Botham	2	(6)	not out	62
DW Hookes	c Taylor b Pringle	53	(5)	c Willis b Cowans	68
RW Marsh†	b Willis	53		lbw b Cowans	13
B Yardley	b Miller	9		b Cowans	0
GF Lawson	c Fowler b Miller	0		c Cowans b Pringle	7
RM Hogg	not out	8		lbw b Cowans	4
JR Thomson	b Miller	1		c Miller b Botham	21
Extras	(lb 8, nb 19)	27		(b 5, lb 9, w 1, nb 3)	18
Total	(79 overs)	**287**		(96.1 overs)	**288**

Australia	O	M	R	W	O	M	R	W
Lawson	17	6	48	0	21.4	6	66	4
Hogg	23.3	6	69	4	22	5	64	3
Yardley	27	9	89	4	15	2	67	0
Thomson	13	2	49	2	21	3	74	3
Chappell	1	0	5	0	1	0	6	0

England	O	M	R	W	O	M	R	W
Willis	15	2	38	3	17	0	57	0
Botham	18	3	69	1	25.1	4	80	2
Cowans	16	0	69	2	26	6	77	6
Pringle	15	2	40	1	12	4	26	1
Miller	15	5	44	3	16	6	30	1

Fall of Wickets:

	Eng	Aus	Eng	Aus
1st	11	55	40	37
2nd	25	55	41	39
3rd	56	83	45	71
4th	217	89	128	171
5th	227	180	129	173
6th	259	261	160	190
7th	262	276	201	190
8th	268	276	262	202
9th	278	278	280	218
10th	284	287	294	288

13

IN HIS OWN WORDS

This chapter presents some examples of Bob's own writing, on the life of a cricketer and on other matters close to his heart. It starts with extracts from three books that were published in diary form (all in collaboration with Alan Lee). These are followed by an article written by Bob for *The Times* in which he talks about his fascination with **Bob Dylan** and gives his verdict on his hero's many albums. Finally, another side of Bob is revealed in selected passages from the **Father of the Bride speech** he wrote, in verse form, for his daughter, Katie.

The first book, ***Diary of a Cricket Season***, was published in 1979 and is an entertaining record – full of his beloved nicknames – of the **summer of 1978,** when Bob is a senior figure at Warwickshire and plays in two successful three-match Test series for England. In the first, he takes 13 wickets as Pakistan are beaten 2–0, while his 12 wickets contribute to a 3–0 win against New Zealand.

As the extracts reveal, in addition to a first-hand account of the cricket, the book offers an insight into the everyday challenges facing a professional sportsman, both physical and mental. One recurring theme is the toll that fast bowling takes on Bob's feet and his constant search for the perfect boot. We also see his attempts to deal with pre-match nerves and his perennial problems with sleeping. In the dressing room, where his annual haircut leads to much mickey-taking, he paints a picture of the different personalities, while on the field he welcomes the arrival of a young David Gower and applauds the all-round performances of Ian Botham in peak form.

The two other books, both called *The Captain's Diary*, were published in 1983 and 1984 and cover Bob's two tours as England captain. The trip to **Australia and New Zealand in 1982–83** features the first Ashes series since the dramas of 1981. The drawn first Test at Perth, which sees Terry Alderman injure himself rugby-tackling a pitch invader, is followed by a convincing Australian victory at Brisbane. Any chance England have of bouncing back is then thrown away by putting Australia in at Adelaide, a decision Bob is to rue for many years.

The stresses of captaincy inevitably colour Bob's account as he dwells on the headaches of selection, the attitudes of the younger players and the difficulty of coping with the poor form of the hero of 1981, his friend Ian Botham, while fending off press stories about a rift. The lighter side of touring, however, is still much in evidence.

Bob's second tour as captain, and his last as an England player, is to **New Zealand and Pakistan in 1983–84.** On the New Zealand leg, much to his annoyance, England fail to press home a winning position in the first Test at Wellington, which ends in a draw. A dominant all-round performance from Richard Hadlee then brings victory for New Zealand at Christchurch, which leaves England facing the almost impossible task of winning at Auckland on a pitch destined to produce a draw, and New Zealand duly celebrate their first ever series win against England. The series in Pakistan is also lost 1–0, but Bob's account is interrupted when illness forces him to return home early to England after playing in only one Test.

Diary of a Cricket Season – 1978

Monday, 1 May 1978. With no cricket for two days, I have a chance to catch up on a lot of jobs. The first was accomplished this morning when I visited a pal at Winit's to be fitted with new boots. That may sound a simple task, but it's always a massive headache for me.

My left foot takes size 11½ and my right foot size 11. The arch on my left foot has fallen, but not on my right. Both feet are narrow in body but splay at the toes. If you add all that together, it can be appreciated that any bootmaker has troubles in creating the correct shape to support my feet and my strange, heavy bowling action. Nobody yet has completely succeeded.

Wednesday, 24 May. David Gower looked good in his first match of any sort for England, but he must stop wafting at the ball outside off stump if he gets a chance in the Test side. At this level, it will get him out more often than not.

Friday, 26 May. How do you feel when you wake up to be told that you are captain of England [in the second ODI v Pakistan at The Oval] – if only for a day? That was my unexpected privilege this morning, following Fiery's [Boycott] sudden withdrawal with a thumb injury.

I've captained the side before, but only in New Zealand. This, before an England crowd and on the ground where I began my career, seemed different ... more significant, more stimulating.

Alone in the Great Western Hotel, after being given my news, my thoughts were dominated by the toss. Oval pitches are so flat and benign that I felt we must win it, bat well and set them a target as close to unassailable as it is possible to get.

The first wish was rejected – I lost the toss. But amazingly, for no reason that I could fathom, Pakistan's captain Wasim Bari put us in to bat. David Gower made a marvellous unbeaten century [114] and my target of 260 was realised. This time, we didn't bowl Pakistan out, but the result was still never in doubt. They made so little effort it was almost embarrassing, and I even brought on one or two joke bowlers at the end, more to keep the crowd amused than anything.

Tonight the Pru's reception seemed a brighter affair. Tannoy and Grummidge* and the rest of the family were there, proud of their boy I hope, but the reunion was all too brief and I was soon heading back up the motorway to Birmingham with England physio Bernard Thomas, complete with brand-new MGB GT.

As the car was still being run in and the drive more a crawl than a dash, I had plenty of time to chat with Bernard, and to appreciate once again what an important part he has had to play in my life, and the lives of so many cricketers.

I recall exactly when I met him first. It was 22 November 1970, the day that I arrived in Australia as a fresh-faced twenty-one-year-old, having been summoned to join the England tour as replacement for the injured Alan Ward. I checked in at the

---

* 'Tannoy' was the nickname Bob gave his father, Ted. It came from a combination of 'Pa' as in 'father' and 'PA' as in 'Public Address'. 'Grummidge' was a nickname originally given by Bob's father to Bob's mother, Anne. It started as 'Mrs Gummidge', after he joked that an unfashionable raincoat she used to wear made her look like the scarecrow character Worzel Gummidge, and with Bob's help the name evolved to 'Mrs Grummidge' and just 'Grummidge'.

Park Royal Hotel in Brisbane at seven in the morning, but Bernard was up to meet me and supervise my needs after a gruelling flight. He helped me through the problems of that first England tour and was then instrumental in my move from Surrey, where I was desperately unsettled, to Warwickshire, where he had long been physiotherapist.

Tuesday, 30 May. The day echoed to the sound of Barnsley's [David Brown] grumbles, having heard that Barry Richards, in his new book, was proposing that cricketers over thirty-five should take a drop in wages and be phased out as they were no longer of use to the game. D.J. Brown, at thirty-six years of age, didn't agree.

Wednesday, 31 May. There is a ritual feel about the eve of a Test match. It may not necessarily be looked forward to; the nervous may dread it. But nobody questions the value of what we are asked to do.

Today was the first such day of the summer, and consequently carried the most stress. My stomach was unsettled as soon as I got up – and that wasn't last night's alcohol. I spent the morning washing up the debris from the party, tidying the house, anything to keep my mind and body active.

At two o'clock, I left for Edgbaston. The ritual had begun. Birthday cards and letters had arrived for me in some numbers, and I filled in time reading them – some amusing, some touching, some just stupid – until the rest of the side began to arrive.

Something was not quite right in the changing room. It wasn't much, and perhaps I've been spoiled by the unbelievably good spirit that has been maintained since the tour of India four years ago, but I'm sure we weren't quite so happy. It's hard to define, this hint of slightly less camaraderie, and the one reason I can think of is that John Lever is not playing.

We miss JK badly, there can be no doubt about that. He is a very talented and essentially international bowler – a great performer all round the world. He is unlucky not to get in the side, for he is more than an on-field contributor. Off the pitch, in dressing rooms and hotels, he is a character, a cheerful and amusing guy who lifts morale by his sheer presence. I hope he will be back soon.

Thursday, 1 June. Sleep is elusive, and trying to sleep just irritating, so I'm up early. The guts are turning over quite violently, but I would be more worried if they weren't. The nerves have become part of my own ritual, and if they don't make themselves known, something must be wrong.

I'm not good company on mornings like this and I prefer being alone with my thoughts and my shakes. Those who don't know me would probably never suspect that I suffer from nerves like this. It's at its worst on the first day of a Test, and particularly the first Test. Today, perhaps, it is still more acute because for me it is a home Test. There are more people to let down when you play at home.

Outside, it is bright and sunny. But it rained overnight, and there is still the hint of a storm in the air. That could prove interesting later.

After just a few minutes of pacing I turn for comfort to my stereo, and the music of Bob Dylan. He can be soothing as well as stimulating; just as Scagg [Brearley] hums a Rasoumovsky cello passage to himself when batting, I can sing Dylan in my mind to divert my brain from what is to come. I've been known to imitate him rather more demonstratively, too!

It's a relief to get out on the pitch. Almost ninety minutes remain before the start, but the seats are beginning to fill. The sun by now is blazing – it's getting hotter by the minute.

I bowled a few balls at Bob 'Chat' Taylor just to get myself loose, then went through my exercise routine with Bernard Thomas. One of the stretches involves me putting my legs on Bernie's shoulders – one at a time. It's not quite as difficult as it sounds, because Bernie is about a foot shorter than me, but it made such an odd sight that the cameramen latched on to it straight away.

The captains tossed early, fifty minutes before the start. Wasim Bari won it and made the natural choice to bat first, so I had three-quarters of an hour to build myself up to bowling. Instead of improving, the nerves got steadily worse, only easing as I burst out from behind the captain and sprinted onto the ground at 11.25. That part has become habit since the time of Tony Greig as captain; at one time there were about six of us in the side who would sprint past the captain, fanning out into a pattern. It might upset the theorists, but it does release some of the tension.

I feel better as soon as the first over is past. The tension eases quite noticeably. Chris Old bowls from the Pavilion End, as tidily and competently as ever, but from the other end I find it hard to collect my rhythm. I know things are not quite right.

Before lunch, we picked up two fairly fortunate wickets, and during the break it was decided that I should switch ends for another burst. The change worked marvellously. Suddenly, the punch and the tempo was back in my bowling, and the pace naturally followed. Three good bouncers began to sort out the Pakistan weakness. Mohsin Khan was taken aback by the first and dismissed by the second; the third accounted for Haroon [Rasheed]. Those who say bouncers are not part of the game should have been here today – the crowd loved it, too.

Friday, 2 June. Some people are born to be Test cricketers; on today's evidence, David Gower is one of the lucky few. His first scoring shot was an arrogant hook for four; he had one lucky escape and went on to play like a young master, an innings [58] full of beautiful shots. A lot of people are going to travel a long way to watch this fellow bat in years to come.

I'm edgy and fidgety in the dressing room. Whereas some of the lads can turn off completely – Phil Edmonds has a sleep, several others play cards – I'm a permanent wanderer. I can't even sit and watch the game for long. I'm probably the worst spectator in the world. I don't want to bowl again too soon, because I need time to recover energy, so I'm desperately hoping that the batsmen do well.

Saturday, 3 June. Rad [Clive Radley] battled on to a typical hundred [106], and by being the first England centurion of the series he won a hundred bottles of champagne. For the crowd, however, the best entertainment came from Ian Botham, now nicknamed 'the Master Butcher' by Phil Edmonds and myself as a tribute to his batting style.

The Butcher carved the attack into tiny pieces and ate them for breakfast in a century [100] as devastating as any I've seen in recent times. It can't rank with the best, because the bowling was by then so demoralised, but to have a fellow like this coming in at number seven is the ideal bonus for any captain.

Monday, 5 June. Controversy has always tended to follow the fast bowlers around. Today it was my turn, and I didn't enjoy the experience.

The story in its crudest form is that I hit Pakistan's night-watchman, Iqbal Qasim, in the face with a bouncer and made quite a mess of him. The press appear to be turning it into a full-blown scandal, suggesting in some cases that I deliberately set out to hit the fellow, and in others that Scagg [Mike Brearley] should apologise on my behalf. The Pakistanis are furious and are threatening to complain to Lord's about it.

Personally, I think it's all been exaggerated nonsensically – and that does not mean that I'm callous enough to have no feelings for the batsman who got hurt. There are bowlers around who have caused a considerable stir by stating publicly that they occasionally bowl with intent to injure. I would never like that to be said of me, because I get no pleasure at all from the sight of anyone being hit in the face, particularly when I am the bowler.

The after-match champagne tasted a bit flat; I was tired and hungry, and the news that several of the national newspaper 'hatchet-men' wanted to see me for a quote on Qasim did little to improve my mood. I said nothing to them, and simply couldn't understand the fuss. It upset me, nevertheless.

From one disturbance to another . . . two drunken supporters in the social club were causing a menace, so I bundled them into the car and took them home. The good deed done, I retired to the White Swan with a few friends, anxious to get away from accusing eyes and just as anxious to get some sleep.

Monday, 12 June. I have never bowled better in my life. That was the opinion of Mike Brearley and myself after I had taken five for 38 to bowl Middlesex out a second time and set us up for a precious victory [in a three-day County Championship match at Edgbaston].

There is a fine borderline between success and failure for fast bowlers; days when the harder you try, the worse you bowl, and others when everything functions so smoothly that the job seems easy. This was one of the latter occasions. I bowled very fast indeed to a seven-two field (seven fielders on the off side and only two on the leg), and seemed able to dictate my line and length far better than ever before. Naturally, I was delighted, even elated, especially as our openers put on 70 without being parted before the close. I celebrated in style with orange juice and soda water at the White Swan.

Thursday, 15 June. No sooner had I completed my loosening routine at the Nursery End of the ground than rain began to fall. It did not relent for the rest of the day. The ground was full, the perennial first-day feeling at a Lord's Test was growing – and all anyone could do was shelter from the rain. I felt very sorry for all those who had paid for tickets, as there is no such thing as a refund in this game.

The Long Room and the bars in the pavilion are well populated, but I slipped down the side stairs and ran the gauntlet of schoolboys waiting at the door as I headed for the guests' enclosure for a chat and a drink (soft) with Tannoy.

Over lunch, Mike Brearley spoke to me about bouncers. The captains had consulted, he explained, and drawn up a list of five non-recognised batsmen who should at no time receive a bouncer. The list is Hendrick and myself of England, and Liaqat Ali, Sikander Bakht and Iqbal Qasim of Pakistan. I repeated to Mike that I completely disagreed with this system and still felt that everybody should get bouncers, although obviously some discretion must be shown against those less capable. But as all this had come about after the Pakistanis' anger over Qasim's injury at Edgbaston, I suppose it must be accepted.

Mike also said that he thought I should show more sympathy to anyone that I might hit with a short ball. I know he took a lot of stick over the fact that I walked away after hitting Qasim in the face, and he was concerned that I gave the impression of being callously uncaring for my victim. I do care, and Mike accepts that. But I can also see the public's point. My reason for not getting involved when I have injured someone is that showing too much sympathy will detract from my concentration. I need to feel right to bowl at my best, and if I stand tending to a bloodied batsman I am not likely to have much fire left in my belly.

After lunch my priority was to acquire some tickets for the Bob Dylan concert at Earls Court tonight. Anyone who knows me at all realises that I have a passion for the music of Dylan, and his long-awaited return to this country was something I did not intend to miss.

Before that, though, we all had another appointment to keep ... with the Queen. We were introduced to the Queen and Prince Philip in the Long Room at five o'clock – it was to have been on the pitch, but the rain was still falling – and I was one of the privileged few invited on into the 'inner sanctum' afterwards for a drink and a chat. I didn't get much of a word with the Queen, but Prince Philip chatted happily about racing, which he follows slightly less fervently than his wife, and said that he was glad that the cricket at Lord's did not clash with Royal Ascot, as he liked to watch both.

From the tea party with the Queen to a concert with Bob Dylan might seem from the sublime to the ridiculous, but I managed to enjoy both enormously, even though the acoustics at Earls Court were poor – a pity, because the man and his band were brilliant.

Monday, 19 June. The other subject that the press are, quite naturally, finding it difficult to ignore is that of the captaincy. In terms of results gained, there should be no argument that Mike [Brearley] must be the right man; he still hasn't lost a Test as captain. But his complete loss of form with the bat has brought the vultures crowding round, some of them calling for Boycott.

I know my feelings on the matter, and I believe most of the players feel the same. However much we respect Geoff for his batting and his dedication, we would rather be led by Mike Brearley. Perhaps he took some of the pressure off his head today by leading us to yet another win; although, to be honest, most of us were able to sit back and watch 'Sobers' Botham win it for us.

I had a burst from the Pavilion End, which is unusual for me, and rapidly gained in confidence about the cramp-inflicted leg. Mohsin Khan fell to me early on, and the rest surrendered to Botham's magnificent spell. The ball swung more for him than I have ever seen at Lord's – and it did so without any assistance whatever from cloud cover.

It was all over just before lunch, and it had all happened so swiftly that I don't think it sank into anyone's head that we had won the series. Any celebrations were fairly minor, and I found myself in the odd position of not knowing what to do with the next thirty-six hours.

I solved that problem by heading for Earls Court and another evening with Dylan, this time without a ticket. My intention had been to spend some of the win money on lining a tout's pocket, but when I discovered they were asking £40 for a £5 ticket, I rapidly withdrew.

Just as I was despairing of getting in at all, one of the security guards recognised me and I found myself being smuggled through a side door into a place twenty feet from the stage. There are not many occasions when I enjoy being recognised in public, but this was one on which I had no complaints.

Thursday, 22 June. Woke soon after seven to the sound of the traffic on the wet streets outside my hotel window. There had been more rain during the night and a prompt resumption was out of the question. Rather than return to the boredom of the ground, I spent the morning shopping in Derby, and visited about fifteen shoe shops in search of a pair of size 11½ shoes!

The weather improved enough to allow a restart soon after lunch, and we never seriously threatened to challenge Derby's final total of 203 [in the Benson & Hedges Cup semi-final]. The ball went through the top of the wicket, which is a disgrace in a one-day game, and I was altogether unimpressed with everything about this match. It has also left us with an undoubted problem in lifting the players now that the carrot of a Lord's cup final has been snatched away.

Having bought the new Dylan album [*Street Legal*] on my morning's shopping expedition, I cheered myself up before bed with a first spin.

Friday, 23 June. To start the day in the right mood, I played the Dylan album five times in succession. After that I felt fit to face the world.

Friday, 7 July. To many people who watch the game, I suppose I have always been 'that one with the long, curly hair'. My locks have become something of a trademark over the years, especially as I grew them fashionably longer at about the time that I overcame my fitness problems of 1976 and got back into the England side.

The fact is, I like my hair long, and although it has excited one or two bitter criticisms from traditionalists, it has certainly never adversely affected my career. Today, though, I decided that enough was enough, and duly paid my money for the annual operation. Quite a severe cut, actually, and there was no way I would escape the mickey-taking in the dressing room when I reported to the ground at midday.

There are a number of very humorous individuals in the Warwickshire dressing room, but in attempting to describe them I've found that cricket humour does not translate well from the spoken to the written word. Much of it can be vulgar, though not obscenely so, and almost all of the laughs are gained at the expense of another member of the team. It is sharp, instant wit that loses everything in repetition. Today I was a heaven-sent target for the jokers, with most of my curls left on the barber's floor.

Saturday, 29 July. 'The train now standing at platform 5 …' brought me into the woken world at quite an early hour, cursing the noises of this hotel [the Charing Cross]. Despite the supposed soundproofing, there isn't much goes on in the station below that we don't know about. The day dawned humid, and our fifty minutes batting at the start of play [in the first Test v New Zealand at The Oval] was a very sticky experience. I managed to hang around for a while with Goat [Phil Edmonds] and added some useful runs.

I enjoy batting, especially with the knowledge that nobody is allowed to drop the ball short at me. Like Pakistan's Sarfraz, I have a very long reach, and although I have never made a great deal of runs, my Test record proves that bowlers often find it difficult to get me out. Even for a number eleven, I have a very high proportion of not-outs.

Monday, 31 July. The rain began just before the scheduled start, and soon after lunch, puddles, turning quickly into lakes, extended across the outfield from end to end.

Without any cricket to restrict my appetite, I would normally have got stuck into a sizeable lunch on a day like this. But it didn't quite work out like that. If only the catering at The Oval was as good as that at Lord's, where the friendly Nancy does such a marvellous job, I might really have enjoyed it.

A typical lunch menu for a Test day at Lord's would be: soup; roast lamb, roast potatoes and two vegetables; hot fruit pie and custard; variety of cheeses and biscuits; tea or coffee. For a drink with the main course, I usually have a glass of orange or lemon squash, certainly nothing stronger, and if possible nothing too fizzy, as I find that can upset me when I start bowling again.

Most of the England lads enjoy their food and eat heartily whenever possible. I say that because, for the bowlers at least, there are clearly occasions when to wade through a four-course lunch would be asking to be sick on the field. If we are bowling at the time, most of the seamers will stay in the dressing room and order something light and easy to digest. I normally choose cheese in a roll or sandwich – although at Edgbaston I have a slice of ham or tongue – and follow up with some plain ice cream.

Today we were at least able to dally at the table, compared with the normal rush to bolt our food in half an hour and be back in the dressing room in time to follow the umpires out. But with the rain lashing down outside, we were a fairly deflated bunch of players.

Wednesday, 6 September. A touch of déjà vu . . . a rainy morning and no play before lunch – just like April and May all over again.

Took the opportunity to breakfast in style at The Towrope and returned for the afternoon start against Derbyshire to find myself bowling with an Australian 'Kookaburra' ball. Each county is having to use these balls a certain number of times this season as an experiment. Personally, I think it's a failure, but then I might be influenced by the fact that I can't get a wicket with them. They all seem to be soft, losing their bounce after a few overs and their shape soon afterwards. Spectators often barrack when a fast bowler complains about a ball to the umpires, but they can't realise just how important it is to have one that stays hard and keeps its shape.

The Captain's Diary – 1982–83

Tuesday, 26 October 1982. Packing can be one of the hazards of any tour. One hardly gets settled in a room, clothes spread about in splendid confusion, when it is time to move on. Some have the process under control better than others. Derek Randall makes a habit of packing away his uniform travelling shirt and having to wear a brown or a green one under his blazer. I have also known him to be hailed by a fretting porter just as we are boarding a coach, because he has left a bagful of laundry in his room – so that eventually he does the journey with cricket flannels over one arm, sports-shirts over the other and that hysterical laugh of his sending everyone into fits of amusement.

Thursday, 28 October. I have trouble with my boots each time I come to Australia. This year, so far, nothing too serious, but I was in some pain at Brisbane [v Queensland] because my studs were not sharp enough. So today helpful organisers of the Newcastle match [v Northern New South Wales] found some-one to sharpen and shorten the studs. Hopefully I am now better equipped to get by on the rock-hard surfaces which never fail to take me by surprise.

Wednesday, 3 November. For the first time in almost a week [because of illness] I bowled in the nets today. Only gently, and only for an hour, but progress is certainly being made. I also had a bat against the machine, and the bloody thing got me out three times in six balls, all pitching on the same spot. I always said nets did my batting no good.

Thursday, 11 November. I announced the side to the squad [for the first Test in Perth] and showed the appropriate, heartfelt sympathy for those left out. Everyone builds towards this moment, early in a tour, and to have it confirmed suddenly that you will not be part of the Test team can't be easy.

The tension is getting to me now. After joining the lads in a store appearance for [tour sponsors] JVC, I went back to my room and played the hypnosis tape, followed by a cassette of lute music by Julian Bream. I was much more relaxed by the time I had to get ready for our 6.30 p.m. team meeting.

Saturday, 13 November. Quite early in the day [the second day of the first Test], sitting on my dressing-room chair and waiting to bat, I commented to no one in particular that the group of youths who had begun chanting in the style of soccer fans, on the bank away to the left of us, were bound to make trouble of some sort after a few more cans of beer. I am not proud that the prediction came true, because the trouble they did cause was about as sickening as anything I have seen on a Test ground, and totally unexpected in its repercussions.

We were eight wickets down when it happened, the old boys Taylor and Willis together at the crease again. About twenty of the chanting mob came over the fence and began running towards the middle. More lumbering, actually, because they had plainly mixed heavy measures of sun and grog and discovered the powerful chemistry. It was not something I like seeing on any ground, but we have all grown used to it over the years and like most unwanted folk, if you ignore them long enough they usually go away.

I find it hard to be rational in relating this incident because it certainly disturbed everyone. But I can't escape from the conclusion that Alderman was at fault on two counts. First, he pushed one of the invaders quite violently away from him, although he had not seemed to be posing him any kind of threat. Then another, trotting away from the pitch back towards the boundary, raised his arm as he passed Alderman, whether with the intent of hitting him or just grabbing his sun-hat I am not sure. What is certain is that he connected with a cuff to the back of Terry's head, and suddenly the frustrations of five sessions in the field for only one wicket visibly boiled over. Terry Alderman forsook the sensible course of turning the other cheek and leaving the mob to the police, and gave chase in most determined style.

It was hardly a contest. The youth, doubtless carrying an overweight of Swan Lager, survived for about 20 yards. Then Alderman, who plays Australian Rules football in his spare time, brought him down with as good a tackle as I have seen in a long time. I found it all hard to believe, standing there leaning on my bat and watching what was becoming a dangerous style of farce.

As soon as Alderman hit the ground he rolled over in apparent agony, while Allan Border and Dennis Lillee, who had both sprinted to the assistance of their team-mate, pinned the outnumbered youth in a commanding arm-lock until the police regrouped to take charge.

Alderman's condition was now causing rising panic, and it was not long before a stretcher was summoned. It transpired that he had dislocated his shoulder on landing from his flying tackle. Nerves were also damaged and the initial prognosis is that he will not be fit for a month. What a way to go! There are quite enough opportunities for a fast bowler to injure himself, but this was one I had never considered and don't intend to try.

Saturday, 20 November. We are showing a sad shortage of discipline and ambition in state games, and it happened again today. It mystifies me, but the current trend certainly seems to scorn full effort until the big occasion comes along. What some of our guys do not seem to appreciate is that they cannot expect to turn on their best like a tap when the occasion demands it. The other matches may not be as important in terms of results, but they are there to be used for form and confidence. One or two of our batsmen find concentration elusive because they are so confident of playing the next Test anyway. It is a situation which concerns me even more now, following another unimpressive batting display today.

In the team-room tonight, Ian Botham – who had been absent from the ground with his wife for much of the day – asked Derek Randall how he was out. 'I played one of your shots,' said 'Arkle', and the room collapsed in mirth.

Saturday, 27 November. Hookes looked dangerous for a while and Ian helped him on his way with a dreadful over of short stuff. He still believes this is the way to dismiss Hookes, who took 15 off the over. Fortunately, he was given out caught behind in the next over, bowled by Geoff Miller, and I took the opportunity to tell Ian he was bowling rubbish. It worked as I had anticipated, and he angrily retorted, 'Why don't you bloody bowl if you can do better?' But at the end of that over he

This time it's Viv Richards who comes out on top in his long-running duel with Bob, driving him for four on his way to 189 not out in an ODI at Old Trafford in 1984.

'Why aren't all these people at work?' The Queen is surprised by the size of the crowd at Lord's for Bob's first Test as captain, against India in 1982.

Bob admires a poster of the man who caused havoc with his O levels, his lifelong musical hero Bob Dylan.

Cricket fan Elton John jokes for the camera with David Gower before joining Bob and team-mates for lunch in Sydney in 1983.

His Greatest challenge? In 1984, Bob tries to teach Muhammad Ali the secret of a batting technique that brought him a then record 55 not-outs in Tests – as perplexed Warwickshire team-mate Dennis Amiss looks on.

Enjoying a bottle of Rioja with his great mate Paul Allott on holiday in West Sussex in 2013.

Tennis was another sport Bob loved. Here he is moved by the unexpected applause after being presented to the crowd at Wimbledon in 2012.

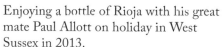

Hamming it up with David Lloyd in a live performance of 'Bumble and Grumble', shown on Sky in a lunch interval during England's Test against India at Southampton in 2018.

Discussing boyhood heroes and the 'Spirit of Cricket' with Sir John Major in an interview for *The Guardian* about the former prime minister's book *More Than a Game* in 2007.

Despite playing without the protection of central contacts, Bob and Ian Botham are still among England's top four leading Test wicket-takers. Here they mark their achievement with the current top two, James Anderson and Stuart Broad, at Headingley in 2017.

Behind the scenes with Sky colleagues Michael Atherton, David Gower and Ian Botham at Edgbaston in 2017. Making his friends laugh was something that came naturally.

Joining James Anderson, Joe Root and David Gower at Edgbaston in 2018 as a member of England's all-time greatest XI, as voted by fans – part of the celebrations for the 1000th England Test match.

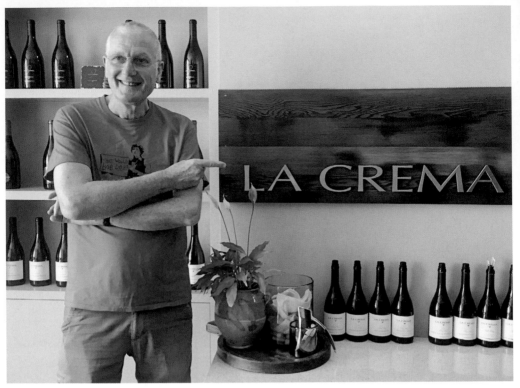

'A day without wine is a day without sunshine.' All set to taste Russian River Valley Chardonnay at one of his favourite wineries – La Crema in Healdsburg, California – in 2016.

With winemaker Geoff Merrill, one of his many close friends in Adelaide, at Geoff's daughter's wedding in 2017.

'Cricketer, Wine Lover, Mate.' Bob's resting place at Geoff Merrill's winery in McLaren Vale, commemorated in February 2020.

'The Adelaide contingent' – many of Bob's Australian friends gather to toast his memory on the day of his funeral in London in December 2019.

Lauren's cubist tribute to Bob.

Bob and Lauren on their wedding day in Richmond in 2014.

Smiles all round – with Katie, Lauren and good friend Louise Moran at Lord's in 2015.

grabbed the ball, marched back to his mark and ran in full of righteous indignation. This method of psychology often does have the desired effect with Ian, and he was certainly very effective for the next few overs.

Sadly, it did not last . . .

Monday, 29 November. Before the customary rest-day morning conference, I needed further surgery on my toenails as they were extremely tender overnight. This is becoming something of a saga, and a painful one at that, but after six trips to Australia I am well used to suffering problems with my feet.

Went to the cinema tonight to see *Monty Python Live at the Hollywood Bowl.* I had seen all the sketches before on their TV shows, but still laughed hysterically. They amuse me even more as I have met John Cleese and Eric Idle at cricket matches – they are both great fans – and Terry Jones was school captain of RGS Guildford when I was in the first year.

Thursday, 2 December. Bystanders and fellow passengers watching us arrive at Brisbane airport this morning probably took pity on Norman Cowans. On his feet he wore only his cricket socks, and the conclusion that he was suffering the effects of a hard Test was natural . . . but very wrong. In fact he had no shoes to wear, thanks to his pal Derek Randall.

'Arkle' and 'Flash' have formed an unlikely pairing on this trip; they roomed together during the second Test and Derek's fidgeting humour was probably good for Norman, who was extremely tense about his debut and suffering some virtually sleepless nights. So when, on the last night of the Test, Derek realised he had packed all his shoes in his case (not for the first time) he asked to borrow Norman's for an evening out.

All would have been well, but late that night 'Arkle' unpacked his own shoes and packed Norman's instead. The cases disappeared at 7.15 a.m. on the baggage van, and although Derek now had shoes to wear, Norman did not! Hence the rather odd sight of an England fast bowler wandering through an airport departure lounge in cricket socks.

We arrived in Melbourne at lunchtime and gathered at the ground in mid-afternoon. There seemed little to be gained from a strenuous training session the day after a Test, so I got Ian to organise a fielding game and the lads loosened up for forty-five minutes.

My troublesome toes prevented me joining in. Instead, I had half of one of the nails removed, and the rest taped up to hold it together – a messy business, but progress is apparently being made, although there is no way I could possibly be fit to play in Saturday's match against Victoria, even if it was desirable.

Friday, 3 December. I heard today that the London *Sun* has carried a story claiming that there has been a serious rift between Ian Botham and myself. It made me extremely angry, because this is just the sort of malicious, unsubstantiated rumour-spreading that I feared. For the record, the whole idea is nonsense. Ian and I have a friendship which is unlikely to be affected by either of us falling out of form, and although we have had some serious chats during the trip about the way things are going, we are on extremely good terms, as ever.

I again did not bowl in the nets today, but went instead to see Melbourne's famous bootmaker, Hope Sweeney. He is in his sixties now, but his skills have not diminished, and I wanted him to fix up Messrs Hemmings, Pringle and Cowans, each of whom have been having footwear problems. Hope's boots are hand-sewn in kangaroo skin and feel as comfortable as slippers. For someone like 'Flash', who misguidedly came on this tour with one worn-out pair of boots, he could be a life-saver, but he has also measured me for a pair which might alleviate some of the pressure on my toes.

Spent a relaxing couple of hours this afternoon at the Australian Open tennis tournament. I had met Sue Barker at the Hilton and she kindly arranged tickets for myself and one or two others – tickets, I discovered, which involved a shaded courtside seat and a constant supply of wine and edibles.

Rather surprised that when Martina Navratilova finished her match, a clinical win in the quarter-finals, she looked across at us and imitated a cricketer. I would never have suspected such interest from a Czech-cum-American.

Thursday, 9 December. I had a preliminary look at the [Adelaide] pitch after practice. It was surprisingly wet, and unless the sun broke through the thick cloud cover I could not imagine it drying out properly before the start. If it remained damp, then our best chance clearly lay in bowling first, and I expressed this view at the press conference which followed our selection meeting [for the third Test].

As it transpired, the sun did break through this afternoon, and at four o'clock I returned to the ground to make further inspection. It was already appreciably drier, and I considered another few hours of sun would make it a very good batting surface. My inclination to put them in began to seem wrong.

Tomorrow morning's final inspection will be decisive, but I see no reason to relinquish first innings on a good strip – if I can call correctly this time!

Friday, 10 December 1982. I stand to be branded as another foolish gambler who blundered away a Test match by putting Australia in. The truth of it is I was strongly in favour of batting first, but found myself outvoted in the committee and within the team.

I have seldom felt so angry about a day's cricket, but most of the anger is directed at myself for not being strong enough to insist. Now I am faced with trying publicly to justify a decision I thought absurd.

The pitch had dried completely by this morning. When we gathered on the ground at 9.45 a.m. I could not move the surface at all with my thumb. Nothing suggested it would be other than a perfect batting strip and, although silently regretting my forthright remarks about damp wickets and insertions at yesterday's press conference, I decided we should certainly bat first if I won the toss.

It would be an understatement to say I was surprised when I discovered I was in the minority, but every player I consulted came up with the same view – we should bowl. In my heart I knew we would be doing it for all the wrong reasons, negative reasons, because the batsmen plainly did not fancy batting first against the pace bowlers. That disappointed me. I had hoped there might be more appetite for the battle. I wondered whether to use my authority and overrule everyone, but what frame of mind would the batsmen have gone out in then?

I was pretty upset in the dressing room and it probably showed. My usual pre-match talk, aimed at motivating the lads, may not have sounded very convincing, because I could certainly not convince myself that what we were doing was right. The least I could do, though, was to try to make the best of it and I ran in well for my first spell, avoided bowling any no-balls and felt pretty good. But, as I had feared, the pitch gave us no help at all, and it was soon patently obvious that we faced a long and tiring struggle for wickets.

Ian took a wicket either side of lunch, both the openers going for 44, but [Greg] Chappell and [Kim] Hughes were ominously assured and steady, Chappell hitting anything loose for four. The lads bowled well, definitely better than at Brisbane, but there was no movement and little bounce to trouble the batters. All day long, I can recall only three balls beating the bat.

Chappell scored 115, which turns out to be his first Test century in Adelaide, his home town, but we had a break just before the close when he cut me to gully and David Gower took a great catch, tumbling backwards.

They ended the day at 265 for three and, although we can console ourselves that it could have been considerably worse, it is hardly reason to celebrate. I really can't see us getting them out for under 500 if Hughes stays in long tomorrow, and I am afraid I view our decision as a cockeyed way of going about winning a Test.

I left the ground almost straight away, feeling angry and depressed. Back at the hotel, things still seemed against me when I tried to have a soak – my en-suite bath is about five feet long and wholly inadequate for one of my size.

Gradually, after some silent minutes of meditation followed by an hour of chatting in the team room, I calmed down. But I still cannot relax completely. I feel pretty foolish, and it will only get worse if this game goes badly wrong.

Thursday, 16 December. Played tennis this afternoon, and at six o'clock we all gathered for a meeting run by the 'Mafia'. Each of the twenty players and officials drew a number and had to do the corresponding forfeit from a list drawn up by Messrs [Geoff] Miller, [Robin] Jackman and Botham. The forfeits ranged from acting the part of a drunken man trying to mount a horse to reciting the first five books of the Old Testament. Mine consisted of eating six Ritz crackers within a minute and whistling the first four bars of 'Colonel Bogey'. The crackers I managed easily, but whistling has never been among my strong points.

We met Danny la Rue at a hotel cocktail party later this evening and, after a pleasant seafood meal, I wandered briefly into the gaming rooms and noticed, without surprise, that many of the lads were partaking of the delights of the table.

Saturday, 25 December. Christmas Days on tour follow a familiar pattern and, while they can certainly be enjoyed at the time, I am invariably glad when they are over. It is impossible to enter fully into the spirit of things, especially as a Test match is very often scheduled to begin on Boxing Day.

I had slept well again, courtesy of the tablets, and on waking at 8.30 a.m. the priority was a hasty attempt to compose and rehearse my sketch for the party. Last-minute panic as usual! After the customary drinks with the press at 10 a.m., the players were all ushered away by Miller's Mafia to don costumes. A parade for the cameras followed, and then down to the serious business of lunch and entertainment.

The food was not very exciting and took a dreadfully long time to come as courses were punctuated by sketches and cabarets from each of the lads in turn. The new tourists, for instance, performed a skit of a Chas and Dave song (words altered, of course) and Doug Insole had taken enormous trouble to write a script for his management team. 'Lubo' Gower and I did a recital in rhyme, we all sang 'Partridge in a Pear Tree' to more topical lyrics and a band of carol singers appeared, to serenade us.

Wednesday, 5 January. There has never been a moment on this tour when I have wished I wasn't captain. I can say that despite the depression of Adelaide, in particular, and the constant knowledge – not always welcome – that every move I make, every word I say, is being monitored. It adds more pressure and I have found it mentally as well as physically demanding. But I have never lost confidence in myself, never felt I am simply no good at the job and should give it away. Perhaps I take it all too personally, and certainly I have sometimes sat back and wondered whether anyone else sees the whole thing in as serious a light as I do. But at my age, I am not going to change.

Friday, 7 January. I managed to be pretty philosophical at tonight's press conference [after the drawn fifth Test at Sydney], I think, and answered as honestly as I could. It appears every beaten captain is always going to be asked about his future, but I could only reply that I would go on as captain, and go on playing, as long as I was wanted.

I had a glass of flat champagne, ironically suitable for the occasion, discharged interview after interview and finally returned to the hotel around eight. A night of jazz in some of my favourite Sydney haunts. Thoughts of endless one-day matches to come. Wonder if we can get our game together. Wonder if I will now sleep better. Wonder why losing never comes any easier, even at thirty-three.

Sunday, 16 January. We had somehow stuttered to 182 [in an ODI v Australia], but Brisbane is not the biggest of grounds and that total would have been difficult to defend even bowling at our best. When [John] Dyson was joined by [Greg] Chappell the scoring rate accelerated, and the job was finished in quite brutal style by [Allan] Border and [David] Hookes. It was obvious that we were beaten some time before the end, but I wish Hookes had not taken quite such a hungry liking to my final over.

It was another disappointing performance and it leaves us in an unenviable position at the foot of the competition table [in a tournament also featuring New Zealand], but even in defeat there was a moment of high humour which sustained us through the evening. While we were batting there was a commotion in one section of the packed crowd and suddenly a pig emerged onto the outfield – a particularly fat little pig. Attached to its tail was an Australian flag; painted on one of his sides was 'Botham' and on the other side 'Eddie' [Hemmings]. Everyone in our dressing room collapsed laughing while the pig was captured and escorted from the ground (I can only guess someone smuggled him in in a freezer box) and even the subjects of the joke took it all in good part. Much later tonight, all of us were gloomy about the day's result, but we could still smile at the thought of that pig grazing at midwicket.

Monday, 17 January. Today was Monday so it had to be Sydney ... Lunch in Kings Cross at one of their endless restaurants, then a trip to the Opera House to book tickets for the performance of *Tosca* on the 25th. My interest in opera is young, and stems from going to a performance in Vienna last year which, much to my initial surprise, I enjoyed tremendously. I am trying to broaden my knowledge of the subject, but it is hard with so many cricket commitments ...

My more regular entertainment in Sydney is jazz, and tonight – after the team meeting and a cocktail party given by the Lord's Taverners – a group of us went to the popular Basement Club, where the star of the evening was Georgie Fame, playing with an Australian backing band. Some members of the band were old friends, and I met the others with Georgie afterwards. A good night.

Friday, 4 February. We held a team meeting and I repeated, in slightly less heated fashion, everything I had said in anger at the end of last Saturday's match. Now is not the time for a repeat of that type of complacency. If we win tomorrow, we are in the finals. If we lose, we have to rely on New Zealand beating Australia the following day. I would rather we kept our fate in our own hands.

Saturday, 5 February. My head has not entirely been turned by opera and the classics, and I spent half an hour this morning listening to Bob Dylan in order to put myself in the right mood for our crucial match. I had eaten a substantial breakfast as I had been on a relative famine since Wednesday, and although the weather outside the Sheraton Hotel was dry and sunny, showers were forecast for later in the day. As a weather forecast, it was a masterpiece of understatement.

In the middle of the 18th over, with Gower and Randall together and the total 45, light drizzle turned into persistent rain, which quickly became one of the most torrential downpours I have seen in this part of Australia. It had the intensity of a tropical storm but the stamina of November rain in Manchester. The ground became dotted with ever-widening lakes and with every minute that the rain continued so our chances diminished.

It rained for almost an hour and a half, the 16,000 spectators huddling under any cover they could find and, if they could find none, abandoning the affair and heading home. Surely, with the ground in such a waterlogged state, abandoning the game was only a matter of time.

Apparently not. Channel Nine summoned their newshounds' helicopter, which proceeded to hover over the water in absurd style, succeeding only in sloshing it around. A fire engine turned up and some of the water was pumped off the outfield. The ground staff bustled around with squeegees, which was rather like wielding a cosh against an armoured tank. I sat still and waited for the inevitable decision.

At ten past three it came. The umpires looked into the dressing room and announced that play would restart in half an hour.

To say I was surprised does not meet the case. I was flabbergasted. The reaction next door was much the same, and Geoff Howarth and Glenn Turner immediately went out on to the ground, returning to say the decision was 'a joke' as water was still lapping around their feet.

I did not blame the umpires. They were under pressure from all sides to satisfy the audience – both on the ground and in front of their television sets at home – and if there was any conceivable way they could restart play, they had to do so. But the ground was never fit, and the rest of the match became a fiasco.

The conditions ruined our chances and ruined an excellent pair of boots, as I came off with both soles peeling off due to waterlogging. It was an entirely unsatisfactory day, but at least we had not brought this one upon ourselves. I could afford to be a little more philosophical than I was a week ago as I faced the cameras and the microphones and the notebooks.

The Captain's Diary – 1983–84

Saturday, 31 December 1983. Light rain was falling on Fiji as we disembarked at 4.10 a.m., which was a surprise to us. It was, however, extremely sticky even at that ungodly hour, which was no surprise at all.

A welcoming reception had been set for mid-afternoon, at which [manager] A.C. [Smith] and I had to toast our hosts with the traditional local drink, a non-alcoholic concoction known as 'cava', made by dissolving the powdered root of a pepper plant in cold water and then straining it through the bark of the vau tree. It has a texture like muddy water and has to be swallowed in a single gulp, but tasted surprisingly good. The proceedings included a formal ceremony in which we were presented with a whale tooth, but as the afternoon wore on the clouds dispersed and there were rapid signs of overheating on the brows of many of the lads.

At dinner tonight I was introduced to another of the local delights – the mosquitoes which attack in swarms. More pleasantly, the villagers put on a colourful routine of dancing and singing, which I managed to enjoy before surrendering to drooping eyelids and retiring to bed shortly before nine.

I woke, startled, and lay listening to drumbeats and fireworks. I struggled out of bed to the window in time to see people jumping into the swimming pool. Glancing at my clock, I saw that it was precisely midnight, and as sleep left my brain I realised what the fuss was about. I had quite forgotten it was New Year's Eve.

Sunday, 1 January 1984. There was a relaxed atmosphere this afternoon. Some of the boys had flown to a neighbouring island for lunch, while others dispersed around the pleasant beaches. Being a confirmed anti-sun man, I stayed in the hotel. At dinner this evening the main topic of conversation was the voracity of those local mosquitoes. They seem to have taken a particular fancy to the ankles of A.C. and Nick Cook and the backside of Allan Lamb, of which I entirely fail to see the attraction.

Sunday, 15 January. We were 370 runs at stumps [v Northern Districts at Hamilton] and as I lay in the bath listening to Bob Dylan on my tape machine I could reflect on a happy position. There was also a hilarious evening to come – the first meeting called by our new social committee. Fines were imposed on almost everybody, in order to raise funds for our later parties, and this evening's business brought in 86 New Zealand dollars. Those who were fined for their misdemeanours included the entire management, for booking the lads into a hotel with no bar; Norman Gifford, for an excessively sunburned face; Bernard Thomas, for driving his borrowed car the wrong way round a central reservation in Auckland; and Chris Tavaré, for his custom of wearing pyjamas. Messrs [Vic] Marks, [Neil] Foster and [Graeme] Fowler have entered into the spirit of their position and done well. With so few gaffes being missed, however, I think they are now unpopular team-mates!

Tuesday, 17 January. I made it clear that the lads could enjoy themselves tonight and it was good to see that spirits were high in the team room. 'Arkle' was in one of his uninhibited, comic moods as we recalled the pig which was set loose on the Brisbane ground last winter, 'Botham' painted on one side and 'Eddie' (Hemmings) on the other. I was able to take the tale a stage further as I had subsequently met the guys responsible – a pair of vets, who put the pig in a freezer box with an apple in his mouth. Apparently the gateman, having insisted that the box be opened, prodded the animal dubiously and said it didn't look very well cooked!

Friday, 20 January. Today I became England's leading wicket-taker in Test history. For all my misgivings about the value of statistics, all my protestations that I am not a records man, I found that I was very conscious of counting down to the record as I took the three wickets necessary and, perhaps more surprising, I also found that I was very moved by the whole occasion. For a change, I really did savour the moment as it happened, relishing the genuinely enthusiastic congratulations of the other lads, appreciating the gesture of Richard Hadlee in coming to meet me and shake my hand as we left the field, and enjoying the taste and the meaning of the champagne which Alan Smith had poured in readiness. In some ways I would consider it the highlight of my career. A lot of work and a good deal of pain has gone into the taking of 308 wickets and it was especially good to share the moment with Ian Botham and Bob Taylor, two friends who have been very much part of the scenery while I have taken the majority of them.

Fred Trueman held the record for twenty years, but I doubt if whatever mark I set will stand for anything like another twenty. I.T. Botham is hot on the trail and no one will be more pleased than me if, having passed my total, he goes on to break Dennis Lillee's world record.

Saturday, 21 January. Gradually, from the brink of crisis [in the first Test v New Zealand], we achieved respect and then strength. By the close Ian [Botham] and Derek [Randall] had put on 178.

At five o'clock, Vic Marks, as acting twelfth man, had taken out the drinks. Ian was in the 80s and 'Skid' asked if I wanted to pass on any messages. 'Yes,' I replied. 'Tell him to concentrate, play straight and think how many players have scored thirteen Test hundreds.' A few minutes later I had my reply: 'He says you know he can't concentrate, he's never played straight in his life and he couldn't give a damn how many blokes have got thirteen hundreds.' It was a typically irrepressible Botham answer, but maybe some of the message got through. As 'Skid' remarked thoughtfully at the end of the day, he did play straighter and he did get his hundred.

I played Van Morrison in the bath and enjoyed it enormously. Every player came to the team room for a hilarious twenty minutes of in-jokes. Touring can seem a good life while things go well on the field.

Sunday, 22 January. [Lance] Cairns removed [Nick] Cook and [Neil] Foster was given the treatment by Hadlee – a series of short balls which he negotiated, then one well up which he edged to third slip.

I made my entry in a helmet borrowed from Mike Gatting, who had taken to his bed suffering from a chest infection. I was soon glad I had taken the precaution. For reasons best known to himself, Hadlee set about me with five bouncers in one seven-ball over. One of them crashed into my left temple and, but for the helmet, it could have been my lot. To my mind this was a pathetic piece of cricket by Hadlee. It is true that I dug one in at tail-ender Ewen Chatfield yesterday . . . but five in seven balls is taking vengeance a little far, especially as Hadlee had not run in at our early batsmen with anything like the same venom. I have said before he is a complicated mix as a cricketer; it now seems that may equally apply to his character. We contented ourselves with taking a silently dim view of the episode, which did in any case have its funny side. During the barrage I was attempting to employ the duck rather than the sway as an evasive tactic, bearing in mind the occasion in 1982 when, again clad in a helmet, I had done a good deal of swaying against Imran Khan and consequently ricked my neck and missed a Test. In ducking rather rapidly, however, I succeeded in putting a twelve-inch split in the backside of my trousers. Dear old 'Flash' Cowans came to the rescue with a surprisingly nimble needle and thread during the tea interval.

Thursday, 2 February. Our fractured, anxious build-up [to the second Test, at Christchurch] finally reached crisis point today and we had to resort to finding a replacement seam bowler. At the height of the negotiations, I learned that I am the father of a healthy daughter. For a time, everything else seemed suddenly unimportant, but this was such a frantic pre-Test day that I had regrettably few minutes to dwell on it.

It was A.C. who broke the news. I had just returned from a courtesy visit to the company supplying our cars here when the manager appeared at my door, demanding to know how long I had been back. When I said 'five seconds' he looked relieved and congratulated me on the arrival. Everything is evidently well with Juliet and the baby, although delivery was induced. I wanted to phone, of course, but A.C. told me that Juliet was under sedation and I would have to wait until tomorrow.

No sooner had the news sunk in than I had to drag my thoughts back to cricket for our evening tactical team meeting – but before we began, A.C. insisted that everyone should have a sip of champagne.

What with one thing and another, it was pushing 11 p.m. when I got to bed, later than my usual hour for the night prior to a Test.

Wednesday, 8 February. Today's post was interesting. I opened an air-mail package addressed to me and found some sour grapes in it . . . real ones. The sender announced himself as a war veteran who had spent much of his life fighting so that the likes of me could play cricket and wanted to know why we moaned in defeat [England had lost the second Test] – noble sentiments, but quite irrelevant. I also received a couple of poisonous telexes, including one saying that even Yorkshire, in their current disarray, could play better than us. I shall treat that with the disdain it deserves.

Saturday, 11 February. The bowling [in the third Test at Auckland] wore a tired, deflated look in the last session and New Zealand, on 354 for six, have virtually ensured that our chance of levelling the series is dead.

My words to A.C. in Wellington [during the first Test] came flooding back. 'If we don't nail them now,' I had said, 'we will really be struggling to win this series.' It looks as if I was right, but I can take no pleasure in that. Tonight, I feel pretty depressed, not to mention weary after the best part of two days' fielding.

I ate some smoked snapper and mussels which Hedley Howarth [brother of Geoff] had sent to the dressing room, then returned to lie in the bath and console myself with Bob Dylan's latest album [*Infidels*]. Confining myself to a glass of water in the team room, I then spent the evening with Hedley and his wife Louise. They are great hosts, not just for the food they cook and the drink they provide, but because they were sensitive enough not to mention cricket all night ... and I certainly didn't prompt them.

Sunday, 12 February. With the rest-day oasis tomorrow, I indulged in escapism tonight. The Crowe brothers had thrown a party for us at their house and I was delighted to find they had laid on not only copious supplies of food and drink but a lot of vintage Bob Dylan music. I parked myself next to the speaker and sang along, with accompaniment by G. Howarth.

Monday, 13 February. Having failed to eat between Dylan songs last night, I downed some egg and hash browns – my first cooked breakfast for some weeks – before joining about half the playing strength of the party on a trip to Corbans, a winery owned by the Test sponsors here, Rothmans. On the way we bought some wedding cards to dispatch to Elton John, who gets married in Sydney tomorrow. He came to support us in Australia last winter and we are due to run into him again during the one-day series later this month when his concert tour coincides with some of our matches.

Corbans had laid on the perfect rest-day relaxation. A marquee had been erected on their lawns, next to the vines, and I sat in the shade sampling an excellent choice of reds, whites and vintage port before devouring a portion of one of the three lambs they spit-roasted for us. We all ate well, none better than Mike Gatting, who has become known as 'Jabba' after a character in *Return of the Jedi* which eats everything it comes across!

Friday, 17 February. Bob [McArdle] had been good enough to take Ian [Botham], Norman Gifford and me to see one of the top training establishments in the trotting scene this afternoon. Not only that, he had also arranged for us to try our skills driving the 'sulkies'. To my untutored eyes, the horses in trotting races had always seemed pretty slow from the stands, but when I set off, Beefy in the opposition 'sulky', I honestly had no idea what my destiny might be. Beyond being fairly confident that the horses ought to know their way around the track, I had no idea whether I should be steering, whether the horses should slow down at bends or even how to make them stop. Despite all that, it was a very exciting experience, and when Beefy gave up his 'sulky' for Giff to have a try, I went round another couple of times with him.

While we were enjoying this unusual experience, Bob had been videoing the entire episode and tonight, after dinner, he showed us the evidence of our efforts in glorious Technicolor.

I had told the hotel where I could be contacted and a phone call came through from Elton John. Beefy and I both had a chat with him and it transpires that he is going to come and watch us play tomorrow and, by way of return, invite us to his concert on Sunday. I've no doubt most of the lads will snap his hand off.

Sunday, 19 February. As we have three clear days before the second of the limited-overs matches, we gave the lads a rest today. As usual, they each used the free time in their own way. Having lent Ian Botham my car so that he could go fishing, I busied myself at the hotel and made the arrangements for tonight's Elton John concert. In all, they are supplying us with twenty-three tickets, which is more than generous.

A fleet of cabs transported our party to the concert, where we were met by one of the promoters and taken to the VIP area backstage. Elton and his wife Renate were there to chat to us and I couldn't help but be struck by Elton's relaxed conversational mood with a performance only a matter of minutes away. I compared this approach to a big night with mine on the morning of a Test and decided that, in this respect at least, we must be complete opposites.

There were 21,000 in the audience, virtually all standing, and although my unusual height enabled me to see the stage without much difficulty, some of the other lads struggled – especially when blokes in front of us lifted their ladies on to their shoulders. It was, however, a memorable night; when Patti Moyston, Elton's press secretary, said we would be welcome at the next concert, which happens to coincide with our stop-over in Wellington, the response was enthusiastic. We had a long, cold wait for taxis but nobody seemed to mind, and even that inconvenience was cut short when the obliging promoter organised cars for us.

Wednesday, 22 February. Elton John came into the dressing room for a beer and a chat after the game and, tonight, four of us went to see him in concert again. 'Beefy' [Botham], 'Skid' [Marks], 'Foxy' [Fowler] and myself made up the party and, this time, we watched the performance from backstage, standing ten feet away from the band in the wings. It added a new dimension, being able to see the reaction of the audience to each song, and by the end of the night I was croaky from singing along.

Friday, 24 February. Elton is in town again. It seems that his tour could have been planned to coincide with ours – but none of us are complaining about that. The four of us who have attended both concerts to date went to dinner with the man and his entourage tonight, and a convivial and animated evening was had by all. Sitting next to Elton, we compared the problems of cricketers with footballers, about whom he is well qualified to talk through his position with Watford, and also compared the pressures of sportsmen and entertainers. I found myself being fascinated by his appetite for work after fifteen years at the top of his profession. Not many cricketers could claim such a record and Ian, for one, freely admits that he would find enthusiasm impossible after such a long run. Elton's thoughts on I.T. Botham also made interesting listening: having studied him on two overseas tours now, he feels we gave Ian too long a lead in Australia last winter and ought to have kept him more under the thumb. Perhaps he is right.

Saturday, 25 February. At seven o'clock, we said farewell to the New Zealanders for the last time, wishing them well for their forthcoming trip to Sri Lanka and accepting their good wishes for our journey into Pakistan.

Ian and I then went to our third Elton John concert – just as good as the previous two – before rejoining the rest of the lads for the party Elton was throwing for us in his suite. He certainly gave us a fine send-off. I certainly enjoyed myself. And I am not exactly sure what time it was when I struggled off to bed.

Sunday, 26 February. My head reminded me of last night. Rapidly and painfully. But after two months away, and with virtually a week before our next competitive cricket, a hangover seems no great sin. Just an inconvenience.

I ate some breakfast before taking a call from the Elton John suite. Remarkably fresh, the entourage were now serving buck's fizz. It would have been churlish not to join them ... so another humorous and convivial few hours got underway, various of the players and management dropping in as we chatted through funny events during our matches and their gigs.

They all call each other by their job rather than their name. So Patti is known as Publicity, Elton as Artiste, Bernie Taupin as Scribbler, and others as Producer, Promoter etc. This emerged as we ate a delicious English-style Sunday lunch to the strains of Elton's uncompleted forthcoming LP.

The kindness of Elton and his crew, especially to Ian and me, has been quite staggering. I think they enjoyed having us around and the feeling was certainly mutual. Too much high living on a tour is obviously to be discouraged, but this past twenty-four hours has been a perfect way to end the New Zealand leg and prepare us for the more spartan existence to come [in Pakistan].

Tuesday, 20 March. After bowling off three paces for a while and still feeling shockingly weak, I asked Bernard Thomas if he could find a doctor to examine me. I went to the local hospital [in Lahore] after lunch and the doctor told me he thought my condition was the result of loss of fluid in hot weather. This certainly seems to happen every time I come to the subcontinent, and sometimes in other hot climates. He took a blood test, which I was pleased to have just in case it showed anything positive.

Wednesday, 21 March. My tour is over. The doctor from Lahore General Hospital arrived just after eleven this morning and advised me to sit down. He then said I had jaundice. I pressed him for more details and he explained he suspects a mild form of hepatitis, which took me completely by surprise. Although I was aware my condition was something more severe than flu, we had been inoculated against hepatitis before leaving New Zealand, so I had never considered it a possibility. I was soon told that I would be going to Rawalpindi tonight, then returning to London on a British Airways flight early tomorrow morning.

I set up camp in the team room. One by one, the lads came in to say goodbye. I tried to give each of them a word or two of thanks and encouragement but it was the type of occasion when it seemed impossible to choose the right thing to say – I felt so disappointed at having to leave them.

Why I changed my name to honour my hero

I REALLY hated rugby at school and never made any representative teams. Instead, my Saturday afternoon entertainment was football for the school Old Boys Second XI. In goal I could pretend to be my boyhood hero, Manchester City's Bert Trautmann. After the matches there was a special attraction for a fourteen-year-old – under-age drinking! While the rugger buggers stood in a circle singing their bawdy songs, the more sophisticated soccer crew imbibed in a quiet corner talking sport and music.

Our centre half had recently been to a Peter, Paul and Mary concert and waited to meet the trio afterwards. They told him that he had to listen to this young singer-songwriter who had written their hit 'Blowin' in the Wind'. He rushed out to buy his albums and soon after lent me *The Freewheelin' Bob Dylan*

and *The Times They Are a-Changin'*. As a paid-up member of the Beatles fan club I was thinking that 'Love Me Do' was a great work of musical composition.

Dylan hit me like a sledgehammer. Everything went out of the window – girls, booze and homework. My folks had a radiogram and I was forced to listen to Bobby prostrate beneath the machine with my ear pressed to the speaker because they could not stand his voice. Their biggest mistake as far as my O levels were concerned was the purchase of a portable record player for my bedroom so they wouldn't have to listen to 'that strangled cat'. Hour after hour, Dylan's songs permeated my brain instead of my eight GCE subjects.

My new school briefcase was defaced with that five-letter word in four inch-high ballpoint and I added a third initial to my forenames (always a good idea if one wanted to be an amateur England cricket captain). The added name stuck and the next passport read Robert George Dylan Willis.

After feasting on *Another Side of Bob Dylan* in late 1964, the news came through that Dylan was to tour the UK. As release dates of his albums became more important than teenage birthdays, so concert dates took on more significance than Christmas. The Royal Albert Hall shows of 1965 and 1966 defined the journey Dylan was starting in the second stage of his career. The dressed-in-black troubadour of the first year was replaced by the nattily suited rock singer in '66. The folk fans detested the change, of course, and many, including our centre half, gave up on him. But I sensed something special was developing and, as Bob ploughed on through the boos and catcalls, I learnt every word of these new songs.

Bringing It All Back Home, *Highway 61 Revisited* and *Blonde on Blonde* are his best three consecutive albums. Dylan, as we know, is full of surprises and no sooner had we got used to his electric excellence than he veered off on a more traditional course with *John Wesley Harding*, *Nashville Skyline* and *Self Portrait*.

After the chastening '66 tour it was no surprise that Bob did not return to these shores until the Isle of Wight Festival in 1969. By now

my dad could tolerate 'Mr Tambourine Man' and 'All Along the Watchtower' (Hendrix hadn't got hold of it by then) and he bought me a ticket.

What a shambles! I was in the middle of a cricket match for Surrey at The Oval. Sunday was a day off so I took a train to Portsmouth Harbour and the ferry to Ryde. There were so many people at the site that the closest I could get to the stage was half a mile away. All I could see of the man was a bright white dot. His set and the sound system were appalling, as was the exodus afterwards. It was to be my first and last pop festival.

The release of *New Morning* in 1970 coincided with my first England call-up. Australia was a long way from my bedroom in south-west London and without the portable cassette player that was to become a constant companion on future tours, it was back to beer and birds for post-match entertainment. By the time of my next tour to Oz in 1974–75, Dylan had written the soundtrack for *Pat Garrett and Billy the Kid* and released the most agreeable *Planet Waves* with The Band. But as Lillee and Thomson were pounding us into the dust on the field, relief came with the release of arguably Bob's greatest album, *Blood on the Tracks*. The themes of relationships falling apart echoed his own marriage disintegrating.

A year later *Desire* was released, with the memorable 'Hurricane' describing the dreadful treatment of the boxer Rubin Carter – was this a return to the 'protest song'?

Dylan's 1978 world tour spawned the album *Street Legal*. I was fortunate to catch dates in Auckland, Melbourne and Earls Court during my cricket commitments. I even dragged Ian Botham to the Auckland gig and we went again together to St James's Park, Newcastle, in 1984, sitting right beside the stage.

The singer was continuing to frustrate some fans by changing not only the arrangements of his songs but also the words. He refused to stay in one place and give the people what they wanted. My own fanaticism was immovable. I loved the introduction of backing singers and instruments like the electric violin. The following ten years, however, were to sorely try my loyalty.

The 'born-again' albums *Slow Train Coming*, *Saved* and *Shot of Love* had some memorable tracks, not least Mark Knopfler on the first of the trilogy, but they were patchy and the overall religious message was not one I wanted to hear. *Infidels* in 1983 was an improvement, but it was not until after *Empire Burlesque*, *Knocked Out Loaded* and *Down in the Groove* had come and gone that Dylan hit top form again with *Oh Mercy*. Daniel Lanois's production enabled Bob to shine on tracks like

'Ring Them Bells' and 'What Was it You Wanted'.

It was a difficult act to follow and *Under the Red Sky*, *Good as I Been to You* and *World Gone Wrong* saw Dylan at his most self-indulgent. He was testing my patience now and after three dreadful shows into a five-night residence at the Hammersmith Odeon in 1991, I was at my lowest. But nights four and five were brilliant and he won me back.

My resolve has been solid ever since and although the albums appeared at less frequent intervals, each one has been a triumph.

Time Out of Mind started the string of successes, with the amazing 16½-minute *Highlands* to finish the album, then came *Love and Theft* and, what seemed like an eternity later, *Modern Times*.

His voice was seriously beginning to go by the time *Together Through Life* appeared in 2009 and there seemed to have been some sandpaper on the tonsils for *Christmas in the Heart*. Still I went to every UK show I could get to. Newcastle, Brighton and Brixton spring to mind, and most recently I was back in Hammersmith for three nights last November – all terrific, with his band as tight as ever, led by the bassist Tony Garnier, who's been with him since 1989.

This article on was originally published in The Times *on 5 September 2012.*

Selections from a Father of the Bride speech, Barbados, 8 April 2015

Our story begins back in 1984,
    Mum in Birmingham, Dad away on tour.
A new arrival in the UK's second city,
    Immediately blonde and incredibly pretty.
Obviously must have taken after father;
    'No,' you say, you think the mother rather.

A few little accidents she had to survive,
    All part of growing up and staying alive.
The boiling hot coffee spilt down her arm,
    Thankfully from that came no lasting harm.

Then Uncle Bhuna dropped her on her head,
    An egg-sized bump, but happily not dead.
Then it was Dad's turn to drop his little treasure,
    On the pub floor, much to Mum's displeasure.

In her high chair, at home or away,
    She would never spoil other people's day.
Any semblance of sound would bring out a bread roll,
    Which was quickly stuffed – down her cakehole.

Soon back to London the family moved down,
    To Fitzwillingham Road in Clapham Old Town.
Then off to Wimbledon, to the cottage in West Place;
    The arrival of Poppy put a smile on her face.

Education now in the hands of Wimbledon High,
    Quite pleased to go there usually, there was rarely a sigh.

There was hockey and netball and all kinds of japes,
    And endless visits to the Fox and Grapes.

Trips abroad too, to follow her dad,
    To Oz, SA and even Trinidad.
Then the serious business of the dreaded GCSEs,
    And applying for places at universities.

It was back to Brum, for Sport Science and booze;
    Just as well Selly Oak had separate loos.
Despite Rachel and Annie leading her astray,
    She somehow made it to graduation day.

Around this time, although memory deceives,
    Onto the scene appeared someone named Reeves.
A fine upstanding young man, if ever there was,
    But a gap year was pending and she went off to Oz.

With Sally in Sydney near the Harbour Bridge,
    Cold beers and white wine clogging their fridge.
No slumming or backpacks for this trusty two,
    Just the bars of Kings Cross and Wooloomooloo.
Even the jobs they got were on Bondi Beach,
    With a chilled bottle of bubbly always in reach.

Employment in Canary Wharf at the same time,
    The pleasure of commuting on the Jubilee Line.
He, changing jobs, was all very manly,
    While she couldn't shift from Morgan Stanley.
Mugged on her doorstep, she didn't explode;
    It didn't put her off living in Sugden Road.

Sharing with Rachel was always lots of fun,
    But then along came Charlie and off she did run.
Time to size up Brett in Armoury Way:
    Could she really settle down with him one day?
'Yes' seemed to be the answer to that,
    So it's back to Sugden, to their own lovely flat.

But no sooner had they got through the door,
    They're deserting us for the humidity of Singapore.
Brett's soon the locals' Standard Chartered guru,
    While she's taking all the visitors around the zoo.
Keeping very fit in gym and on tennis court;
    Netball too, she's always been a bit of a sport.

So now we've all come to this Caribbean isle,
    To follow her laughter and engaging smile.
She's always travelling the globe with someone or other,
    Maybe Brett, the girls, or her very special mother.

So the ring's on now, the bride's been kissed,
    It's nearly time to all get pissed.
Yes, the alcohol has addled this particular brain;
    I've missed lots out, which is a bit of a shame.
But thank you for listening to this little rhyme.
    I know you're all having a cracking good time.

Later we'll all be straining to have a chance
    To witness the newly-weds share their first dance,
And while, on the dance floor, Katie will twirl,
    We'll all be thinking, 'What a very special girl!'

14

CHAINSAW BOB

In his roles as TV commentator and pundit, Bob became known for his forthright opinions and acerbic putdowns – a selection of which are included below. As the comments from fellow broadcasters make clear, however, at heart Bob was always an England supporter who wanted nothing more than to see his team succeed, and there was a big difference between the persona that was presented on the screen and the off-air character they knew as friends.

Bob set high standards on the field and expected others to maintain those standards, both in the teams he played in and commentated on. Some of his comments may have sounded harsh, but I think they all came from an inbuilt passion. His Sky persona evolved.

It was a mixture of entertainment, passion for the game and for England to do well. We knew that if England had had a bad day, the chainsaw would be warmed up. He had many nicknames and 'Chainsaw Bob' was one of them.

David Gower, *The Times*

The one thing I found out very quickly when I started working with Bob at Sky was that he was desperate for England to do well. He was England through and through. He absolutely loved it when they won games.

He was a model professional around the commentary box, too.

He would turn up early, do his prep and research and always gave the director and producer great 'grabs' to work with. I can remember him building up towards the first ball of the 2005 Ashes as if it were a boxing contest and he found the perfect words to describe Brian Lara's history-making batting against us in

Antigua. He would nail the theatre of the moment.

And he made such a niche for himself on the *Verdict* and *Debate* programmes. In recent years when England had been having a bad day I just had to look at social media to see so many people saying, 'I can't wait to hear what Bob Willis has got to say about this.'

Nasser Hussain, *Daily Mail*

WHEN he really got into his own on *The Verdict*, the players would wither. He started everything with the same two words, 'Well, Charles . . .' It was an act and he was brilliant at it. He was a massive England supporter. He didn't mind giving the players a serve but we would say to them, 'Meet the guy once and you will have a mate for life.' That's what happened with lads like Steve Harmison, Andrew Flintoff, Stuart Broad, Jimmy Anderson. Also, technically, he was as good a commentator as you could ever work with. At calling the moment, he was absolutely bang on.

David 'Bumble' Lloyd, Sky podcast

YOU would arrive an hour or two early – and he would always be earlier. You would jovially chat away about all sorts beforehand and then the camera would start rolling and he'd be into his schtick. Charles Colvile would send a question Bob's way and he would fly into people. But the key was that no one else would know what he was going to say – not even Charles. I found it incredibly hard, as he came off his long run, not to crack up. You knew it would be gold, but you also knew he was such a nice man – it would shock you every time. That anticipation was unforgettable: knowing something was coming but not knowing what it would be. Then Charles would turn to me and I'd have a look as if to say, 'How am I supposed to follow that?'

Rob Key, *Evening Standard*

The following brief collection of quotations from Bob's broadcasting career begins with one that was made while he was still a player – a complaint about the press that came as a shock to many, made as it was so soon after his finest hour, in a post-match interview on the BBC with a bemused Peter West at Headingley in 1981.

'The standard of journalism in this country has gone down the nick completely. People have to rely on small-minded quotes from players under pressure for their stories. Whereas they used to write about cricket, they don't seem to be able to do that any more.'

> Bob reveals one of the sources of the anger that contributed to his 8–43 match-winning performance.

'Well, huge shout, and he's gone as well. Stewart goes first ball and England are looking like a village side on the village green at the moment.'

> Bob despairs as Alec Stewart's wicket leaves England struggling at 2–4 in their first innings at Johannesburg in November 1999.

'There it is … And there it goes. Put the cheese in the trap, in walks the mouse and off goes his head.'

> Darren Gough, out for a duck, proves no match for the wiles of Shane Warne in the first Ashes Test at Edgbaston in July 2001.

'Oh, he's gone this time. Down the track, a huge mow across the line. What on earth went through Ramprakash's head then? England needing a period of calm – and that's what Ramprakash produces!'

> Mark Ramprakash decides to take on Warne and is stumped by Adam Gilchrist in the third Ashes Test at Trent Bridge in August 2001.

'Daryl Harper – hopeless. Billy Bowden – a show pony. Steve Bucknor – past his sell-by date.'

Bob offers his opinion of the elite panel of umpires in 2005.

'No he hasn't got a clue, Charles. He shouldn't be umpiring school cricket. He's one of the worst umpires I've ever seen in any level of cricket. And the second worst is standing at the other end: Daryl Harper. These are the two worst umpires I've seen in Test match cricket since they brought in the so-called "elite" panel.'

Russell Tiffin and Daryl Harper receive some feedback for their umpiring of the fifth Test between the West Indies and England at Port of Spain in March 2009.

'Let's be honest, England was the only country that had decent umpires. We heard all about Indian umpires, Pakistan umpires, but I can tell you: Australian umpires were cheats, there was no doubt about that, and you ask Michael Holding about New Zealand umpires. They were absolutely shocking as well: bias in the extreme.'

Prompted by some decisions that went against England during their 2011–12 series with Pakistan in the UAE, Bob reflects on the umpiring in his own playing days.

'There should be three sets of stocks in the town square in Leeds: one for Andy Flower, one for Alastair Cook and one for Jonathan Trott. And a great big barrel of rotten tomatoes to hurl at them.'

> Bob finds England's negative tactics hard to take in their laborious victory against New Zealand in the second Test at Headingley in May 2013.

'I have never had a Jägerbomb. Maybe Australian beer is even worse than it used to be.'

> Bob gives a damning assessment of David Warner's reported choice of drink before the altercation with Joe Root in the lead-up to the 2013 Ashes.

'I don't think he's leaving with his head held high at all, I mean, we'll remember Graeme Swann for being the deserter, getting into disguise and creeping into the lifeboat on *The Titanic* with the women and children. Appalling decision.'

> Bob is not impressed by Graeme Swann's retirement from the sport in the middle of the 2013–14 Ashes whitewash.

'If you look closely, Charles, Ishant Sharma [is] a great student of the game, and that black-and-white archive back in India, and he's quaking in his boots just at the sight of this action. And the very next ball, what happens? Cook mops him up!'

> Bob basks in the moment when Alastair Cook takes his only Test wicket while mimicking Bob's distinctive action: India's Ishant Sharma, caught behind, in the first Test at Trent Bridge in July 2014.

'Would I have liked to have played T20? Not half, only four overs a day? Wouldn't mind getting smashed around for the sort of money these guys are earning these days.'

Bob reveals some of his feelings about Twenty20 cricket.

'I've seen fewer hookers in Soho on a Saturday night than I saw at Lord's this afternoon.'

Remarking on England's approach to India's short-pitched bowling in the second Test at Lord's in July 2014.

'Well, I'm very flattered, Joe, that you likened me to Albert Einstein – quite a good impression of the late Brian Clough, I thought. But, young man, when your little purple patch comes to an end ... *I'll have you back in the dock!*'

Tongue firmly in his cheek, Bob responds to Joe Root's impersonation of him, wearing an Einstein mask, after regaining the Ashes at Trent Bridge in August 2015.

'Well, he isn't an international wicketkeeper, is he, let's be honest about it. You know, I called him a stopper standing back. I mean, standing up he looks like a performing seal at feeding time ... flapping away there!'

Jonny Bairstow's performance in the first Test at Durban in December 2015 fails to win Bob's approval.

‘Once the onslaught came he didn't have an answer: short, wide, full, half-volley, wide … this is garbage.’

> Bob gives his verdict on the performance of South African bowler Chris Morris against England in the second Test in Cape Town in January 2016.

‘In terms of cricketing disaster, this is right at the top of the tree. England demeaned Test match cricket by picking a reduced side. It was nothing short of disgraceful … Is Gary Ballance's goose cooked? It certainly should be. He should never have been picked for the tour; he should have been dropped after Chittagong. He and Rashid should be on a charter flight back to Leeds-Bradford airport as soon as possible.’

> A first ever Test loss to Bangladesh, in Dhaka in October 2016, prompts a withering assessment of England's approach to the match.

‘The last idiot to put Australia in at Adelaide in an Ashes Test was yours truly, R.G.D. Willis. I thought Joe Root might have learned from that mistake, but apparently not.’

> Reflecting on the lessons of history after Joe Root's ill-fated decision to bowl first in the Adelaide Test during the 2017–18 Ashes.

'This "umpire's call" has got to disappear. If the ball's hitting the stumps, the batsman's out. If the ball's hitting the stumps, he's out, isn't he?'

> Bob struggles to see the justification for one aspect of the Umpire Decision Review System.

'England are careering headlong into those dark, dismal days of Hussain being booed at The Oval and Duncan Fletcher being appointed to come in and rescue the team. It's just getting worse and worse. We thought perhaps that Auckland, 58 all out, might have been a blip, but it's not looking that way now. I think complete structural change is needed in the English game to try and produce better cricketers.'

> Following defeat to Pakistan in the first Test at Lord's in 2018, Bob pulls no punches in his assessment of the state of English cricket.

'Now, what birdbrains over there thought that Ben Foakes wouldn't score more runs than Jennings, Sam Curran wouldn't score more runs than Jennings, Chris Woakes on one leg hopping around wouldn't score more runs than Jennings, and Jack Leach wouldn't score more runs than Jennings? That excruciating innings by the left-handed opener just was . . . embarrassing, absolutely embarrassing. Why the guy was anywhere near the team . . . He looked as if he was embarrassed being out there.'

> Bob expresses a few doubts about Keaton Jennings's place in the England side after his 43-ball eight in the third Test against the West Indies in February 2019.

'Certainly not. I don't go with all this "resting players". You know, Stokes and Buttler were in the IPL, weren't they, filling their wallets in April and May – why are they "resting" during a Test match?'

Bob responds to the suggestion that England's struggles in their Test against Ireland in July 2019 could be put down to a World Cup hangover.

'That was abject, Charles, absolutely pathetic. Apart from Joe Root and Ben Stokes, these guys cannot bat, it's as simple as that. The Ashes have now gone, it's going to be all over inside three Test matches, and if the penny hasn't now dropped with England's cricket administrators about the programme of four-day cricket . . . if they want the primacy of Test-match cricket, if they want to keep the best form of the game alive, they're going to have to do something about it and pretty damn quick, because this was totally unacceptable.'

Bob gives the England players both barrels after they are bowled out for 67 in the third Ashes Test at Headingley in August 2019. Two days later they pulled off a dramatic one-wicket win.

'I guess some guys are just naturally built for comfort rather than cricket.'

Bob Willis (90 Test caps) reflects on the physical attributes of his colleague at Sky, Rob Key (15 Test caps).

15

UPON HEARING
THE NEWS

In the following piece – written with Mike Dickson in May 2019 as part of an introduction for a planned new autobiography – Bob describes the moment he heard his diagnosis and reflects on how it made him look back at his eventful life.

———

I guess you never know how you are going to react to being told you have cancer. It is not something you ever want to find out, but now I know. It was April 2016 and I was seated, as an apparently healthy 66-year-old, opposite a doctor in a hospital in west London when he gave me the results of a biopsy on my prostate. There is a scale of one to ten, with the worst scenario being upwards. I was a nine, and there was worse to come. The cancer was not confined to the prostate but had spread, to a degree.

At this point it feels like you are coming in on the hat-trick ball.

Fortunately I was to hear that there are treatments for my particular version, and these are evolving all the time. Thanks to some excellent medical care, I have been able to continue living a largely normal life in parallel with ongoing treatment. These days the scorecard I follow most closely is the one with the results of my frequent blood tests. From the moment you are told, you know things are never going to be quite the same again.

I recall being reasonably stoic upon hearing the news, although it did feel something akin to sustaining a huge blow to the solar plexus. I was stunned for the next two or three hours, until I started to come to terms with what I had been told. It takes a while to sink in and then you start working out the best way to proceed. Nor did I feel much in the way of self-pity, although you inevitably ask yourself why it is you whose number has come up. I have, by and large, looked after myself in life. While always an enthusiastic drinker – of wine and beer, not the hard stuff – I have not been prone to too many other vices and I have kept myself in reasonable shape, always taking plenty of vigorous exercise. My diet has been decent enough. Going back to my days as a cricketer I have, for many decades, even had a personal rule that I eat nothing but fruit until lunchtime. These days I am a 24/7 vegetarian, and have found that regime unexpectedly agreeable.

But here I was, being given the kind of news that everybody dreads, trying to work out how to soften the blow for those I care about the most. One thing you find out quickly enough is that there are always people worse off than yourself. You wonder, inevitably, if it could have been spotted or investigated sooner, and there were indeed a few warning signs for me that I was assured at the time were not overly concerning. But there is no point trying to turn the clock back, and being over-emotional is not my style. If anything, I surprised myself with my relatively phlegmatic response to this life-changing event and how I have come to terms with it, especially as I have suffered plenty of depressive episodes over the years.

Perhaps it helps that my life has been one of abrupt twists and turns, with events rarely turning out as I expected them to, whether in the personal sphere or as a cricketer and broadcaster. I certainly never grew up thinking that I would make it as a high-profile athlete in international sport, as there was precious little indication in my childhood or teenage years that my dreams would swiftly become reality. By the time I left school at eighteen, after a somewhat less than blissful time at grammar school, I was shaping up to be a half-decent bowler with hopes of a county contract, while also being a non-league football goalkeeper. At twenty-one, having only recently broken into the Surrey team with a handful of games behind me, I got a call telling me to get on a flight to Australia to join the England team, the flight leaving in thirty-six hours. A few months later I had featured in four Ashes Test matches in a winning England team. Having gone on to play for England over a fourteen-year period – much longer than I ever thought possible – I then never envisaged such a lengthy career in sports broadcasting, thirty years of them with Sky.

So when I was given my diagnosis, on that spring day, it was another tale of the unexpected to be reckoned with. When something like this happens, you take stock and reflect upon all the things that have happened: adding Dylan to my name as an unconventional teenager, in homage to my musical idol; roaring down the hill at Headingley in 1981, in something of a trance, to knock over the Australians; the sleepless nights while captaining England (I have always tended towards insomnia); the fantastic friendships and lifelong bonds that anyone lucky enough to play professional team sports will establish. In my case, I wonder if I allowed myself to enjoy it all enough. And then a second life as a former cricketer, for which I am also grateful, commentating on and analysing the game I love while visiting fascinating places and meeting a huge array of people. As a participant in 35 ferociously competitive Tests against Australia, I never thought I would come to be so fond of that country and its people.

My original mentor as a broadcaster was one of the greatest Australians of them all, Richie Benaud. I was first employed by the Beeb in 1985, the year after my body finally gave up on me as a cricketer. Like most players-turned-commentators, I wasn't given much in the way of formal training; you're just put in the seat next to the lead person and off you go. In my case it was Richie, the master. In his very understated way he was tremendously helpful when I started. I began, like a lot of people who have just left the dressing room, by making excuses for my friends when they fouled up or played a bad shot. Richie told me I had to be more critical and not just put a superficial gloss on things.

As it happened, I never wanted to be able to go back into the dressing room after a day's play to socialise with the likes of David Gower, Allan Lamb or Ian Botham when they were still playing, friendly though I was with them. So by the time I joined Sky four years later my style had evolved. The birth of Sky's cricket coverage came with what was perceived as a success in covering the West Indies tour of 1989–90. Tony Greig was working for us on that tour and he was then persuaded to front the programmes when the channel got its first exclusive cricket package the following summer, which was the Sunday league.

He had long been involved with Channel Nine in Australia and I had worked with them on previous Ashes series, becoming familiar with their way of doing things. When I worked for them in both Australia and England their executive producer was David Hill, a no-nonsense character who had pioneered Kerry Packer's TV coverage of World Series Cricket. This was very different from the BBC, although Richie was so good he could lend himself to any style of broadcasting. He gave me a lot of tips, and it was particularly useful for someone like me who did not have an especially melodic delivery. I was a bit laconic and monotone, you might say, and somebody called me 'Mr Mogadon', I recall. It was the influence of Channel Nine that moulded the way I would approach broadcasting.

Being plain-speaking came naturally, but it was a conscious thing in that I thought I had to do something different if I was going to stay in the job. I resolved to be fairly blunt in expressing what I was thinking. I didn't want to be like Fred Trueman, asking what was 'going off out there' or banging on about what it was like back in my day. I wanted to tell it how it is and talk as if I was in the pub with a mate: 'Why on earth have they picked him?' What I was determined to avoid was falling in with a lot of what you heard, and still hear, on football, as in the 'He'll be disappointed with that' approach. I prefer to say that something is not good enough or is unprofessional; it's not just 'disappointing'. Contrary to some perceptions, I am also keen to hand out praise when I believe it is merited, and I hope that, by the same token, this carries more weight.

Perhaps it can come across as personal, although it is not intended that way. For example, I felt obliged, when watching Keaton Jennings play for England, to ask why he could not learn to avoid getting out in the same way all the time. Maybe

I should not have called him a 'robotic stick insect', but that was the image that came into my head. When James Vince, clearly a naturally talented player, was batting for England in Tests, he would hit three glorious cover drives before getting caught at second slip – so frustrating for the watching fan, and you had to point it out.

Being blunt can have its drawbacks, because I am also aware we are all human and make mistakes. When, as part of the England management, Andrew Strauss and Paul Farbrace asked me to go and meet the team in 2015, I will admit to a little trepidation, because I have never sought favour with the England team of the day. I had given a few of them some fearful stick, people like Adam Lyth and Adil Rashid, but I found myself welcomed and cordially received by the company. I gave them a lot of respect for that. Trevor Bayliss had told them that they would all end up being poacher-turned-gamekeeper one day, and that I was just doing my job and they ought to do theirs. It had become part of Strauss's philosophy to try and bridge the schism between the commentary box and the dressing room by hearing from the likes of myself, Mike Atherton and Nasser Hussain. He had been in the commentary box himself and knew what we had to offer, although we cannot get involved in coaching in any formal way.

Anyway, to my surprise, nobody looked to punch me on the nose.

16

FAREWELL, BOB

The announcement of Bob's death in December 2019 prompted an outpouring of grief and affection that was both moving and unexpected. Below is a selection of the many tributes and messages from friends, colleagues and admirers that appeared in the press, on television and on social media. Also included are some of the personal messages from friends that were sent to Bob in his last few days.

'Such sad news that Bob Willis has passed away. A true friend to so many. An outstanding man. God, we will miss him.'

David Lloyd

'He was a fine man and very, very fine bowler – one of the best England fast bowlers there has ever been. Everyone who knew him will miss him hugely.'

Mike Brearley

'Oh no, not Bob Willis . . . what joy he gave, and what a marvellous man. That eight for 43. Used to lunch with him occasionally to talk cricket, Wagner and Bob Dylan, his three great passions.'

Stephen Fry

'I will remember Bob Willis for many reasons, but most importantly as a very loyal and supportive friend. There are so many memories off the field, so many times on tours where, after that inevitable glass of wine, we would have such good times. The Bob Willis laugh was as distinctive as any. Once you had taken off the restraints of the public persona, the laugh would echo around the night for quite some miles and for quite some hours. I will miss that, I will miss him. We will all miss him.'

David Gower

'He was incredibly kind, with his time and with his advice. He was one of those people who made you feel better about yourself. Bob was one of the funniest, if not the funniest I've ever met. I can't remember a time I spent in his company where I didn't either laugh uncontrollably or gain some insight into the game or into life itself. If only he could have seen the outpouring of affection he's received.'

Rob Key

'Bob was my neighbour, and I remember one day he was sitting in his car waiting for the main gates of our block to open when I walked up to the pedestrian gate feeling a bit flustered. I'm in my eighties, and as soon as Bob saw me he rolled down the window. I told him that I had just got off the bus and realised that I'd left my handbag on it. Bob said, "Jump in," and we started chasing down the bus! Somehow he managed to get in front to make it stop, then he climbed aboard and found my handbag. That's my memory of Bob.'

Sheila Thompson

' Such a sad time for cricket fans all around the world. You shall be remembered forever for what you have done on the pitch!'

Sir Vivian Richards

' Through good and bad in the Bothams' family life you have always been there for us, Bob. Reassuring words and gestures have given us strength when times were tough. We've laughed and danced over the years and had such great times. Becky will never forget your babysitting rules all those years ago. Thank you for your friendship, lover.'

Ian and Kath Botham

' I have always thought of you as family. I have some great memories as a child through to now. All our trips away, the huge laughs will stay with me and it actually brings a smile to my face thinking of them. I also put my love of good wine partly down to our long lunches and evenings out. But also your teaching and educating me on them. You taught me a lot about life and even now you are not complaining, as always you are simply getting on with it in your own way. You are a fantastic person, family man, friend.'

Liam Botham

'I am in total shock. I love Big Bad Bob. He was an incredible man with a great sense of humour and a very generous human being. The many tours I did with Bob were always fun between the cricket we played and I always enjoyed having a glass or two together, which I am going to sadly miss!!!!'

Allan Lamb

'I woke up in Adelaide to the sad news about Bob Willis. I spent many glorious times with him and the England team in Australia. A funny and gentle soul, except when you had to face his bowling … #RIPBobWillis, you legend. Love, E xx'

Sir Elton John

'Today, one of my true heroes passed away. Bob Willis was one of the main reasons that cricket became such a lifetime passion of mine. His Herculean exploits in the famous 1981 "Botham's Ashes" series, alongside his great mate Beefy, electrified the nation and me, then just sixteen. To my joy, I got to know both men well in later years, sharing some hilarious times.

Bob and I bonded over our firm "better-out-than-in" belief that if you've got something to say, say it loudly, proudly and preferably in a way that winds up a lot of people. Yet beneath his apparently glum and inflammatory commentary style lay a man of fierce intelligence, wonderfully acerbic humour and tremendous loyalty.

RIP Bob. They say never meet your heroes, but I'm so glad I met you.'

Piers Morgan

'Each player's career is defined by performances over a long period of time, but what sticks in the minds of cricket fans the world over are certain pivotal moments or brilliant individual performances, and for Bob Willis, it was Headingley 1981. Without his bowling we had no chance of winning that game. He was not seeing anything else other than the batsman and the stumps. He had blinkered vision, a bit like a racehorse galloping towards the finishing line. None of us needed to speak to him. There was no point anyway as his focus, emotion and passion all came together in that moment and he blew the Aussies away with some breathtaking fast bowling. Bob gave everything for England.'

Sir Geoffrey Boycott

'An icon of English cricket has sadly departed us, someone I looked up to when I played in the England teams of the late 1970s. The standards Bob set as a player, as a leader and above all as an ambassador for his country will be unsurpassed.

At an unearthly time in the mornings I remember him training and running round the field outside the South Terrace travel lodge in Adelaide on my first England tour in 1978–79 – driving himself hard so that he would be ready to lead our attack for the six Test matches in front of us, against the old enemy.

To me he will always be one of my heroes.'

Graham Gooch

'He was an inspiration to many of us on the field of play; his passion and pride when playing for England were second to none. He led by example and that taught us youngsters many good lessons. His friendship off the field of play was always warm and humorous. An England great and a good friend.'

Mike Gatting

'Willis had no right to be such a successful pace bowler. He possessed sparrows' legs and wonky knees, which were frequently visited by surgeons; he had a pigeon-chest that was inhabited by half a dozen measly hairs and he was seemingly devoid of any biceps. Not even Heath Robinson would have had the gall to design a fast-bowling machine like this. Yet he adorned the England side for more than thirteen years.'

Vic Marks

'He was a super man, and I had so many wonderful times with him, both on and off the field. He will be sadly missed and, I assure you … never forgotten. His character will live on.'

Geoff Miller

'Willis was a terrific fast bowler, with a run-up that was unique. Not a fluent run-up, but once the ball left his hand it was terror for the batsman. I never heard Willis swear at a batsman, never saw him argue with the umpire. He did not believe in talking. He wanted his ball to speak for him. A true legend he was.'

Kapil Dev

'I always enjoyed our battles out on the field and especially looked forward to sharing a beer and a chat away from the game! Stay strong! AB.'

Allan Border

'A remarkable human being. Bob, you were truly one of the greats of this beautiful game. RIP #BobWillis.'

Brian Lara

'Please thank him for selecting me to tour with him to Australia in 1982–83 and for the reasons that he wanted me there. It was the ultimate in my career and I will always remember him for his input. I am so pleased that I managed to share a few glasses of wine with you both last June and recall that although Bob couldn't have been well, he chose to walk me all the way to the station to catch my train onwards.'

Robin Jackman

'There have been many tributes paid to Bob and I wanted to add mine from someone who had known him as a teenager at RGS Guildford, then his early days with Surrey, followed by his career with England and Warwickshire and finally with Sky TV. Professional cricket and football brings you into contact with a great cross section of society – some good, some not so good! – and I can tell you, Bob was one of the best.'

Micky Stewart

'There will not be many who came across Bob Willis without liking him. He had the time of day for everyone, whoever they were, and he never took himself too seriously. Those who knew him will not have a bad word to say about him and that is the perfect tribute.'

Nasser Hussain

'RIP Bob. Such sad news to wake up to. A hero of mine. Great cricketer. Incredibly entertaining pundit. More importantly, an unbelievable bloke!!'

Michael Vaughan

'Gutted to hear the news of Bob Willis passing. A lovely person with a great humour who was so proud of England cricket. Legend.'

Stuart Broad

'Incredibly sad to hear the news about Bob Willis. He was a true great, generous in sharing his knowledge about the game and a lovely man. RIP Bob.'

James Anderson

'Rest in peace Bob. A true England great. Fantastic player, pundit and a lovely man with a great sense of humour. #RIPBobWillis.'

Joe Root

'Hurtling to the wicket like a man possessed, Bob Willis was the greatest English fast bowler of my generation. His uncompromising, fearless, agenda-less approach to cricket or punditry gave us all the confidence to do it our way or to speak our mind. He was a trailblazer, an irresistible force of nature, and yet off the field or off camera he was sympathetic, wry and self-deprecating. A lionhearted bowler, a brilliant pundit, a hilarious storyteller and loyal father and friend, he is a colossal loss to our world.'

Simon Hughes

'Just received the saddest of sad news. Bob Willis, great fast bowler, opponent, team-mate, room-mate and wonderful bloke, has passed away ... The great flapping Goose. Such tales to tell. Good times. Some of my happiest memories.'

Mike Selvey

'Bob Willis was a great man with a wonderful, wonderful dry sense of humour. Almost thirty years ago we spent two summers driving round England together while working for Sky. What fun and laughter we had and what excellent wine we drank! I shall miss him very much.'

Henry Blofeld

'As a player he had a big heart, he'd run in and hit the pitch hard. At his peak, he was one of the best three bowlers in the world. He was hugely admired all around the world. In his company, over a glass of wine, he would make you laugh all night.'

Darren Gough

‘Saddened to hear that Bob Willis has died. One of our greatest fast bowlers. Met him on many occasions and he was always great company, with a sense of humour that was as sharp as his bowling.’

Gary Lineker

‘Bob Willis was completely different off air to the man "off his long run" on air! Very, very funny man and loved life! He will be missed . . .!’

Kevin Pietersen

‘Had the pleasure of working with him for @SkyCricket and off air I loved listening to his great stories on how they played the game back in the day. RIP Great man.’

Allan Donald

‘Such sad news. Bob was an English legend, inspired a generation of fast bowlers around the world and was a good bloke. RIP mate.’

Glenn McGrath

‘In the 1970s and early 1980s, when English cricket was beset by regular crises, offset by the occasional moment of outrageous glory, there was one sight to gladden patriotic hearts: Bob Willis – all 6 ft 6 in of him – charging towards the stumps . . . Bob was a true son of the game and cricket will miss him.’

Matthew Engel

'With his death, Bob Dylan has lost one of his most devoted fans, wine growers everywhere a serious connoisseur of their art and English cricket one of their greatest ever players.'

Charles Colvile

'Consider myself very fortunate to have spent time with Bob Willis in the @SkyCricket studios. Fantastically funny with a generous nature, Bob will be missed by us all.'

Tom Moody

'Ralph Waldo Emerson once said "It's not the length of life, it's the depth of life that matters," and Bob's life had depth beyond measure. His achievements on the cricket pitch and in the studio were only a part of the Bob Willis story.'

Rod Bransgrove, Hampshire Cricket chairman

'One of the few videos I had as a kid was *Botham's Ashes*, so I was just a little bit in awe of meeting the big fast bowler who'd whirled in and knocked over the Aussies in that famous Headingley Test! I'd also seen you countless times as a commentator and analyst tearing strips off subsequent England teams, so half expected you to be some kind of irascible schoolmaster, ready to give me a dressing down.

Of course, as it turned out, the opposite was true. Your warmth, kindness, authenticity and humour are the characteristics that make you someone who I've grown to dearly love and care for.

Whether it's been chewing the fat over many a glass of good wine, watching you hit shot after shot on the golf course shouting "******* ****" at yourself or your golf ball, or seeing you from the stage towering above the rest of the crowd at one of my shows, you've been a very fine and steady presence in my life. I'll be so sad when that's no longer the case but it's been an honour to know you and to call you a friend.'

Tom Chaplin, lead singer of Keane

'I've never thought that the number of years one lives defines people, but rather they are defined by the imprint they leave on people at large and particularly their family, friends and community. You've ticked all those boxes big time!! Cricket was your signature but cricket alone didn't define you.'

Jack Clarke, friend and former Chairman of Cricket Australia

'He cared so passionately for the game and its future, our conversations were always about protecting it and growing it at all costs, words which I hold very dear. Bob was a true great of the game, a giant on the field, and a wonderful man off it.'

Tom Harrison, Chief Executive Officer of the ECB

'The man I admired from afar as a kid I have admired from the chair next to me. I'll never forget the big smile on your face as Ben Stokes was winning that game at Headingley this summer. At that moment it said everything about you that I already knew. We had our moment there, here is another one and you were delighted that it had happened.

I've always admired your poise, intelligence, ability to put your view on any matter across in the perfect way and your judgement of when to stick and when to twist on the acerbic wit to brilliantly sum up a situation.

You're a truly great man, Bobby. '

Ian Gade, Sky

'I remember thinking how surprising (and brilliant) it was that someone so talented and successful couldn't give a **** about trophies and memorabilia. You have always favoured good wine, good friends and a good giggle. '

Alex Hakes, Sky

'Having just done ten *Debates* in a row without you, I can honestly say that neither Nass or Keysie have got what it takes when sitting in your chair. There was a total lack of pithy one-liners and withering looks! It is an honour and a pleasure to have been a colleague and friend over the last twenty years, plus you are 50 per cent responsible for my first cricketing memory, yes the miracle of '81. '

James Lawson, Sky

'Bob, you have provided us all with so many great memories that I will cherish for ever.

I'm proud to have been your friend. As you put the Winit's up one last time, red instep and all, know that you'll forever be remembered, forever talked about. You are one of life's few and precious great people. Rest well, see you in the Comms Box up on high one day. '

Barney Francis, Sky

'Bob was an absolute pleasure to produce. Never, ever can I remember a hint of ego. From all the "talent" I have ever worked with I can safely say that he was the most caring, kind and compassionate to the production staff. He was loved by everyone who worked with him.'

Graeme Brown, Sky

'Every time I think of you – you make me smile.

You make me smile because you care. You care about life, about love, about family, about friends, about the world. You care deeply about cricket – the love of a game that brought us and so many great people together.

You care about commentary. You care about television coverage. You care about music. You care about Manchester City . . .

This may be your last innings, your last spell, a few more overs, steaming in, legs pumping . . .

I want to say thank you. I want to thank you for caring. I want to thank you for being my friend. And I want you to know that your friends and colleagues care about you too. Very much.'

Bryan Henderson, Sky

'I was lucky enough to work closely with you on *The Verdict* for several years, you kept Charles in check and delivered some famous knock-out lines on the players! Talking of soundbites, your grabs have long been a lesson to the new breed of commentators on how to nail the moment – you're a true Sky Sports legend, Bob!

One thing we've all really appreciated is how you've always made the effort with the team – you are first at the bar, always attend Christmas parties and leaving drinks and are very generous with your time – always going above and beyond.'

Robin Reeve, Sky

'When I turned up then as a youngster fresh out of school and massive cricket fan I was blown away when first introduced to you. You made me feel so welcome and I quickly realised what a top bloke you were and since then I've felt very close to you and had immense respect for you.

You are a brilliant commentator but my best memories are of your fantastic company over a bottle of red and of countless singing sessions paying homage to the great Bob Dylan.'

Will Sawrey-Cookson, Sky

Acknowledgements

The Willis family is profoundly indebted to Bob's many friends, colleagues and team-mates from around the world in the preparation and writing of this book. Mike Dickson has written an elegiac biography which reflects not only detailed study and research but a friendship going back over a quarter of a century. The warmth of this relationship shines through his prose throughout.

Tim Waller, our talented and diligent co-editor, has worked tirelessly to tease out interviews and contributions from all over the globe, tracking down some important, but hard-to-find, contacts and checking all the facts and statistics with care and precision.

The list of contributors could have been much longer and is testament to the range and variety of the many obituaries which appeared following Bob's death. These people had a special place in Bob's heart and memory and, following their words included here, they will all enjoy a warm place in ours too.

Paul Allott, Michael Atherton, Benedict Bermange, Scyld Berry, Sir Ian Botham, David Brown, Charles Colvile, Michael Henderson, Michael Holding, Paul King, John Lever, David Lloyd, Rod Marsh, The Rt Hon Sir John Major, Geoff Miller, Piers Morgan, Mark Nicholas, Sir Michael Parkinson, Sir Tim Rice, John Snow, Martin Tyler.

Barney Francis, Bryan Henderson and Bob's colleagues at Sky, who clearly loved him as much as he loved them.

Dr Lisa Pickering and all who cared for Bob at Cancer Centre London and Parkside Hospital.

Special thanks to everyone who has supported Bob and Lauren, especially Peter and Frankie Altman, Dr Maggie Blott, Patrick Barclay, Phil and Dawn Collins, Alex Hakes, Karen Holden, Bob Holmes, Andrew and Louise Jameson, Ed and Kim Lewis, Leon McEvoy, Geoff and Annie Merrill, Paul Monk, Louise Moran, Michelle 'Mitzi' Piccioni, Alyson Rudd, Johnny Sandery, Dot and Ian Wallis, Geoff Walls, Jessie Willis.

We would like to give particular thanks to the Bob Dylan Music Company. Bob Dylan was a very important figure in Bob's life and it means a great deal to us that they have shown their support for this book by allowing us to reproduce lyrics and use song titles as chapter headings.

And finally we would like to thank Roddy Bloomfield, who has helped us produce this beautiful tribute to Bob's amazing life.

Copyright Acknowledgements

Photographs
The editor and publisher would like to thank the following for permission to reproduce photographs:

Section One: Allsport UK/Getty Images; Ken Kelly/Popperfoto via Getty Images; Graham Wood/Hulton Archive/Getty Images; Patrick Eagar/Popperfoto via Getty Images; Gerry Armes/*Birmingham Mail*/Popperfoto via Getty Images; Patrick Eagar/Popperfoto via Getty Images; Patrick Eagar/Popperfoto via Getty Images; Adrian Murrell/Allsport/Getty Images; Adrian Murrell/Allsport/Getty Images; Adrian Murrell/Allsport/Getty Images; Patrick Eagar/Popperfoto via Getty Images; Adrian Murrell/Allsport/Getty Images; Ken Kelly/Popperfoto via Getty Images; PA Wire/PA Images; Ken Kelly/Popperfoto via Getty Images.

Section Two: Patrick Eagar/Popperfoto via Getty Images; Ken Kelly/Popperfoto via Getty Images; Russell McPhedran/Fairfax Media via Getty Images; Ken Kelly/Popperfoto via Getty Images; Clive Brunskill/Getty Images; Sky Sports; Richard Saker/GNM/Courtesy of Eyevine; Gareth Copley/Getty Images; Visionhaus/Corbis via Getty Images; Gareth Copley/Getty Images.

All other photographs are from private collections.

Songs
The editor and publisher would like to thank the Bob Dylan Music Company for permission to use the titles of a number of Bob Dylan's songs as chapter titles and to reproduce lines from the following songs:

'Not Dark Yet' © 1997 by Special Rider Music; 'Forever Young' © 1973 by Ram's Horn Music; renewed 2001 by Ram's Horn Music.

Books

The editor and publisher would like to thank the authors and publishers of the following for permission to reproduce extracts:

Paul Allott (contributor), *Wisden Cricketers' Almanack*, 2020; Allan Border, *An Autobiography*, Methuen, 1986; Ian Botham, *My Autobiography*, Collins Willow, 1994; Tony Greig, *My Story*, Stanley Paul, 1980; Ray Illingworth, *Yorkshire and Back*, Queen Anne Press, 1980; Allan Lamb, *My Autobiography*, Collins Willow, 1997; Dennis Lillee, *Menace: The Autobiography*, Headline, 2003; Derek Randall, *The Sun Has Got His Hat On*, Collins Willow, 1984; Derek Randall, *Rags*, Sport-in-Print, 1992; Viv Richards, *Sir Vivian*, Michael Joseph, 2000; Bob Willis, *Diary of a Cricket Season*, Pelham, 1979; Bob Willis, *The Captain's Diary*, Collins Willow, 1983; Bob Willis, *The Captain's Diary*, Collins Willow, 1984; Bob Willis, *Lasting the Pace*, Collins Willow, 1985.

Newspapers

The editor and publisher would like to thank the following writers and newspapers for permission to reproduce extracts:

John Arlott/*The Guardian*; Michael Atherton/*The Times*; Scyld Berry/ *The Observer*; Henry Blofeld/*The Guardian*; Mike Brearley/*The Guardian*; Brian Chapman/*The Guardian*; Matthew Engel/*The Guardian*; Paul Fitzpatrick/*The Guardian*; Pat Gibson/*Daily Express*/Reach Licensing; David Gower/*The Times*; Nasser Hussain/*Daily Mail*; Frank Keating/ *The Guardian*; Rob Key/*Evening Standard*; David Lloyd/Sky Sports Podcast; Keith Miller/*Daily Express*/Reach Licensing; Piers Morgan/ *Mail on Sunday*; Mark Nicholas/ESPN Cricinfo; Bob Willis/*The Times*; John Woodcock/*The Times*/News Licensing.

Television commentary

The editor and publisher would like to thank the BBC for permission to reproduce a transcription of part of the television coverage of the 1981 Ashes Test at Headingley.

Every reasonable effort has been made to trace the copyright holders, but if there are any errors or omissions, Hodder & Stoughton will be pleased to insert the appropriate acknowledgements in any subsequent printings or editions.